CONTENTS

Betty Hugo

"VERY INNOCENT EPISTLES": THE LETTERS OF ELINOR HUDDART TO SHAW

Elinor Huddart was an obscure late-Victorian novelist, a spinster who lived with her mother and family on a large country estate in Fareham. Her father lived in London and spent his days at the Carlton Club, visiting his family occasionally. Her grandfather was Captain Joseph Huddart (1741–1816), who worked for the East India Company as hydrographer and manufacturer. Only one of his five sons, Elinor's father Joseph, survived him, according to the *Dictionary of National Biography*. According to Elinor's letters, however, her grandfather had seven daughters and two sons, one of whom survived him.

Miss Huddart wrote six novels, the first three of which were published under pseudonyms: *Cheer or Kill* (1878) as Elinor Aitch; *Via Crucis* (1882) as Louisa Ronile (changed to Rouile); *My Heart and I* (1883) as Elinor Hume; *A Commonplace Sinner* (1885); *Leslie* (1891); and *A Modern Milkmaid* (1892). The term "novelist" is actually a misnomer: her work is no more than an effusion of sentimental melodramatic situations presented in the form of a story.

At 13 Victoria Grove in 1878, Elinor met the young George Shaw. He was living with his mother. She was one of Mrs. Shaw's many singing pupils. Shaw was twenty-two at the time; Elinor admitted two years later to being "close to forty."

None of Shaw's letters to her have survived. Since he does not mention her or her letters in any but the most dismissive way, interpretation has been largely a matter of conjecture and inference, supported by what is known about Shaw himself. He kept 170 letters from her all his life, these now in the Shaw Archive in the British Library. They encompass the years 1878 to 1894. Presumably Shaw wrote about the same number of letters to her, as most of her letters which Shaw kept respond to his letters.

Why Shaw continued to write to her remains puzzling. On at least two occasions he initiated the correspondence, and Elinor herself often wonders why he bothers to write (especially toward the end of their association, when he was beginning to be irritated by her). She was more than a little bit "in love" with Shaw, but there is no question of an affair of any kind. On a professional level (their association began when Shaw offered to "look over Elinor Huddart's work" when novel writing was his own abiding interest), the association is even more puzzling. He must have realized very soon that she was not a serious artist: she often complains that he scolds her for not wanting to revise, for not *working* to improve her style.

They met each other six or seven times. The first time was in 1878 at 13 Victoria Grove (she refers to his judging her by her "manner and appearance" and asks him for a photograph so that she can recognize him if she sees him again). Between October and November 1881 she suggests a visit, and another one in March 1883, although this visit is not confirmed. They met in July 1883 and again in October. She sends him a ticket for a play and discusses this meeting in October 1882, and he visits her in October 1884. These meetings did not appear to have improved their relationship.

Elinor frequently tells him that he is a genius, but also that he is "arrogant" and "cold"; that in his novels he does not attempt to "win" his readers and that his characters talk too much. Yet she insists that "some day the world will acknowledge you a genius."

To a man in his early twenties, even a supremely confident and determined man, this must have been flattering. Her references to the "savageness" of his nature, the "strain of barbarism" in him, and his "satanic" qualities probably urged him to develop rather than curb these characteristics: she was the very kind of reader he had set out to convert. Their views on almost everything were essentially different. It is possible that he saw in her a challenge. Could he convert her? He certainly tried.

She often talks about his brilliant dialogue and advises him to write a play, offering him the plot of one of her novels (an offer he turned down). Coincidentally, this happened at about the same time that William Archer, whom Elinor had never heard of, was doing the same thing with Shaw. Her sense of humor must have appealed to Shaw, and he must have known that she was in love with him. Almost certainly she was the first "older woman" in his life. And she was "safe": a Victorian spinster who lived far away, made no demands, and was entirely devoted to him—on paper! Toward the end of this paper romance she says: ". . . the quintessence of your living has come out into your face. It is the face of an outlaw." Shaw probably did not mind this remark at all.

Why Elinor continued to write to Shaw is not difficult to understand. She was lonely; she had nothing to do. She indulged herself by writing novels. Then she met a man who encouraged her to write, who read her stories and gave her his to read in return, and who seemed to want to go on writing to her. That his letters were lively and interesting cannot be doubted. She could argue with him, try to change his views, encourage him, tell him all about herself—and he responded to all of this. Although, by her own admission, she learned nothing from him and the association ended rather sadly for her, the years 1882–84, at the height of their correspondence, were probably the best years of her life. His friendship meant a great deal to her, so much, in fact, that she seems to have been pleasantly horrified when he suggested that their letters would one day be made public: "The picture you drew in your last of the complications that may arise from these our very innocent epistles was dramatic and appalling. Almost thou persuadest me to write to thee no more." Was Shaw teasing her? They *are* very innocent epistles.

When Elinor met Shaw, he had already acquired the habit of writing five pages a day, and she had just written her first novel. She was neither an established nor a successful novelist: she just happened to have written a novel and paid to have it published. Shaw had written little more than *My Dear Dorothea*, a curious piece of satirical writing that took the form of a long letter of advice to a girl of five, and an abortive "passion play" in blank verse.

Why *did* Shaw continue to write to Elinor? What could he possibly have derived from the association? Why did he keep her letters? The personality that emerges from the letters is an interesting one, but intellectually there is nothing that could have attracted him. The first letters are formal, without any indication that either party intended entering into a regular correspondence. Yet the subsequent flood of letters—thirty-two in 1881, forty-four in 1882, forty in 1883, twenty-nine in 1884—reveals a marked change in tone and subject matter. Elinor discusses literary matters, her novels and his, but she includes a great deal of personal and family history. Shaw responded in a like manner, or so one may presume from her comments.

Elinor's first letter to Shaw (21 July 1878) expresses her gratitude to him for having given her his views on her work. As indicated, Shaw had told his mother that he would "look over" her work, and from her

comments it is clear that Shaw did not attempt to spare her feelings:
"You have made me see its faults too clearly to allow me even to dream
the work can, or ought to succeed." Shaw had evidently called her
heroine a "preposterous creation" and used phrases such as "destitute
of simplicity," "not true to nature," and so on. About a month later she
sent him a short story of hers, "Bargie," assuring him that the plot had
been drawn from fact. He replied promptly, again giving her a frank
opinion, and she replies: "How you manage to pick my work to pieces
from end to end, and yet never hurt me (and I am easily hurt) I
cannot conceive. . . . I wont subscribe to your stricture on woman's
reasonableness. It is too sweeping. . . . A woman never displays more
inventive faculty than when engaged in this, her special province . . ."
(16 September 1878).

During 1878 Elinor wrote only three letters to Shaw, all of them
friendly but formal and signed "Elinor Huddart." The correspondence might well have ended there, because there are no letters from
her to him in 1879. One can assume that, if there had been, Shaw
would have kept them too, since he meticulously kept all the others,
even dating them in his easily recognizable, neat handwriting when
she had carelessly left out the date.

Then, suddenly in January 1880, there is another letter from Elinor:

> I do not at all resent the spirit of inquiry that prompted your letter. I
> am only sorry that I cannot further satisfy it, and flattered that you
> care in the least into what paths my mind (genius is a quality of which I
> know nothing) has wandered. That the paths have not been profit-
> able, scarcely even pleasant, yet fatally magnetic, is surely enough to
> know.
>
> I am afraid I am unstable. I am afraid I am not worthy to follow, even
> at a distance, the steps of those "who have overcome in literature."

He appears to have told her about his own novel (he had written
Immaturity in 1879) because she asks to read it ("turn about is only fair
play") but adds that her critical faculties are poor ("I cannot pay you
back in kind"). She is candid about her moods ("very much out of
temper with myself . . . self-disgust is not pleasant") and tells him
something about himself ("you are far too independent a writer to
succeed at first . . . you would make not the smallest concession to
public taste"). However, she says something interesting about her own
work: "My novel had all the faults that circulating library readers
usually adore." This letter, like the others, is signed "Elinor Huddart"
and addressed "Dear Mr Shaw."

On 12 April 1880 she again asks to read Shaw's novel ("what is keeping it so long?"), and in response to his urging her to write a few pages every day, she says, "I have not so much self-control as you." In this letter she also admits that she is "close to forty" but adds that literary ability cannot be judged by "manner and appearance" and that "if a woman argued from a like impression, you would have been the first to laugh at her."

On 4 January 1881 she asks again about the manuscript of *Immaturity* ("I have already a profound respect for it called forth by the fact of its having so often bearded publishers in their dens") and refers to it as a "travelled and valiant manuscript." Once again, one can assume that it was Shaw himself who reopened the correspondence after a break of about eight months: he had obviously told her about his manuscript. She tells him that she cannot write according to "prescribed rules" and that her "leisure invites" him to send her the "other tale" that she is likewise keen to read. This "other tale" must have been *The Irrational Knot,* which Shaw was working on in 1880. Shaw must have repeated what he says to "Dear Dorothea" about being selfish when necessary, because Elinor says:

> I am glad I am not entirely selfish. I would rather miss "completeness" than become so. Unselfishness is the quality above all others I admire most. All the noblest acts of humanity have it for foundation. One can love greatly, yet not well without it. . . .
> George Eliot is dead, but I am not the prophet on whom her cloak has fallen . . . your intellect is akin to hers.

She tells Shaw that he is "almost as sharp as a woman" and speaks about religion as a "purifying and ennobling influence . . . so there again we are at variance."

About Shaw himself, she says (8 January 1881): "Most of your opinions I totally disagree with. There is much in you I do not know—much I cannot sympathise with, yet never anything I can despise. . . . You need encouragement . . . not that I imagine you very much care what feelings, antagonistic or otherwise, you excite." She signs this letter: "Exit Miss Aitch."

The Irrational Knot, in manuscript, duly arrived, and on 15 January 1881 she let Shaw know what she thought of it:

> I like your sketch. I think its defect is the one you are conscious of. Namely the way in which it ends, the spoilt interest. Readers are not fond of being laughed at any more than are authors, for they are both

human, and though beyond doubt the latter are all geniuses, yet genius albeit divine tends only to make the human more intensely human (how aesthetic I get!). Remember your business is to win them. You are too arrogant. There is a certain coldness in your manner of narrating which is easy to feel but difficult to define. It affects one at times like a silent sneer.

More than a year later (6 September 1882) she was still berating him for the unattractiveness of his leading characters in *The Irrational Knot.* Conolly was a monster of "super-human selfishness"—a finding to which Shaw would object. She replies: "I love to make you sneer. Then it is that the latent savageness of your nature betrays itself: the strain of barbarism that lurks in you. . . . Your characters as a whole are very true to nature—too true . . . they talk too much . . . what an abominable set they are."

She would repeat her concern that Shaw's fiction lacked warmth in a letter (10 March 1881), again expressing her feeling that *Immaturity* was full of good things—more of them, is the implication, than *The Irrational Knot:* "Immaturity is a work to be proud of. There is enough thought in it for a dozen novels and not enough emotion in it for half a one." About the characters in it she says, "how they talk!" and "I hear you talking when I am meant to hear Scott, or Mrs Scott, or Smith . . . I dont like any of your women . . . you are a satirist . . . the love that you depict is chilling."

The relationship had reached the point that Shaw sends her a photograph of himself and tells her about a bedridden boy who has written a novel and asked him to read it: "By all means read it, and be gentle to it. How angry that last injunction will make you! 'At the expense of truth,' you will exclaim, 'never!'—and then you will calm down and smile bitterly, remembering that I am only a woman" (22 January 1881).

Having discovered the efficiencies of Pitman shorthand, Shaw suggests it to Miss Huddart, but she has no need for economies of time:

> I must confess to you my shortcomings and then you will see how pitifully I contradict the promise you are pleased to see in me. I have not even begun to learn short-hand. I have not sufficient energy, nor time, nor anything that is of any real solid force, at my disposal to enable me to attempt it. After all, what particular use would it be to me? Except as an exercise to the brain, and as a discipline to the imagination, I fail to see how it would benefit me. (5 February 1881)

The phrase, "the promise you are pleased to see in me," indicates that part of the reason for Shaw's keeping up the correspondence was that he believed she had promise as a writer. Could he really have seen her as a second George Eliot? Or was it that he believed so absolutely in hard work, in self-discipline as agents of art? "My mind," she responds on 5 March 1881, "is not cast in a logical mould."

Now and then we hear Shaw's authentic voice, as she quotes him directly about her own fiction. "You *can* scold," she writes on 22 March 1881. And three days later,

> Oh! Why has not my MS a "fibre in it that lifts it above criticism?" This sentence is from the heart, not the brain, for I know, alas! very well why it has not. No. It gives me no consolation to learn the adverse criticism that Charlotte [Bronte] met with, for her book was out and being read by half the world when it encountered . . . the swine who would have trampled . . . its genius underfoot.

Although Shaw and Miss Huddart had very little in common, both shared an interest in Shaw's wayward, dipsomaniac friend (and sparring partner) Pakenham Beatty. She had friends at 9 Philbeach Gardens, she wrote to Shaw (19 May 1881), whose

> peace has been much disturbed by Mr and Mrs Beatty. They are commonly suspected to be insane, Mr Beatty having thrown one of his servants, a boy, downstairs and broken his arm and Mrs Beatty being at times in terror of her life and limbs from her husband's violent behaviour. . . . You had better be on your guard when you visit this poet. His father is in a lunatic asylum. His servants are afraid to stay with him (Pakenham Beatty's, I mean) for so more than one of them have informed the servants at No. 9.

There is nothing in "Aitch's" letters about Shaw's fourth novel, which boxing inspired, *Cashel Byron's Profession,* but she was caustic about Shaw's third novel, *Love among the Artists,* and one wonders why he interrupted his efforts to sell his manuscript novels by lending them to her for weeks and even months at a time. In fairness to Shaw, Elinor Huddart's comments do not take into account that Shaw's seemingly conventional "love triangles" have as their purpose not a romantic happy ending—or melodramatic yet equally romantic unhappy ending—but a statement about characters in novels who learn independence and self-respect and who do not conform to conventional notions about people.

She has some queries (2 October 1882) about *Love among the Artists:*

> Why didn't you make Mary marry [Owen] Jack? One's sense of fitness
> demands all through the book, loudly demands that she should. After
> she had married Hoskyn, a nonentity, I still lived in hopes that he was
> to die shortly and make way for the unique and always entertaining
> Mr Jack. But no, he disappears into the night, misunderstood by the
> rabble, and mightily true to himself, to the last.

Elinor's reactions are typical of her own "solutions" in her novels. In
My Heart and I the two "obstacles" to the heroine's union with her
"hero" both die to allow the lovers to "wander home through the
twilight land." If she rejected Shaw's character Jack ("mightily true to
himself"), would she, one wonders, have understood, about *Candida,*
why Marchbanks "flies out into the night" with a "secret in his heart"?
Hardly. It is possible that Elinor's reaction was one of the many that
would strengthen Shaw's conviction that realism should replace sentimentality in fiction. "Do you remember," she had written to Shaw (19
January 1882), "taking me severely to task not many years ago, for
always writing about love[?] Try and construct a tale without that
sickening sentiment or at any rate keep it well in the background, was
your constant cry. And now how about the title of your last?"

It almost seems as though Elinor had something to do, then, with
the unsentimental title as well as the content of Shaw's last completed
novel, *An Unsocial Socialist,* in which the rationalist Socialist of the title,
Sidney Trefusis, is wickedly cynical about love and other human weak-
nesses, yet succumbs himself, for reasons which he unpersuasively
rationalizes. She found "nothing to laugh at in it," so she explained on
10 August 1883, and a week later after—reluctantly, she claimed—
finishing it, she added, "I have read the Socialist. It is dull. Ditchwater
is bright in comparison." His polemic about equality failed to move
her:

> Rich and poor are "races" that are built into man, as race-horses and
> cart-horses are built in. For thousands of years this difference of
> fibre and form has been growing, in man as in beast. It cannot be
> checked now. The work that suits the cart-horse would kill the race-
> horse. The socialist wants to level up, not down, he says. He wants, in
> short, to make the population aristocrats in form and feeling. Well, it
> will, when everything is ready to begin which it isn't yet, take some
> hundred years so to *level up* to the race-horse. My sympathies are a
> good deal with the "cursed aristocrat," as the French communists had
> it. My grandfather was one, a French one. He could not help his

superiority—a superiority which made him free of the guilt of idleness and saved his "position." The lower class . . . are the strength of the earth, but not its salt.

The letters from Shaw became fewer, but they did not cease altogether. Still, we find Miss Huddart writing (24 March 1884),

I think you might write me a line, if you are not dead, or if your influenza has not developed dangerous symptoms. . . . The Unsocial Socialist's [concluding] letter is a masterpiece of cool egotism and if the woman whose heart it cuts were a woman worthy of such refined, ultra-refined cruelty, one might feel for her to the right extent.

Later (9 July 1884) she comments on *An Unsocial Socialist:* "Trefusis, as I read him, is rather a mild type of male flirt, his wife is a woman without pride, and the rest are schoolgirls."

From the Kent countryside she talks again (11 July 1884) about settling in the suburbs of London, even about Shaw's meeting her sisters. Trefusis, she says, wants to "bear the burden of all the oppressed" but deserts a woman who "has the misfortune to love him." She adds that even socialism has its "reiterated phrases, its pet adjectives, its overused words, its pig-headed disciples and its false prophets."

The letters continue, Shaw confiding even more about his private life than he might have had Elinor lived in London. He mentions women friends, and "Aitch" asks him when he is going to marry Eleanor Marx. He talks about his street-corner speechmaking and his participation in debates. His "vocation," she tells him on 17 August 1886, is in his voice: "Speechifying is all in your line. Eloquence is probably your major talent."

When his most important speech turns into *The Quintessence of Ibsenism,* she uses it late in 1891 to revive a correspondence apparently moribund for six years. Finally in from the country, she writes from Earl's Court Square (16 November 1891), having discovered his new book, "You are yet alive, I fancy! . . . My hair is snow-white now, and my gait is tottering."

Rather than describe himself, Shaw sends a new photograph, and three days later has a reply: "Thanks for the photograph . . . the quintessence of your living has come out into your face. It is the face of an outlaw. . . . I dislike Ibsen . . . he repels me . . . he may be a pioneer but I'm damned if he is an artist." On 29 November she discusses Ibsen again ("Brand is a tragic Sidney Trefusis"), and on 6 December she mentions a new edition of her *Modern Milkmaid,* slyly suggesting that she dedicate it to him since "it is a work you would absolutely disapprove, I think."

Four months later she sends him a copy of her novel and a photograph of herself, to which Shaw must have responded rather irritably because on 26 May 1892 she writes, "I will trouble you no more. I *can't* swim 'into your ken.' Farewell."

Her old pen-pal is gaining notice now, producing *Widowers' Houses*, his first play, and she cannot relinquish her faint claim, writing again on 31 December 1892:

> You do not enclose a prospectus of the Independent Theatre. I am sorry the performance of your play is over. I wanted much to see it. . . . I was able to gather (from the Illustrated London News) that your play ran upon the same lines, the same sordid emotions, the same low-type of character as have all your novels. Nevertheless these uninteresting ignoble characters as depicted in your books are splendidly drawn, drawn without one false line or smudge. The press appears to be of this mind as regards the people in your play.

Elinor's last three letters to Shaw are dated 20 June, 5 July, and 8 July, and the year must have been 1894 because she refers to tickets for his next play and to her having been to one of the performances. (*Arms and the Man* was the second of Shaw's plays to be performed.)

Elinor's last letters are rather pathetic. She asks (20 June 1894) for tickets for friends and discusses *Arms and the Man:*

> Brilliant, clever, faultless in a way, but lacking, always lacking . . . that touch that means genius. . . . Intellect of the finest order, humour, insight, energy, originality, self-assertiveness—all are yours. Go, mon ami, sell all these and buy the one thing needful without which you will never be truly great . . . never immortal. . . . To win the world you must love with its love, hate with its hate, die, if need be, for its truth. But you find no truth in it.

Some days later she sends a card, asking for more tickets. Then (5 July 1894), another card:

> What is the matter? Have I offended you? oh great and mighty one! I hope not . . . was I wrong to ask for those free tickets? I hate my friends, they are always wrong and therefore I, whenever I do their bidding, I also am in the wrong. I am not even as nice as I was in the old days. I am more lazy, more untruthful, more selfish. Go up higher still, oh man of iron mind, but in the meantime, forgive me.

A last card three days later:

> "I am not mad, most noble Festus." The reason why I "cherished misgivings" is simple, even classical. You made no answer to my appeal either by writing or sending tickets. Hence these tears. ELH

The line from *Twelfth Night* is "I am not mad, Sir Topas" (Feste is disguised as the curate Sir Topas in this scene).

Shaw may have said no more than that she must be mad to think that he was a fountain of ticket largesse. But the apparent brusqueness in answer to her appeal was evidence enough that Shaw had again, and now finally, tired of the correspondence. He had begun it as a nonentity, still new in London. He was now known to a wide public. Elinor Huddart had long faded out of his life, but her surviving letters mirror the aspiring young Shaw on his way to becoming "G.B.S." And possibly she was even more than that. On 20 September 1883 she had written to him from Kent. The country, she says, "is not peaceful, it is only dull: it is not quiet, it is only slow." Mirroring the cadences of that line is the striking litany by Don Juan, responding to the Devil in the Dream Interlude of *Man and Superman:*

> Your friends are all the dullest dogs I know. They are not beautiful; they are only decorated. . . . They are not artistic; they are only lascivious. . . . They are not loyal, they are only servile; not dutiful, only sheepish; not public-spirited, only patriotic; not courageous, only quarrelsome.

Elinor Huddart's rhetorical device is exactly that of one of the great speeches in Shavian drama. Was she indirectly responsible? Shaw's long memory may have retrieved it from the correspondence already forgotten. It would be good to think that she made a literary impact after all.

Robert G. Everding

SHAW AND THE PALACES OF VARIETY

In Edwardian England the variety palace and the one-act play burst into commercial prominence, with one result being that established playwrights turned a large portion of their creative energies to the playlet. Eighteen short plays were written by Barrie, twelve by Sutro, four by Galsworthy, and four by Barker (in addition to his translations of *Anatol*). Even Pinero, who had not written a short play since 1880, completed six one-act pieces, including *Mr. Livermore's Dream,* which premiered as a vaudeville turn at the London Coliseum. Shaw also responded to the siren call of this new economic opportunity, for between 1909 and 1918 he completed a dozen one-act plays and only four full-length works. To understand Shaw's newfound enthusiasm for the playlet and the place of these works in his canon, it is necessary to examine first the theatrical conditions that created a commercial demand; then to explore the artistic, financial, and sociopolitical considerations that drew Shaw to the shorter dramatic form; and, finally, to assess Shaw's achievement in this area.

At the turn of the century, the palace of variety challenged and supplanted the music hall as the most popular form of Edwardian entertainment. The halls were still primarily the workingman's neighborhood retreat and offered a raucous evening of ribald jokes, satirical songs, and sing-along choruses. This Rabelaisian atmosphere was intimate, mingling liquor and laughter to create a bonhomie which was captured in the paintings of Walter Sickert and the poems of Arthur Symons. In the following decade, however, big business capitalized on the halls' commercial potential by establishing large, elegant facilities that presented two, three, and even four daily programs of international talent and innovative spectacle. A typical bill might include performing animals, a French singer, living pictures, Japanese acrobats, a Tyrolean giantess, an American lassoist, Spanish dancers, and a bioscope of the Derby. Such varied programs were immensely popular and generated large profits. In 1909, for example, Oswald Stoll, chairman of the Coliseum Syndicate, reported that he oversaw a £200,000,000 organization that paid annual salaries of £497,000 and that employed nightly more than 3,000 artists.[1] Shareholders of the Coliseum, Palace, and Empire theaters enjoyed that year a tax-free return on investment of twenty percent. As one of the characters in *Press Cuttings* accurately assesses, "Theres no Music Halls nowadays: theyre Variety Theatres."[2]

The 1908 appearance of Maud Allan demonstrates the drawing power of a single turn. This Canadian dancer created a sensation with her rendition of "The Vision of Salome," which *The Times* critic graphically described as "a dance of many passions, the sheer intoxication of movement to music, allurement, exhaltation, rage, fear, despair, even exhaustion."[3] The subsequent debate whether this barefooted, barelegged dancing was a new art form, mere sensationalism, or outright immorality produced the predictable result that "for a year all London, high and low, swarmed to the Palace."[4] Such notoriety captured the Edwardian imagination and appealed to a broad cross section of the population that voiced its approval by filling nightly the city's various variety palaces.

"This change in the composition of the music-hall audience," noted George Rowell, "called for corresponding changes in the bill of fare, amongst which the popularity in the Edwardian era of the sketch and short play was particularly striking."[5] The Theatre Bill of 1843 guaranteed theaters the exclusive production rights for plays. When music halls introduced short sketches (a term invented to circumvent the 1843 legislation) into their programs, a Select Committee of the House of Commons was formed (1892) and recommended that sketches be allowed without license if the piece did not exceed a forty-minute length, had fewer than seven performers, contained a plot unrelated to events in another sketch offered that evening, and allowed at least thirty minutes between sketches. The theater and music-hall managers agreed to abide voluntarily by these rules, but soon competitive vaudeville owners tested the concordat's limits. By 1903 the encroachment into theatrical fare became such an economic threat that the Theatrical Managers' Association initiated a series of court actions against London's leading variety houses. The Palace was fined £50 for staging a truncated version of the opera *La Toledad;* the Oxford paid a £120 fine for presenting *Belle of the Orient,* which contained three scenes and ten speaking roles.

These prosecutions led to a more restrictive agreement (1906) that limited an evening's offering to two sketches—one running no longer than thirty minutes and containing six or fewer speaking parts, and another restricted to one scene, four speaking roles, and fifteen minutes. The short play grew in popularity, however, and within months managers were again risking legal action to protect lucrative ticket revenues. In fact, the variety stage became bolder in its offerings, moving beyond the traditional music-hall staples of lightheaded farces and musical pastiches to the presentation of dramatic recitals and playlets. By mid-1909 not only did the thirty-minute play head many variety bills, but the nature of the material expanded to include serious work like the feminist melodrama *A Woman's Revolt* and the realistic piece *Magusse*. Moreover, variety managers produced several short works that had recently been successful at West End theaters. The London Hippodrome presented Fannie Ward in *The Flag Station* during the same season in which she appeared in it at the Aldwych Theatre, and the Empire staged *Feed the Brute* with its original cast only days after the play completed a run of eighty-three performances at the Royalty Theatre.

The defection of theatrical performers to the vaudeville stage enhanced, if not stimulated, the growing stature of the short play in the variety theater. By 1908 established actors like Rutland Barrington, Mrs. Lewis Waller, Fanny Brough, Lewis Calvert, Arthur Roberts, and Yorke Stephens appeared on music-hall stages as well as in commercial theaters. In December this migration received an added impetus when the Palace announced that actor-manager Seymour Hicks and his wife, Ellaline Terriss, would make their debut in the aeromusical *The Fly-By-Night*. Within months music-hall appearances were recorded by Herbert Sleath, Ellis Jeffreys, Allan Aynesworth, Herbert Waring, and Charles Hawtrey. Theater managers resumed prosecutions, but found little legal or legislative support for what the public embraced enthusiastically. Indeed, the 1909 Select Committee on Stage Plays (Censorship and Theatre Licensing) concluded in November that music halls should be granted a theater license. This recommendation (parliamentary action had yet to be taken) removed what few professional prejudices remained against either the halls or the short play and generated a deluge of first appearances as variety owners scrambled to sign the theater's leading luminaries. Henry Ainley, Suzanne Sheldon, and Winifred Emery were featured at the Hippodrome; Cyril Maude at the Coliseum; Lewis Waller at the Tivoli; Arthur Bourchier and Violet Vanbrugh at the Palace; and Cyril Keightly at the Empire. The Coliseum announced also that

Sarah Bernhardt had agreed at last to appear on the English variety stage and would receive the astounding fee of £1,000 a week for her performing appearances in addition to expenses and her company's salaries. It was soon reported that "almost every actor and actress of any eminence had at some time or another appeared on the music hall stage."[6]

By 1909, therefore, few would dispute the contention that "in the last ten years the advance of the music hall compared with the theatre had been 100 per cent, to 10 per cent."[7] London's variety palaces had earned a reputation for respectable, quality entertainment and consequently were attracting large audiences from all levels of society. Theatrical luminaries (many of whom had appeared in productions of Shaw's plays) were now engaged by vaudeville managers who possessed the funds to secure suitable dramatic vehicles and to mount attractive productions. The short play was a major feature and found an audience willing to experiment with a wide range of material and themes. The center of theatrical activity was opening out, a transformation that presented opportunities for Shaw at precisely the moment when he was ripe for the exploration of new possibilities.

In 1907 Shaw sensed an end to the demand for the kind of drama that he had written for the Court Theatre. He informed Barker that "the Shaw boom, in its novelty phase, cannot last longer"[8] and that "it looks as if my plays will be homeless in London in 18 months time!"[9] In 1908 London witnessed only the unsuccessful production of *Getting Married* at the Haymarket Theatre and a brief Shaw season consisting of revivals of *Man and Superman* and *Arms and the Man* at the Coronet Theatre. Nor was 1909 kind, for Shaw's January prognostication that "my plays are no longer wanted for immediate use in London"[10] was fulfilled when a revival of *You Never Can Tell* was poorly received in Kensington and the Afternoon Theatre's staging of *The Admirable Bashville* ran for only four performances. Moreover, Shaw's two new plays, *The Shewing-up of Blanco Posnet* and *Press Cuttings*, were deemed offensive and banned by the Lord Chamberlain. In August *The Times* called attention to the unusual fact that of the productions announced for the 1909–10 season, "there is no play by Mr. Shaw on the list."[11]

Shaw had not, of course, abandoned playwriting; rather, he was searching for new directions that would rekindle public interest in his work. Unfortunately, his latest experiment, the disquisitory play, met with considerable critical and popular opposition. *Getting Married* marked a stylistic departure from Shaw's recent work by extending the discussion throughout the play and thereby making debate the essence of the action. The new form was exceptionally long, lacked a conventional plot, and was written in a single act which maintained the unities of time and place. The reaction, as Allan Wade recalls, was that "brilliantly amusing as the conversations proved to be and excellently played . . . London audiences, and perhaps especially the Haymarket audience, accustomed to more conventional comedy, were not enticed to the theatre in very large numbers."[12] Although fortified by broad farcical elements and a plethora of topical references, *Misalliance* suffered a similar fate, running for only sixteen performances and engendering critical disapproval. A disappointing Berlin production, where "unmistakable signs of disapproval followed the fall of the curtain,"[13] compounded the London failure. Arthur Walkley led the attack on the discussion drama with his negative reviews and a feature article condemning the abrogation of the Aristotelian laws of the drama in favor of a format that lacked structural unity and merely distributed "ideas pell-mell among a number of interlocutors."[14] In a subsequent speech on the drama's future, Walkley tolled the death knell for the "rambling conversation on the model of those recent plays of Mr. Shaw" and proclaimed that this was "a model of what to avoid."[15] Shaw retorted with a well-argued defense on 23 June in a letter published in *The Times*, but simultaneously abandoned the disquisitory play in its long one-act form.

These artistic setbacks corresponded with the music halls' emerging need for the established playwright, for, as W. R. Titterton recorded, "it was plain that if the sketch was to remain on the variety stage, expensive dramatists would have to be employed" because " 'cultured' audiences of the West End Halls demanded 'cultured' plays by notorious dramatists as a standing feature of their entertainment."[16] In late 1909 the halls could boast scripts only by writers such as R. C. Carton, William Locke, Malcolm Watson, and George Paston (Emily Morse Symonds). In December 1909, however, the professional playwright's relationship to the halls received added impetus when the Palace announced a new playlet by Henry Arthur Jones. *The Knife* ran for 150 performances and established the variety stage as the commercial home of the short play. Rival managers immediately secured scripts from Gilbert, Sutro, Barrie, Grundy, and other established writers. The degree of this new demand for quality scripts is captured humorously in *Press Cuttings*, when the charwoman's daughter-turned-variety-actress showed little compunction about asking England's Poet Laureate to "write me a sketch, dear."[17]

An improving theatrical market for the short script further encouraged dramatists to turn to the thirty-minute play. While evenings of one-act plays had historically been shunned by patrons and therefore were anathema to professionals, the acceptance of such fare was growing. Commercial ventures like the "triple bill" experiments at the Court (1905) and the Savoy (1906) theaters, the Irish Players' visit (1907), the appearance of Max Maurey's Parisian company in *Le Grand Guignol* (1908), and Lena Ashwell's special matinees at the Kingsway Theatre (1908) contributed to a burgeoning public enthusiasm for bills composed solely of one-act plays. The 1909 plans of two repertory schemes reflect this changed attitude within the legitimate theater. At the Duke of York's Theatre, Charles Frohman proposed a format in which the short play was a prominent feature. He noted that "authors tell me that the one-act play is among the most fascinating forms of writing, and that only the present condition of production prevents their giving of their best to it. I offer them the conditions they want and ask them for the plays. They will be cast and produced as efficiently as the longer plays and no one will be allowed to enter the auditorium during their progress."[18] At the Haymarket Theatre, Henry Trench planned a similar venture and announced that the initial offering of *King Lear* would be followed by a triple bill of plays by Max Beerbohm, Chester Fernald, and Gilbert Cannan, and that the third evening would include a new one-act play by St. John Hankin. What was once the province of the private drama society or a mere makeweight for the commercial melodrama was gradually being recognized as a valuable commodity in its own right.

The playlet offered Shaw an attractive, somewhat less arduous avenue with which to capture the attention of a public that had hitherto ignored him. Previously he had written short pieces to serve the conventional purposes of the curtain raiser (*How He Lied to Her Husband*), the charity benefit (*Passion, Poison, and Petrifaction*), and the *pièce d'occasion* (*The Interlude at the Playhouse*). Now, however, the one-act play was moving into vogue both at the playhouse and at the variety palace, offering Shaw the opportunity to reach not only his former "congregation" from the Court Theatre but also a new public accustomed to music-hall fare. Indeed, the same playlet written for a triple bill at a West End theater might subsequently find popularity on a variety bill. *Press Cuttings*, for example, which was written for the Afternoon Theatre and "which was half-promised for one of the regular evening bills" but was found to be "too long for the honor,"[19] could with minor alterations have been made suitable for the variety stage. Its broad action, topical discussions, and references to the vaudeville world suggest arguably that in its creation some thought might have been given to both a theater and a music-hall audience.

Monetary considerations also prompted Shaw's interest in the palaces of variety. Following the debacle of the Savoy season, Shaw expressed to Barker on 1 July 1908 his disenchantment with the lack of financial rewards from his years with the Vedrenne-Barker management by confessing that he was "fed up with the unremunerative experimental matinee drama."[20] The pecuniary allure of the variety stage must have played a part in this comment because during the previous week Shaw had learned at a luncheon given for Yvette Guilbert that for her current Palace appearance "she is no doubt getting an enormous salary—much more than she can possibly spend."[21] On 4 July Shaw urged Lillah McCarthy to accept an engagement at the Empire and confided that "I have serious thoughts myself of taking to the half-hour play."[22] Within a year Shaw was writing short plays and even distributed to his colleagues in the Dramatists' Club a letter urging support for the music halls' campaign to secure dramatic licensing because "much of our most lucrative work in the future will be done in the variety theatres."[23]

The success of Barrie's *The Twelve-Pound Look* demonstrates the financial rewards awaiting a popular one-act play in a commercial climate that allowed plays by established dramatists to be produced at both theaters and variety palaces. The piece premiered at the Duke of York's Theatre in 1910 as part of a triple bill and was subsequently performed before King George and Queen Mary at the Prime Minister's residence. A revival at the Little Theatre in late 1911 was so successful that the play appeared simultaneously for five weeks at the London Hippodrome and several months later for a four-week run at the Coliseum. In 1913 the playlet served as an afterpiece for the West End production of Houghton's *The Younger Generation* and appeared as a variety turn at the Palladium before embarking on a 1914 provincial tour on a circuit that stretched from Edinburgh to Bournemouth. Playwrights could therefore expect sizable royalties from the multiple opportunities suddenly available at theaters and variety palaces throughout Britain.

Shaw was by no means destitute when he became interested in the variety stage. His work was popular in North America: the previous year Ellen Terry had starred in *Captain Brassbound's Conversion* in New York City; in Toronto four different companies presented four different Shavian plays. Nor did the failures of *Getting Married* and *Misalliance* present a serious economic threat, for Shaw enjoyed continuing royalties from worldwide sources, including English tours of *John Bull's Other Island* and *You Never Can Tell* and long Berlin runs of *Mrs Warren's Profession* and *The Doctor's Dilemma*. Still, the dearth of London productions and the critics' denunciations of Shaw's plays must have concerned the dramatist because of the potential negative effect not only on future London stagings but also on continued foreign royalties.

Shaw must also have been attracted to the short play by the prospect of permeating the most popular form of Edwardian entertainment with his social and political viewpoints. While a contemporary journalist argued that "the variety stage is not a place on which any sane dramatist would attempt the serious discussion of moral problems or ideas,"[24] Shaw had long ago discovered how to use laughter to support his didactic purposes by embedding his serious intentions within a comic experience. Not that he could employ the discussion as he had in *Getting Married* or even in *Major Barbara*—he knew that "if you turned a Tivoli or London Pavilion audience into the Queen's Hall and inflicted Beethoven's Ninth Symphony on them, they would remember the experience with horror to the end of their lives."[25] Ideas and discussion could be introduced into the thirty-minute play, but the dramatic structure needed to meet the technical limitations of the sketch and to satisfy the popular taste of the music-hall patron. These demands required an adjustment to, not an alteration of, Shaw's artistic strategy, for his style already contained elements suitable to the vaudeville stage. Indeed, he had earlier informed Vedrenne that "I have given you a series of first-rate music hall entertainments, thinly disguised as plays, but really offering the public a unique string of turns by comics and serio-comics of every popular type . . . that is the jam that has carried the propaganda pill down."[26]

An increased topicality constituted one of the major elements in this adjustment. A commentary on the daily lives of the people had from the halls' inception been an indispensable ingredient of the vaudeville experience, an ingredient that allowed the spectator to identify himself or herself readily with the action and to dispel through laughter (albeit momentarily) concern over the day's newspaper headlines. Shaw's 1909–14 scripts show a marked increase in the use of timely issues, people, places, and events. *The Fascinating Foundling* contains references to the hunger strikes at Holloway prison, Lloyd George's budget policies, recent divorce legislation, London's leading restaurants, and the latest slang expression. *The Music-Cure* uses for its background the new rage for ragtime music and the current government scandal involving insider-trading of Marconi shares. The play also refers to contemporary details like trained animal acts on the variety stage, a new trick aeronautical maneuver, and the latest medical penchant for pills. Subtitled "A Topical Sketch Compiled from the Editorial and Correspondence Columns of the Daily Papers during the Woman's War in 1909," *Press Cuttings* takes for its main subjects the recent Suffragists' disturbances and the mounting concern over a German invasion; it contains two characters whose names are an amalgam of actual political and military figures. The one-act play employs a plethora of contemporary items ranging from Dreadnoughts to the supertax to *The Times* Book Club. This extensive use of topical material was indirectly noted in the opening-night review of *Androcles and the Lion*, in which the critic expressed surprise that the play "has nothing topical in it" except a single line that "caught the applause of the suffragettes in the house."[27]

While topicality enhanced a play's entertainment value, contemporary references also served Shaw's didactic ends. The social and intellectual level to which the playlets were directed was certainly different from that of the audience at the Court Theatre, and Shaw needed to introduce his sociopolitical viewpoints in a less direct manner. The laughter that accompanied a comment about a specific London neighborhood or a particular legislative bill placed the spectator in a receptive mood and encouraged the acceptance of Shavian opinions, which were embedded in the dialogue rather than comprising the action. Therefore, while the majority of the playlets were written with the taste of the music-hall patron in mind, these short works still convey central Shavian views, many of which had been expressed more directly in earlier plays. *The Fascinating Foundling*, for example, exposes the artificiality of class distinctions and advocates an unromantic approach to courtship. *The Music-Cure* criticizes current medical practices and satirizes the conventional marital relationship. *Press Cuttings* ridicules anti-Suffragist attitudes and attacks the military for its practice of flogging and for the proposed deprivation of the individual soldier's rights under a plan for compulsory service. These short plays were not mere divertissements but part of Shaw's ongoing campaign to address himself to sociopolitical issues and to influence public opinion.

Despite Shaw's July 1908 enthusiasm for the half-hour play, he admitted in late August that "somehow I have never yet succeeded in achieving a sketch."[28] In 1909, however, he worked on at least five short plays. In March he completed *The Shewing-up of Blanco Posnet*, which was to serve as a curtain-raiser for *The Dryad* at Tree's Afternoon Theatre. While traveling to Algeria and Tunisia, he wrote *Press Cuttings*, began *The Glimpse of Reality* "in an idle moment as a star turn for Mr. Harley Granville-Barker,"[29] and planned a sketch on Mahomet for Forbes-Robertson. In August he wrote *The Fascinating Foundling*.

Shaw's efforts yielded few tangible results. While he indicated in July 1909 that he had received several requests for sketches, by year's end he had not had a single commercial production. Nor was Shaw's work sought in the 1910 rush by variety managers to secure scripts from the theater's leading dramatists. Nevertheless, Shaw continued to write short plays, adding *The Glimpse of Reality* to his store of available scripts and informing Barker that he was contemplating "three good historical sketches for Moss Empires."[30] Still, no music-hall engagements materialized. The reality was that Shaw had requests and wrote sketches but was not produced.

The theatrical events surrounding Shaw's vaudeville debut provide insights into this professional predicament. There was in 1909 and 1910 little West End interest in Shavian scripts. In fact, there was considerable prejudice, especially within the press, against Shaw's plays, a prejudice that kept audiences and managers away and that compelled Shaw to wage verbal warfare over this mistreatment. The general mistrust associated with Shaw's name, coupled with (and partly responsible for) the box-office failures of *Getting Married* and *Misalliance,* must have convinced even the most venturesome managers that Shaw's usefulness had ended. In April 1911, however, *Fanny's First Play* opened at the Little Theatre and was an immediate success that "drew London as no play of Shaw's had done before,"[31] even through the sweltering summer of 1911. This success was due in part to its being produced anonymously, a strategy that not only circumvented the rooted critical prejudice but also provided a marketing appeal that played upon the potential patron's curiosity. However, once inside the theater, as C. B. Purdom noted, the spectator was won over by the play itself, for "here was the first Shaw play to open the eyes of the playgoer, accustomed to everyday West End theatrical fare, to the possibility that the Shavian drama was for him. It had a rapturous reception."[32] In October it was announced that the production would move to the larger Kingsway Theatre. The following month Alfred Butt, the manager of the Palace Theatre of Varieties, revealed that *How He Lied to Her Husband* would become the first Shavian play to appear on a vaudeville bill. Shaw was now enjoying his first major commercial success, an experience that finally made his one-act plays valuable properties for the variety manager.

The selection of *How He Lied to Her Husband* rather than one of the unproduced playlets reflects the caution with which the music hall viewed Shaw, even after the success of *Fanny's First Play*. The 1904 curtain raiser was acceptable, in part, because it not only had a record of earlier popularity but also had just completed a series of revivals. In April 1911 the piece appeared at the Court Theatre on a special matinee program of four one-act plays and at the Gaiety Theatre,

Manchester, on a triple bill headed by a new Galsworthy piece. *How He Lied to Her Husband* drew further attention the following month when it was staged at the Little Theatre as a benefit for Gordon Hospital and subsequently was announced by Arnold Daly for a triple bill planned for June at the Criterion Theatre. Butt had therefore secured a script that had recently received considerable publicity and would be readily recognized by his patrons. It is noteworthy that, while playlets by Barrie or Jones routinely received top billing in the variety houses' advertisements, Shaw's one-act work was given the second place, following the Russian ballerina Staasia Naperkowska.

Shaw's debut on the variety stage was an unqualified success. Titterton recorded that " 'The Palace' is packed to-night. The 'best dressed audience in London' has turned out in force to welcome Bernard Shaw, the best-dressed Socialist, to the Halls."[33] *The Times* called the production "a pure delight" and noted that "delicious it proved to an audience which seemed to want it all over again."[34] The playlet ran for two weeks and was then engaged for an additional month, during which time Shaw refined the work by eliminating references to *Candida*. The production moved on 5 February to the London Coliseum for a week of twice-a-day performances. Butt was clearly impressed by this response because he promised "at some future date another play by Mr. Bernard Shaw, the cast of which is not yet disclosed."[35] This statement must have relieved Shaw, who, prior to the opening, had supplied *The Daily Telegraph* with one of his inimitable self-interviews in which he extolled the virtues of writing for the variety stage, called Butt's invitation "a considerable compliment," and assured the public that he would certainly "continue, then, writing specially for the halls."[36]

The promised contract was not soon forthcoming, however, and by June 1912 Shaw's previous praise of Butt turned, in a letter to Barker, into a reference to Butt as one of the "sordid syndicalists."[37] Nevertheless, Shaw continued to write short plays. He began work on *The Music-Cure* (written for Mrs. Patrick Campbell with the hope for a summer variety engagement at the Palace, but set aside days later when she agreed to appear in a revival of *The Second Mrs. Tanqueray* at the St. James's Theatre) and completed *Overruled* (which joined playlets by Pinero and Barrie on a triple bill at the Duke of York's Theatre). The following year Robert Loraine secured Shaw's permission to bring the first act of *Man and Superman* to a variety palace, but this production never came to fruition. On 13 August 1913 Shaw completed *Great Catherine* with the Palace in mind and three days later exuberantly informed his wife that "I am at present struggling with the temptation to begin another sketch—one which I planned long ago for Forbes Robertson—Mahomet in the slave market. I could do that, too, in a fortnight. These thumbnail historical sketches amuse me, and the proceeds at the variety theatres & picture palaces will help to support your extravagance."[38] Butt rejected *Great Catherine*, and again Shaw abandoned the Mahomet project.

Great Catherine was refused "because the cost of it would be too great,"[39] a reasonable objection given the sketch's demands for a large cast, four period settings, and eighteenth-century costumes ranging from Cossack uniforms to elegant court attire to full royal regalia. One can imagine Butt's reaction when he opened Shaw's script and discovered an initial stage direction describing Patiomkin's bejeweled outfit and the extravagant Louis XIV luxury of an Imperial Winter Palace. Such spectacle was not uncommon in the variety theater. The Hippodrome had built its reputation by means of disaster spectacles like *The Volcano* and *The Avalanche*, while the Coliseum had presented Reinhardt's stagings of *Sumurun* and *The Miracle*. In December 1912 Shaw had visited the Hippodrome and was so impressed by the lavish staging of Barrie's sketch *The Dramatists Get What They Want* that he marveled to Barker that it "must have cost enough to mount six Winter's Tales."[40] Shaw may well have had the opulence of this production in mind when he wrote *Great Catherine*. The Palace, however, was not the Hippodrome or the Coliseum, and Shaw miscalculated Butt's willingness to invest the capital necessary to stage the playlet.

It was not until March 1914 that a second Shaw play appeared on a London variety bill. Again it was the Palace, and again it was a piece that had recently achieved public and critical recognition. *The Music-Cure* was finished on 21 January 1914 in order to provide a curtain raiser for the 100th performance of G. K. Chesterton's *Magic*. Shaw's sketch had seven performances and was well received. In late March this production moved to the Palace, where it failed to generate sufficient interest and was removed after one week.

Following his April 1914 success with *Pygmalion*, the war years were not particularly salubrious for Shaw's theatrical ambitions. His pamphlet *Common Sense About the War* reduced the playwright to *persona non grata* with London audiences, which, in turn, rendered him of little use to managers. Moreover, Shaw's four wartime playlets lacked the unqualified patriotism and anti-German feeling demanded by the public. There were for the music-hall owners two programming choices—"some find it best to act on the principle that the audience comes to be distracted from all thought of war; others draw crowds with military or 'recruiting' songs and scenes."[41] Escapist revues like *Chu-Chin-Chow* or propagandistic playlets like *Der Tage* found immediate acceptance, but there was little room for Shaw's balanced assessments and close scrutinies. It was not until the concluding months of the war that another Shavian sketch appeared on a London variety stage: *Annajanska, the Wild Grand Duchess* (the title was altered to *Annajanska, the Bolshevik Empress* upon publication in 1919) opened on 21 January 1918 at the London Coliseum with Lillah McCarthy in the title role. As Shaw had done with *Fanny's First Play*, he stirred interest in the production by arousing curiosity about the author's identity. He suggested that the work was a translation "from the Russian of Gregory Piessipoff" and was "of topical interest, dealing as it does with a certain development of the Russian revolution."[42] The critics were neither confused by the authorship nor impressed by the political revelations, but the play was generally well received and ran for three weeks.

Postwar London brought renewed interest in Shaw's dramatic works, due primarily to the Everyman Theatre. Between 1920 and 1924 the Everyman revived many of his plays, including 1921 stagings of *The Dark Lady of the Sonnets* and *The Shewing-up of Blanco Posnet*, both of which appeared later at London's music halls. *The Dark Lady of the Sonnets* was staged in September 1923 to serve as a curtain raiser for the revival of *Magic* when it was transferred from the Everyman to the Kingsway Theatre. Two weeks after this production closed, the cast moved to the Coliseum for a two-week engagement of the Shaw playlet. Preceded by the music of Rossini and followed by that of Wagner, the sketch achieved "the unusual spectacle of typical Shavian humour appealing to a large general audience" to the extent that it "cheered each prophecy lustily, as though complimenting the author on his apparent perspicacity."[43] *The Shewing-up of Blanco Posnet*, starring Philip Yale Drew, played for a single week at the Alhambra in December 1923 (Maud Allan danced on the same bill) and for two weeks, featuring Sir Martin Harvey, at the Coliseum in October 1926.

It is difficult to conclude that these later vaudeville productions brought Shaw much delight. In postwar England, both the number and the stature of the music halls were greatly diminished. In fact, by 1923 the Tivoli and the Pavilion halls had been converted into cinemas, while the Empire, Palace, and Hippodrome had become legitimate theaters. Moreover, Shaw had again focused on the full-length play and had completed works such as *Heartbreak House, Back to Methuselah,* and *Saint Joan.*

Shaw's flirtation with the short play and with the palaces of variety in the decade between 1909 and 1918 was not particularly rewarding for the playwright. Few of his newly created playlets found their way onto the vaudeville stage or generated the expected popular and financial success. Unlike many of his colleagues, Shaw encountered hesitant managers who in general avoided his scripts or who restricted production choices to works that had already proven their commercial viability. Still, while Shaw's output during this time does not stand among his best work, the plays do represent a distinct phase of his career, a period in which he attempted to capitalize on the commercial emergence of the one-act play and to reach the large, socially-diverse audience that attended London's palaces of variety.

Notes

1. "Stage Plays and Music Halls," *The Times*, 15 October 1909, p. 3.

2. Bernard Shaw, *Collected Plays with Their Prefaces* (New York: Dodd, Mead, 1975), 3:858.

3. "Palace Theatre," *The Times*, 10 March 1908, p. 5.

4. H. G. Hibbert, *Fifty Years of a Londoner's Life* (London: Grant Richards, 1916), p. 110.

5. George Rowell, *The Victorian Theatre: A Survey* (Oxford: The Clarendon Press, 1956), p. 145.

6. "Theatrical Managers' Association," *The Times*, 25 October 1911, p. 4.

7. "Variety Artists and the Censorship," *The Times*, 17 September 1909, p. 6.

8. C. B. Purdom, ed., *Bernard Shaw's Letters to Granville Barker* (New York: Theatre Arts Books, 1957), p. 82.

9. Ibid., p. 102.

10. Bernard Shaw, *Collected Letters II, 1898–1910*, ed. Dan H. Laurence (New York: Dodd, Mead, 1972), p. 826.

11. "The Coming Theatrical Season," *The Times*, 28 August 1909, p. 8.

12. Allan Wade, *Memories of the London Theatre, 1900–1914*, ed. Alan Andrews (London: The Society for Theatre Research, 1983), p. 21.

13. "A Shaw Play in Berlin," *The Times*, 11 April 1910, p. 12.

14. "The Theatres: Got and the New Dramaturgy," *The Times*, 21 March 1910, p. 9.

15. "Mr. Walkley on the Drama," *The Times*, 13 June 1910, p. 12.

16. W. R. Titterton, *From Theatre to Music Hall* (London: Stephen Swift and Company, 1912), p. 115.

17. Shaw, *Collected Plays*, 3:858–59.

18. "Mr. Frohman and the Duke of York's Theatre," *The Times*, 22 April 1909, p. 10.

19. "Forthcoming Season," *The Times*, 28 July 1909, p. 8.

20. Purdom, *Bernard Shaw's Letters to Granville Barker*, p. 127.

21. Shaw, *Collected Letters II*, p. 797. In *Fifty Years of a Londoner's Life*, H. G. Hibbert

reports that Guilbert received £300 a week in addition to revenues from social engagements and extra performances.

22. Purdom, *Bernard Shaw's Letters to Granville Barker*, p. 129.

23. Shaw, *Collected Letters II*, pp. 852–53.

24. "The Theatre of Varieties," *The Times*, 24 January 1910, p. 4.

25. Shaw, *Collected Plays*, 3:667.

26. Purdom, *Bernard Shaw's Letters to Granville Barker*, p. 77.

27. "Mr. Shaw's New Play at the St. James's," *The Times*, 2 September 1913, p. 6.

28. Purdom, *Bernard Shaw's Letters to Granville Barker*, p. 136.

29. Shaw, *Collected Plays*, 3:836.

30. Purdom, *Bernard Shaw's Letters to Granville Barker*, p. 176.

31. W. Macqueen Pope, *Carriages at Eleven* (London: Hutchinson & Co., 1947), p. 196.

32. Purdom, *Bernard Shaw's Letters to Granville Barker*, p. 172.

33. Titterton, *From Theatre to Music Hall*, p. 168.

34. "The Variety Theatres," *The Times*, 5 December 1911, p. 7.

35. "The Theatres," *The Times*, 11 December 1911, p. 6.

36. "Plays at Music-Halls: Mr. Shaw's Tribute," *Daily Telegraph*, 5 December 1911, p. 4.

37. Bernard Shaw, *Collected Letters III, 1911–1925*, ed. Dan H. Laurence (New York: Viking, 1985), p. 95.

38. Ibid., p. 200.

39. Ibid., p. 205.

40. Purdom, *Bernard Shaw's Letters to Granville Barker*, p. 186.

41. "Theatre and Hall: The Pleasure-Loving English," *The Times*, 5 February 1915, p. 11.

42. "The Theatres," *The Times*, 21 January 1918, p. 9.

43. "The Dark Lady of the Sonnets," *The Times*, 30 October 1923, p. 10.

"This tribute to the political actuality and ethnographical verisimil-
itude of my play will, I hope, be a warning to you not to disparage my
historical researches in future."[4]

Years later, in his Preface to *The Shewing-up of Blanco Posnet* (1910),
Shaw repeated the allegation that it was his revealing the "unacknowledged fact" that the Serbo-Bulgarian War had implications beyond
two small countries and was "officered by two European Powers of the
first magnitude" that led to its banning in Vienna.

When news of the English press reports reached Vienna, Trebitsch
was dismayed. The Burg had confided its exchanges with the censorship to Trebitsch with the intent of keeping the matter secret and
avoiding embarrassment. Schlenther, formerly the associate of the
pioneering Otto Brahm in establishing naturalism in Berlin, had pur-
sued a more cautious policy since becoming director of the imperial
Burgtheater. And the business with the censor was more complex
than Shaw apparently knew.

The previous month, on 8 January, the secretary of the Burgtheater, Herr Rosenbaum, wrote to Trebitsch in "strict confidential-
ity" inquiring whether *Arms* was available. Trebitsch no doubt answered yes. And on 12 January, Schlenther sent a copy of the play to
the *Hoftheaterzensor,* the official with special jurisdiction over the court
theaters, and requested an *unofficial* opinion of the work. Schlenther
added that Baron Plappart, the court-appointed General Intendant of
the Burg, had expressed a positive view of the comedy. Shortly thereafter, Privy Councillor Dr. Emil Jettel, of the Literary Bureau under
the Ministry of Foreign Affairs, wrote back that from the standpoint
of censorship he had no objections to the play, but because of the
dissension between Bulgaria and Serbia in the play and the "manner
in which the Bulgarians are made ridiculous," he thought that production at the Burg was "inopportune." Moreover, Jettel remarked, he
found no special delight ("Geschmack") in the comedy. On this hint,
the Burg dropped the play.[5]

Jettel, as a member of the Foreign Ministry, was of course sensitive
to foreign affairs. The Balkans since the early nineteenth century
had been torn with national movements and rebellions against Ottoman rule. By the end of the century, Serbia, Rumania, and Montene-
gro won their independence, and Bulgaria its autonomy. But Macedonia, claimed by Bulgaria, Serbia, and Greece, remained under
Turkish rule and during the 1880s was the scene of peasant uprising
and revolutionary organizing that favored unification with Bulgaria.
Behind the scenes, Austria-Hungary and Russia, and to a lesser degree England, competed for influence and interest in the region.

Austria-Hungary encouraged its vassal Serbia to expand southward while at the same time it sought to supplant Russian influence in Bulgaria. In the autumn of 1902, revolutionary action broke out in Macedonia and was climaxed the following summer in an armed uprising that was brutally suppressed. Efforts by Austria-Hungary and Russia to pacify the area failed. Against this background, Dr. Jettel found *Helden* "inopportune." Seemingly, Shaw agreed: "I had no idea," he wrote to Trebitsch on 1 March, "that there was any secrecy about the action of the Censorship. . . . I hope no harm will come of my indiscretion."[6]

Some months later, Trebitsch placed *Arms* in Vienna with the small, privately owned Theater in der Josefstadt, directed by Josef Jarno. Jarno submitted a copy of the play and a summary of its plot to the Statthalterei (Governor's Office) of Lower Austria, which exercised censorship of privately owned theaters. On 27 May, a reader sent a report to the Präsidium of the Statthalterei summarizing the play's action and locale and explaining the comedy's theme as exposing the supposed ideal of the heroic. The real hero, he pointed out, was the Swiss "free citizen," Bluntschli, in comparison with whom the Bulgarians appeared culturally backward. But they were not presented in a biased, malicious way. On the contrary, true heroism appears at last in Sergius, and the saving of Bluntschli's life by the Bulgarian woman is celebrated. Nevertheless, the reader called attention to several red-penciled passages which bore on Austro-Hungarian foreign relations and thus, against the Balkan Question, perhaps gave cause for concern. It therefore would be advisable, he concluded, to reach some understanding about these passages with the theater management.[7]

The questionable passages were no doubt those which mentioned the role of the Austrian and Russian officers in the Serbo-Bulgarian War, Raina's indignant outcry against the Austrians' setting on the Serbs to rob Bulgaria of its freedom, Catherine's anger at letting the Austrians force peace on Bulgaria instead of annexing Serbia, and Petkoff's rejoinder that he would have had to conquer the whole Austrian empire in that case.

On 10 September, Dr. Jettel, to whom the Statthalterei had turned, wrote an unofficial opinion that there was no objection to the play's production. With Director Jarno's concurrence, the censor permitted the play on condition that the offending passages be deleted and that the name of Petkoff—which happened to be that of the Bulgarian Minister of the Interior—be altered. The decision arrived too late evidently for *Helden* to appear in the 1903–4 season at the Josefstadt, but the play did enter its repertory the following season on 27 December 1904 and ran eleven times—a respectable success. Jarno played Bluntschli; the name Petkoff was changed to Merkoff.

The day after the opening, a member of the censor's office reported on the play and its reception. He noted that the plot was less important than the ironic treatment of the "hero," which appealed to the audience in the first two acts but which flagged in the end. "From the standpoint of the censorship," the report continued, "it is worth noting" that there was loud applause at Sergius's speech on the slavishness of the ordinary soldier and at his declaration that true bravery consists of following one's own will. Yet, the reporter adds, there is no present occasion for censoring.[8] Thus, after a year's delay, *Arms* was introduced to Vienna.

But the Bulgarians were yet to be heard from. Almost two decades later, the Burg, then shorn of its imperial trappings, became embroiled with *Helden* at its associated small, suburban theater that served for summer productions, the Schönbrunner Schlosstheater. The time was post–World War I, during which, despite altered borders and the professed principle of "national self-determination," friction continued in the Balkans. Bulgaria, which had joined the Central Powers, lost some territory to Serbia in the newly created, multinational Yugoslavia. On Saturday evening, 11 June 1921, *Helden* opened at the Schönbrunner Schloss. That afternoon, the theater management learned that the Bulgarian students in Vienna intended to demonstrate against the production. In an attempt to head off the threatened disturbance, the management issued a statement denying that any slur against Bulgaria was intended. Still, as the evening's performance got under way, one sensed, according to the *Neue Freie Presse* (12 June), growing tensions in the gallery, where the students had gathered. When, toward the end of Act 1, Raina mentioned that the Petkoff home contained a goat (!)[9] and a *library,* Bulgarian outrage exploded. Shouts of "Shame," "Scandal," "Stop the show!" rang through the house: "We were allies of Germany and Austria in the war; we won't tolerate this!" Whistles and hoots swept the theater, and in the orchestra a member of the Bulgarian embassy rose and delivered a speech in Bulgarian. Some demonstrators were ejected, and the play continued. During the second act, when Bulgarian washing habits came up, bitter denials were shouted from the gallery. The second curtain finally descended, and Director Phillip Zeska appeared to express the usual thanks to the author. The full fury of the students then erupted. The third act, however, proceeded undisturbed.

The next evening's performance—on Sunday—was allowed to go on peacefully since references to nationalities were cut. The Bulgarian embassy also asserted complete neutrality on the matter of protest and denied that one of its members had delivered a speech on Saturday night.

But the students were only holding fire, and on Monday night about 130 Bulgarian students staged an even more strenuous demonstration than they had on opening night. Reportedly, the Bulgarian colony in Vienna had tried to persuade the Burg to remove the play, and the Burg had agreed only to remove the offending references to the Bulgarians. This, however, did not satisfy the protesters since the characters wore Bulgarian costumes, one even with a military medal! Protesting shouts were countered by shouts from the rest of the audience; police entered and dragged the chief demonstrators out. But outcries continued through the second act, and finally the curtain was dropped and the performance suspended.[10]

On Tuesday, the Burg offered to alter the costumes, but the students now insisted that the names—above all that of Raina, which was specifically Bulgarian—had to go. At that point, the Burg management drew a line and announced that precautions would be taken to prevent trouble.[11]

Nevertheless, the withdrawal of *Helden* from the Schönbrunner was announced on 15 June not only because of the threatened protests but also because of government intervention for diplomatic reasons to remove the play from the state-financed Burg and its affiliate.[12]

That morning, the *Neue Freie Presse* commented wryly on the amazing fact that 130 Bulgarians had actually shown up at the tiny Schönbrunner Schlosstheater to demonstrate against Shaw's play. The Burg management had removed all references to Sofia and the Bulgarians from the text, thereby leaving the play in some nameless never-never land. It is hopeless, the paper continued, to persuade the Bulgarian students that no insult to Bulgarian honor was intended by the Burg and that Shaw had aims other than deriding Bulgarian culture.

Two years later it was the Serbian students' turn to demonstrate. *Arms* opened at the Svanda Theatre in Prague on 5 February 1923 despite a press campaign "agitating fiercely" against the comedy's alleged insult to the Balkan soldier. The Serbian students carried on until ejected by the police.[13]

Berlin was next. Eugen Robert, director of the Theater am Kurfürstendamm, announced *Helden* for 26 September 1924. Before its opening, the Bulgarian embassy, reflecting persisting sensitivity toward Shaw's comedy, requested the theater's management to withdraw the piece as a mockery of the Bulgarian people. The management courteously responded that Shaw's satire was directed not only against Bulgarians but also against Serbians, Russians, and Austrians, and that in other of his works Shaw satirizes his own people with special delight. Nor is he easier on the French Napoleon or the Roman Caesar. It was, the management added, Shaw's artistic privilege not to take human affairs too seriously but to laugh at them. His intent was plainly not to wound Bulgarian sensibilities, and the theater's intent was only to provide entertainment for all good Europeans. The embassy's request was thus politely rejected.[14]

A sensational and scandalous opening night was expected, but the Bulgarian students in Berlin thought better of it. In turn, the theater cut some lines from the text.[15] Shaw, having learned of the dispute, now rose to the challenge. In a letter dated 28 September and published in translation on 6 October in the liberal *Berliner Tageblatt*, which had supported the theater, he wrote (retranslated into English):

> I greatly regret that my play, *Arms and the Man*, has wounded the susceptibilities of Bulgarian students in Berlin and Vienna. But I ask them to remember that it is the business of the writer of a comedy to wound the susceptibilities of his audience.
>
> The classical definition of his function is "the chastening of morals by ridicule." Athens had to submit to the mortification of its *amour propre* by Aristophanes, France by Molière, Norway by Ibsen, Ireland by Synge, and both Ireland and England, to say nothing of the rest of the world, by me.
>
> This means that comedy is possible only in a highly civilized country; for in a comparatively barbarous one the people cannot bear to have their follies ridiculed, and will tolerate nothing but impossibly brave and virtuous native heroes overthrowing villainous opponents, preferably foreign ones. Civilized audiences enjoy being made to laugh at themselves, and recognize how salutary that exercise is for them. Civilized Bulgarians enjoy *Arms and the Man* as much as German audiences do, and indeed more, as they are more directly interested.
>
> Barbarous Bulgarians (Bulgaria, like other nations, has its rustics and its barbarians) behave exactly as my own countrymen behaved when Synge's *Playboy of the Western World* was performed in Dublin: they are infuriated by what seems to them to be a personal insult.
>
> There are evidently many barbarians among the Bulgarian students in Berlin and Vienna (we are all a little barbarous at their age); but as the credit of their country's civilization is in their hands in

Berlin, I appeal to them to sit and smile and applaud like the rest, even if they feel that they would like to shoot me, as many people do in England and America.

They will notice that the brave and honorable Major Sergius Saranoff does not shoot Captain Bluntschli, though he sees well enough that the Captain is laughing at his romanticism, and even forcing him to laugh at it himself. I want the Bulgarian students to laugh at it too.

I know, of course, that libraries and electric bells and houses with more than one floor, and consequently with flights of stairs in them, are no longer the novelties they were in 1885. And the days are gone by when it is possible to assassinate Stambuloff[16] for the reason (among others) that he did not wash his hands often enough.

But I can hardly believe that any Bulgarian student, however innocent, believes that the generation of Bulgarians who were just struggling out of centuries of Turkish oppression were able to enjoy all the refinements which are matters of course nowadays.

When the Bulgarian students, with my sincerely friendly assistance, have developed a sense of humor, there will be no more trouble.[17]

Much earlier, defending the realism of *Arms* against those who accused him of mocking heroism and insulting Bulgaria, Shaw, in "A Dramatic Realist to His Critics" (July 1894), wrote of the historical moment in Bulgaria in 1885–86, "when the need for repelling the onslaught of the Servians made the Bulgarians for six months a nation of heroes. But as they had only just been redeeemed from centuries of miserable bondage to the Turks, and were, therefore, but beginning to work out their own redemption from barbarism—or, if you prefer it, beginning to contract the disease of civilisation—they were very ignorant heroes, with boundless courage and patriotic enthusiasm, but with so little military skill that they had to place themselves under the command of Russian officers. And their attempts at Western civilisation were much the same as their attempts at war—instructive, romantic, ignorant. They were a nation of plucky beginners in every department."[18]

In fact, as will appear, Shaw was mistaken about the Russian officers.

Despite Shaw's rejoinder, not all Bulgarian sensibilities were appeased. The same season that saw *Helden* in Berlin brought *Androcles and the Lion* to the State Theatre in Sofia. In a dispatch dated 31 December 1924 but published in the *Berliner Tageblatt* on 4 January 1925, we learn that the opening of *Androcles* in Sofia was accompanied by whistling—directed obviously against Shaw, not the play—but that the performance continued to the end. The next night, however, the opposition organized to boycott the play. An unusual number of army officers were seated throughout the theater, and before the curtain rose a member of the cast appeared and pleaded that all demonstrations be withheld for the honor of the theater. When the curtain rose on the pretty setting—a desert with palms—all was quiet; so too when the lion roaring in pain appeared, but the moment Androcles began to speak, violent coughing broke out in the auditorium. The curtain fell. Police then warned the public to behave, and the play recommenced with Androcles addressing the lion. Again raucous coughing. This was more than the lion could bear: rearing up on his hind legs, he removed his head, and declared that he would no longer play. The curtain again dropped, and the opposition burst into patriotic hymns, forcing the audience to its feet. The orators then took the floor and harangued the audience fervently. "We won't listen to the play; we are patriots!" cried one person in the stalls. "You are idiots!" shouted one small lady in the balcony. More patriotic songs and heated exchanges followed before the evening was spurred to an end by the explosion of stink bombs. The opposition, led by the officers with whom the police colluded, succeeded, and the play was withdrawn. Shaw, the *Tageblatt* correspondent observed, was more right than he thought.

Five years later, protests by Bulgarian students in Prague against the pending opening of *Arms* on 9 April 1929 at the Vynohrady Theatre led the theater's management to change the setting to Albania! On opening night, police were stationed in the theater, but the feared demonstrations did not occur, "Prague's Albanian population," as the *New York Times* (10 April) dryly noted, "being too small to make trouble."

Nor was that the last effort to appease Bulgarian sentiment by changing the play's scene. In 1941, Gabriel Pascal, Shaw's authorized film producer, left for America with visions of building a studio in the Bahamas, then with plans for a film industry in Canada. At the same time he angled for productions of Shaw in Hollywood and acquired considerable backing for a film of *Arms*. The venture came to nothing, but among the suggestions by would-be backers was a change of setting from Bulgaria to Canada—a change promptly rejected by Shaw. As for Bulgarian objections, Shaw coolly remarked, "The population of Bulgaria is 6 million, the theatre-going proportion of which is negligible. Their feelings may be disregarded."[19]

As we know, Shaw began his comedy before having settled on a particular locale. "Now I am absolutely ignorant of history and geography," he claimed in a self-drafted interview about his new play, and so inquired of his friends for a suitable war as background for *Arms*.[20] On 9 December 1893, he read the "Prologue"—later Act 1—of the play, begun two weeks earlier, to Sidney Webb and Graham Wallas, and presumably then Webb suggested the Serbo-Bulgarian War of 1885— "the very thing," as Shaw stated in his interview. "Put a Republican, say, a Swiss—into the tyrant-ridden East and there you are."[21] And thereafter, in composing Acts 1 and 2 (subsequently Acts 2 and 3), Shaw referred to the Serbo-Bulgarian War (and Bluntschli's Swiss nationality). But having somehow conceived that Serbia won the war, Shaw identified Sergius and the Petkoff household as Serbians and the defeated enemy as Bulgarian.

The following March, shortly after completing the work, he read the play to the revolutionary Russian émigré Stepniak and to a former Russian admiral, Esper Serebryekov, who had commanded the small Bulgarian fleet.[22] Two days later, having learned from Serebryekov that there was no Serbian victory, Shaw consulted the *Annual Register* and maps and outlined the main events of the war and its aftermath in his manuscript.[23] Thanks to the admiral's comments, the play, Shaw wrote to the actor Charles Charrington, "proved impossible from beginning to end. I have had to shift the scene from Servia to Bulgaria, and to make the most absurd alterations in detail for the sake of local color, which, however, is amusing and will intensify the extravagance of the play and give it realism at the same time."[24]

Among the details added were Raina's naïvely proud mention of a staircase in the two-storied house and of a "library," of her father's rank as major, of her going to the opera in Bucharest, and of her having spent a month in Vienna, all intended to assure Bluntschli that he is not among "ignorant country folk" but among "civilized people." Also added were the remarks on Bulgarian washing habits, the "civilized" use of an electric bell instead of shouting for servants, and the like. Necessary alterations included changing Serbians to Bulgarians and reducing Petkoff's and Sergius's ranks of general and colonel, respectively, to that of major, and drastically altering their noble descent to recent ascension to wealth and position. Furthermore, Shaw now specified the battle at which Sergius led his charge as that of Slivnitza, the turning point of the Serbo-Bulgarian War, added details on the peace and the role of foreign officers in the war, entered place names, and altered.or assigned character names. For example, The Father became Petkoff, to approximate Bulgarian. (Shaw retained "Sergius," although he wrote to Richard Mansfield that it was a "very improbable" Bulgarian name.[25] Raina was originally Juana; Louka, Luga; Nicola, Michaeloff.)

Moreover, Shaw grasped the essential social changes that followed the liberation of a backward country, such as Bulgaria in 1878, from centuries of feudal Turkish rule: nascent capitalism and an increasingly important bourgeoisie in an overwhelmingly peasant nation, intense nationalism, and an intelligentsia that inclined to democracy. Turkish influence lingered: peasant homes were small and contained little besides a table and stool; heavy rugs and cushions were used for sleeping, and clothing was homespun. Few homes had running water, and frequently humans shared them with animals. But as capitalism and national consciousness grew, Bulgarian architectural styles revived in the expanding towns. The bourgeoisie now built substantial homes of two or even three stories, protected by heavy walls, with upper stories—the living quarters, as Shaw learned from the Russian admiral—frequently overhanging the lower. Within the wall, one could find lush gardens. As trade grew, clothes and furnishings turned from Turkish models toward Western-manufactured imports. Beds supplanted rugs and cushions, cheaper porcelain replaced copper plates, and knives and forks appeared. Moreover, in a nation only recently freed from Turkish rule and comprising mainly peasants, class barriers between the richer and poorer strata were less rigid than in more developed Western nations.

In the expanded stage directions added after Shaw had revised his manuscript, Raina's room is furnished with an ottoman and opulent Oriental cushions, curtains, and carpets, but with "paltry" Western wallpaper. The rest of the furnishings are simple except for an expensive mirror. Also, there is a bed. Raina wears a rich fur mantle, but her mother, who "might be a very splendid . . . wife of a mountain farmer," is "determined to be a Viennese lady" and so "wears a fashionable tea gown on all occasions." Petkoff drinks Turkish coffee and smokes a hookah; he is "insignificant" and "unpolished" but concerned for his income, as a prosperous farmer, and for his local social standing. Sergius is an amalgam of an imaginative "untamed mountaineer chieftain" and a "civilized type," whose "acute critical faculty . . . has been thrown into intense activity by the arrival of western civilization in the Balkans," with the result that he has turned Byronic. And Louka and Nicola are both determined to rise, she by disdaining servility, he by exploiting it. The "library" also has an ottoman and luxurious cushions, along with a handful of paperbound novels. On one wall is a huge earthenware stove, on the other the newly acquired electric bell.

In sketching his costumes, Shaw sought authenticity through the artist Schönberg, who served on the *Illustrated London News* during the Serbo-Bulgarian War. He also consulted Albert Ludovici, another artist, whose father had recently returned from the Balkans with sketches and photographs of the people. A comparison of Shaw's drawings with Bulgarian and Serbian uniforms and Bulgarian peasant costumes reveals his painstaking accuracy.[26]

Yet in one important respect, Shaw is mistaken. As we have seen, Shaw attributed the Austrian censor's objections to *Arms* to its revealing the "unacknowledged" fact that both sides in the war, begun by Serbia on 14 November 1885, were led by foreign officers, Austrian and Russian, thereby implicating two Great Powers in the touchy Balkan conflict.[27] In revising his manuscript, Shaw added Catherine's remark on the "wretched Serbs and their dandified Austrian officers," Raina's on the "Austrians who set the Serbs on," references to Russian officers in command of the Bulgarian army, and the identification of the friendly officer who enters Raina's room in Act 1 as a Russian. Yet the Austrian government did not favor the independent attack on Bulgaria by its client Serbia, although the Austrian ambassador did encourage Serbian ambitions against its neighbor. And only after the Serbian army, under King Milan, had collapsed and the Bulgarians had entered Serbia and occupied Pirot on 27 November did Austria threaten intervention. The war thus ended after two weeks with the reestablishment of the *status quo ante*. Peace followed in March 1886, marked by one sentence: "Peace is restored between Serbia and Bulgaria." The phrase "and friendly relations" was struck out, as Petkoff mentions, but apparently at Serbian insistence. And Petkoff rightly responds to Catherine that if Bulgaria had tried to annex Serbia, he would have had to fight the entire Austrian army. But the Serbian forces were not led by Austrian officers.

The absence of Russian officers in the Bulgarian camp during the war was even more striking, since the stunning achievement of the Bulgarian army was its rapid victory despite the *withdrawal* of the Russian officers—several hundred—who had hitherto occupied all ranks in the Bulgarian army above that of lieutenant. That anomalous situation arose from a complicated series of events.

Bulgaria owed its liberation to Russia's declaration of war against Turkey in 1877 after Turkey refused to grant Bulgarian autonomy. Volunteer Bulgarian units were formed under Russian command, and after the costly defeat of Turkey in 1878, Russia negotiated for an autonomous Greater Bulgaria, only to have the other Great Powers split Bulgaria into an autonomous principality in the north and an Eastern Rumelia in the south. Macedonia was also lopped off. Russia remained in control of organizing the new principality, and Alexander of Battenberg, a nephew of the Czarina, was elected Prince of

Bulgaria (1879). Russian officers continued to train the Bulgarian army and held all the higher ranks in that army. The Minister of War was also a Russian.

An inevitable collision between Prince Alexander and the Czar developed when the autocratic Prince attempted to gain control over the Bulgarian army. In 1885, Alexander, without consulting the Czar, responded to an insurrection against Turkey in Eastern Rumelia by joining the uprising and proclaiming the union of northern and southern Bulgaria. Angered by Alexander's unilateral move, the Czar ordered the resignation of the Russian general who was the Bulgarian Minister of War and the withdrawal of all Russian officers from the Bulgarian army. Other Great Powers protested Alexander's move into Eastern Rumelia, and against this background Serbia, envious of Bulgarian expansion, invaded Bulgaria on 14 November.

The break with Russia caused great distress in Bulgaria, but it also opened opportunities for junior Bulgarian officers, who had been stymied by their Russian superiors, to advance rapidly. Energetic young men became captains, and the leading Bulgarian officers were promoted to majors. As Catherine complained, there were no native generals (or even colonels). Thus, when the Serbians attacked, the newly independent army was thrown on its own mettle, resources, and courage. Great marches were feverishly made to meet and hold the Serbians at Slivnitza, one day's march from Sofia. And in an heroic three days, the fervently motivated Bulgarians astonishingly turned the tide of battle and sent the Serbians into headlong retreat. The expected Serbian victory turned into a rout.

Strangely enough, Shaw from the start—without any reference to or conscious knowledge of the Serbo-Bulgarian War, which entered his play only after the "Prologue" was written—had conceived an heroic charge against orders by an inexperienced, romantic young officer. Such an unauthorized charge, without Sergius's quixotic folly, actually took place at the battle of Slivnitza (17–19 November 1885). A young captain—not major—Atanas Benderev, after an initial unsuccessful skirmish against the Serbians' rifles and artillery, launched a second attack to delay, despite orders from his superiors, Major Gudzev and Prince Alexander, and carried the day. The next day, Benderev again opposed Alexander and Gudzev, who thought Slivnitza could not be long defended. In the ensuing battles, Benderev's men charged the Serbians with fixed bayonets. The Serbians, dependent on their artillery, were less prepared for hand-to-hand battle. A military band headed Benderev's charges as his men burst into the national hymn, *Schumi Maritza,* and scattered their foes. Benderev emerged as one of the popular heroes of Slivnitza, but Prince Alexander reprimanded him for his premature attack—an insult that Benderev never forgave, even as he did not forgive Alexander's failure to promote him after the war. To Benderev's intercessors, Alexander responded that Benderev's defying orders at Slivnitza almost cost the battle and that such violation of orders in wartime was punishable by execution. In time, Benderev's admirers, who included the wife of the liberal president Karavelov, drew him into a pro-Russian, liberal faction that plotted Alexander's removal.[28]

On 21 August 1886, a band of officers, including Benderev, arrested Alexander and deported him. According to one account, Benderev cocked his pistol at the Prince and exclaimed, "Aha! you see all this comes of your not having made a major of me."[29] A countercoup by the anti-Russian government of Stefan Stambolov, however, returned Alexander to Bulgaria, but strong Russian opposition led shortly to Alexander's abdication on 7 September. Meanwhile, Benderev had escaped into Rumania. The following March, Benderev and a group of officers attempted to overthrow the Stambolov regime, but they failed. Several of the conspirators were captured and executed, but Benderev again escaped into Rumania and from there was deported to Russia. In 1898, all the exiled conspirators received amnesty except Benderev and his close associates.

Some months after Alexander's abdication, Benderev, in exile, published a vituperative letter in the semi-official *St. Petersburg Journal*, denouncing the Serbo-Bulgarian War as "most revolting" and claiming that only his efforts avoided a Bulgarian defeat, such was the "cowardice and incapacity" of his fellow officers, above all Alexander. He reviled as well the Bulgarian Minister of War and another high official as men who "never wash their necks nor comb their hair," another as a "nullity," and yet another as a "moral monster" surrounded by thieves.[30]

The parallels between Benderev and Shaw's disaffected "hero of Slivnitza" (Shaw added the battle site only later) are striking. Sergius leads an unauthorized charge and wins the day, becomes a popular hero, especially with the ladies, is embittered by his lack of promotion, and is disillusioned by the "seamy side" of life glimpsed in the war. Yet Shaw conceived his romantic idealist and his "heroic" charge with no reference to the Serbo-Bulgarian War and with no conscious awareness of Benderev while composing or revising *Arms*. The *Annual Register*, which, as mentioned, Shaw consulted on the war after meeting with Stepniak and the Russian admiral, made no mention of Benderev. What unconscious traces may have entered the conception of

Sergius are only speculative. But we can note the following: the one newspaper which Shaw regularly bought during the Serbo-Bulgarian War and the subsequent conspiracies involving Benderev—November 1885 to March 1887—was the *Pall Mall Gazette,* whose reviewing staff he had joined in May 1885. The *Gazette,* like other papers such as *The Times,* reported prominently on the Serbo-Bulgarian War with no mention of Benderev. The captain first appears in the *Gazette* briefly, with no further identification or details, as one of two officers who arrested Alexander on the day of his deposition (26 August 1886). Then after two eyewitness accounts of the deposition, which do not mention Benderev (27, 28 August), a third, by Prince Louis of Battenberg, was reported (30 August) in which Benderev, in one vivid moment, waves a scrap of paper bearing Alexander's forced abdication and exclaims to the departing Prince, "Look, that is because thou didst not make me major." No explanation of the remark or background of Benderev is given. And he is not connected with Slivnitza until the following year. By then Alexander had returned to Bulgaria only to abdicate formally, and Benderev was in exile. In the unsettled conditions which followed, the *Gazette* supported the Russians against Alexander and, without mentioning names, approvingly referred to the "heroes of Slivnitza" who deposed the Prince (22 January 1887). Then under the rubric "Did Prince Alexander Desert at Slivnitza?" two correspondents debated briefly Benderev's charges of cowardice against Alexander. The first, referring to Benderev's letter in the Russian press (but not reported in the *Gazette*), upheld, without elaboration, Benderev as one of the "real heroes" of Slivnitza; the other defended Alexander against the "traitor," Benderev (4 February). The next day, the *Gazette* reported disapprovingly the arrest in Rumania of Benderev, the "hero of Slivnitza." In rebuttal, a letter on 8 February took issue with the *Gazette*'s characterization of Benderev and, citing the Russian General Kaulbars, alleged—in the first description of Benderev at Slivnitza to appear in the *Gazette*—that Benderev left his troops in the lurch early in the battle and, in an attempt to retrieve his reputation, prematurely attacked the Serbians, thereby disobeying orders and jeopardizing Alexander's plan of battle. In any other army, General Kaulbars is reported to have said, Benderev would have been court-martialed. And in a sarcastic thrust, the correspondent recalls Benderev's "supreme courage" in taunting the deposed Prince with, "This is what comes of not having made me a major." Finally, the writer accuses the captain of craven and treacherous behavior during his arrest after the failed coup. The following month, Benderev briefly reappears in the *Gazette* as one of the ringleaders of the unsuccessful insurrection against the Stambolov government (4–5 March).

Over a period of seven months, only eleven scattered references to Benderev appeared, almost all very brief, identifying him as a conspirator against Alexander and Stambolov. But one highly dramatic moment that is twice mentioned stands out: Benderev flings his failure to be promoted in the face of the departing Prince. And there is another dramatic situation of Benderev's violating orders and rushing into battle, which the hostile correspondent alleges deserved court-martial (a theme famously treated in von Kleist's *Prince of Homburg*). Shaw bought the *Gazette* on the days mentioned above, but whether he read about the volatile Balkan situation and the obscure Captain Benderev with interest we cannot say. Six years later, when he began *Arms*, he had so forgotten the Serbo-Bulgarian War that he did not know who won the conflict, and his "Heroic Lover" entered his fancy without reference to any particular war or place. Moreover, he was not writing an historical drama but a comedy on the clash of "romantic ideals with cold, logical democracy"[31] placed, after a period of indeterminacy and error, in Bulgaria, where, as Shaw put it, "Romantic dreams and Quixotic ideals flourish luxuriantly in the rose valley of that country."[32] Whatever submerged hints may have arisen from Shaw's earlier, forgotten readings, one can still marvel at the power of imagination to mimic life.

Notes

1. *Bernard Shaw's Letters to Siegfried Trebitsch*, ed. Samuel A. Weiss (Stanford: Stanford University Press, 1986), p. 44.

2. Bernard Shaw, *Advice to a Young Critic and Other Letters*, ed. E. J. West (New York: Crown, 1963), pp. 134–35.

3. Marginal note on cutting enclosed in letter to Trebitsch on 1 March 1903, in Berg Collection, New York Public Library.

4. Bernard Shaw, *Collected Letters II, 1898–1910*, ed. Dan H. Laurence (New York: Dodd, Mead, 1972), pp. 312–13.

5. Correspondence relating to the Burgtheater and the censors in the Haus-, Hof- u. Staatsarchiv, Vienna. I am grateful to Director Benna and Dr. Franz Dirnberger for summarizing and citing the relevant letters.

6. *Letters to Siegfried Trebitsch*, p. 44.

7. From the censorship files at the Niederösterreichische Landesarchiv, Vienna, Reg

A, Statthalterei—Präsidium, Theaterzensurakten 1903. I am indebted to the Landes-archiv for copies and use of the relevant documents.

8. Ibid.

9. Raina boasts of a staircase and library, not of a goat, but the reporter evidently misheard *Stiege* (staircase) as *Ziege* (goat). Perhaps the students misunderstood as well, or the actress went Shaw one better.

10. *Neue Freie Presse,* 14 June (Morgenblatt).

11. Ibid., 14 June (Abendblatt).

12. Ibid., 15 June (Abendblatt).

13. *New York Times,* 10 February 1923, 10:2.

14. *Berliner Tageblatt,* 24 September 1924; also *New York Times,* 25 September.

15. *Berliner Tageblatt,* 27 September 1924.

16. Stefan Stambolov (1854–1895), dictatorial Bulgarian prime minister (1887–1894), was savagely beaten by enemies after his forced resignation. He died shortly thereafter.

17. The English retranslation appeared in the *Daily News, Times,* and *Westminster Gazette* on 9 October 1924.

18. *Shaw on Theatre,* ed. E. J. West (New York: Hill and Wang, 1958), p. 23.

19. Valerie Pascal, *The Disciple and His Devil* (New York: McGraw-Hill, 1970), p. 102; also in *The Collected Screenplays of Bernard Shaw,* ed. Bernard F. Dukore (Athens: University of Georgia Press, 1980), p. 124.

20. "A Talk with Mr. Bernard Shaw about His New Play," in *Pall Mall Budget,* 19 April 1894, p. 13. Reprinted in Bernard Shaw, *Arms and the Man,* ed. Louis Crompton (Indianapolis: Bobbs-Merrill, 1969), p. 78.

21. Shaw errs in saying that the play was "nearly finished" when he turned to Webb and other friends. His diaries and the manuscript of *Arms* make clear that Shaw had finished only the "Prologue," begun on 26 November 1893; before consulting Webb and adopting the Serbo-Bulgarian War. See *Bernard Shaw: The Diaries,* ed. Stanley Weintraub (University Park and London: Penn State University Press, 1986), entries 26, 28, 29 November, 2, 9, 16, 18 December 1893. Shaw resumed composition on 2 January 1894 and finished his draft sometime in March; *Arms and the Man, A Facsimile of the Holograph Manuscript* (New York and London: Garland, 1981).

22. *Diaries,* 17 March 1894.

23. In the interview "Ten Minutes with Mr. Bernard Shaw" (*To-Day,* 28 April 1894, reprinted in the *Bodley Head Bernard Shaw,* I:481), Shaw erred in saying that he studied the *Annual Register* and maps after reading his work to Sidney Webb. The diaries, corroborated by the manuscript, establish that he turned to the *Annual Register* on 19 March 1894 after lunching with Stepniak and the Russian admiral on 17 March.

24. Quoted in *Facsimile,* p. xiv; see also "A Talk with Mr. Bernard Shaw" and "Ten Minutes with Mr. Bernard Shaw."

25. Bernard Shaw, *Collected Letters I: 1874–1897,* ed. Dan H. Laurence (New York: Dodd, Mead, 1965), p. 442.

26. See *Facsimile,* Appendix III, and Shaw's self-drafted interview "Arms and the Man," *The Star,* 14 April 1894, reprinted in the *Bodley Head Bernard Shaw,* I:473–74.

27. Shaw suggested that his information came from the Russian admiral (*Letters to Siegfried Trebitsch,* p. 77). But he either misunderstood or was misled by the admiral.

28. On Benderev and the battle of Slivnitza, see Major Alfred Ernst von Huhn, *The Struggle of the Bulgarians,* translated from the German (London: John Murray, 1886), pp. 129–33, 148, 157–59, 160, 192–93; "Servo-Bulgarian War," in *Encyclopaedia Britan-*

nica, 11th ed.; Alois Hajek, *Bulgariens Befreiung* (Munich and Berlin: R. Oldenbourg, 1939), pp. 278, 325; Richard Crampton, *Bulgaria 1878–1918: A History* (Boulder, Colo., and New York: Columbia University Press East European Monographs, 1983), pp. 101, 110f. Benderev's major role in the battle is undisputed.

29. *Times,* 30 August 1886, 5:3. See below for the slightly varying account in the *Pall Mall Gazette.*

30. *New York Times,* 14 January 1887 (datelined 28 December 1886), 3:1; earlier, on 16 December, the London *Times* briefly reported the letter's attack on Alexander's cowardice (5:2) without any of the colorful and scathing remarks. Benderev later published a book on the war, *Serbsko-bolgarskaya voina, 1885 goda* (St. Petersburg, 1892).

31. "A Talk with Mr. Bernard Shaw," p. 13; in *Arms,* ed. Crampton, p. 78.

32. "Arms and the Man," *The Star,* 14 April 1894; in the *Bodley Head Bernard Shaw,* I:475.

Stanley Weintraub

BERNARD SHAW IN DARKEST ENGLAND: G.B.S. AND THE SALVATION ARMY'S GENERAL WILLIAM BOOTH

"What is the use of the gospel of thrift to a man who had nothing to eat yesterday and has not threepence today to pay for his lodging tonight?" So challenged *In Darkest England and The Way Out,* a manifesto which declared that allegedly Christian England was in no condition to compare itself favorably with the horror and degradation of central Africa. (Earlier in its year of release, the intrepid Henry Morton Stanley had published an account of his explorations, *In Darkest Africa.*) The disgrace of a "submerged tenth" of unemployed and down-and-out, with its attendant spiritual degradation, the book charged, could be put down to their moral defects. Salvation was not going to come by prayer but by drastic alteration of the social fabric.

Given the London, 1890, place and date of publication, one might assume that it was the latest Fabian polemic, perhaps written, as were many of them then, by a musical critic and political activist named Bernard Shaw. In actuality he would not get around to reading it until February 1891, and its real author was the feisty "General" William Booth, founder of the Salvation Army. Shaw, however, seems to have never forgotten a line of it. As one-time Pre-Raphaelite painter Edward Burne-Jones remarked a few years later to his assistant, the Army began "at the right end. They begin with enthusiasm and they begin at the poorest [audience]. The very name I like; it's a good one. . . . One thing they did I didn't like; they put outside their meeting house in Hammersmith in big letters 'Blood and Fire'—what did they mean, whose blood and whose fire I should like to know? You can get anything out of mankind by appealing to its sense of beauty and its enthusiasm—but in people's sense of right I have not the least belief. The Socialists will never do anything with it."[1]

Coincidentally, one of the major Socialist headquarters was also in Hammersmith, presided over by another feisty, charismatic prophet, William Morris. Bernard Shaw, often at Hammersmith Terrace, must have also seen the "Blood and Fire" slogan more than once; and he wanted the Socialists to have some of the enthusiasm he saw among the Booth adherents. His *Major Barbara* (1905) seems an attempt to dramatize the possibility—a theatrical *Darkest England.*

Shaw's first acquaintance with Booth's Army was as a young walker of the streets, when he tried to find himself as a new Irish émigré in London. In his first novel, *Immaturity*, written in 1878–79 when he was twenty-two, Shaw includes an obviously autobiographical episode in which Smith, the young hero, new to London, wanders unfamiliar neighborhoods in the quiet of Christmas Day and happens upon an evangelical meeting which has the characteristics of early William Booth. Having broken with Methodism—as being too passive—in 1861, Booth and his wife, Catherine, had established an independent revivalist mission which only received the name of Salvation Army in 1878. At that early stage the Army was one without uniforms and ranks, but with a strong impetus to street meetings, vehement tracts and hymn-happy bands, banners, and the saving of souls. Shaw's acquaintance with chapels of this order emphasized the music and the tracts, Smith finding the tracts neither credible nor interesting, but the music "fairly sung." Although the congregation "either followed the tune or improvised a drone bass which only moved at the cadences, there was a tolerable attempt at part singing; and Smith found no fault in the performance."[2]

The last hymn, emphasizing "We will all be happy over there," with the antiphonal repeat of "over there," is infectious, and Smith joins his "feeble tenor"* to the harmony. "Then there arose a young man, earnest and proud of his oratory, who offered up a long prayer, in the course of which he suggested such modifications of the laws of nature as would bring the arrangement of the universe into conformity with his own tenets. When he was done, several others delivered addresses; but they lacked variety, as the speakers were all very ignorant. The addresses of one or two men who related the atrocities committed by

---

*Manuscript of *Immaturity;* Shaw later changed that to the more autobiographical "colorless baritone."

them before their conversion disgusted Smith; and he watched for an opportunity of retiring quietly."

In 1885 in one of his early music reviews, Shaw, anonymously, wrote approvingly in the *Dramatic Review* of the impetuous "war songs of the Salvation Army,"[3] and a few years later, as "Corno di Bassetto" in *The Star,* he praised "the excellent music" of the "proletarian bands of the industrial North and of the Salvation Army."[4] He liked the way they performed Donizetti's choruses. "These, by the bye," he wrote, "have been discovered by the Salvation Army: I heard one of their bands playing *Per te d'immenso giubilo* [from *Lucia di Lammermoor*] capitally one Sunday morning." In *Major Barbara* he would have the band leave the West Ham shelter playing *immenso giubilo,* Adolphus Cusins giving the time with his drum, and Barbara's father playing a borrowed trombone. It was only after the completion of *Major Barbara,* late in 1905, that he was asked, despite his reservations about the Army, to attend its music festival at Congress Hall in Clapton. Booth thought the play would be good publicity. Shaw was even asked, as a former music critic, to write a confidential report for the Army, not published until forty-five years later, after Shaw's death.[5]

He listened, Shaw explained, as he had done "to some of the best professional orchestras and bands in Europe" when he had been a professional critic. And he found "precision and snap" in the execution. There were no "incompetent conductors" on the podium merely "because they had won a musical degree at a university." But he found their solo instrumental skill often florid, an excess he attributed to the emotional dimension of the Army, the talented amateur's desire to show off a musicianly virtuosity. What he found fault with was not the "joyous vivacity of style and clear jubilant tone" but the monotony of hymnal music. The Army needed, he suggested, more "marches and quick-steps." He understood, he said, that Salvation Army music

> must not be over the heads of the people. At the Festival I sat next [to] a laborer who had probably worked half as long again that day as any man should work at heavy physical toil: at all events he was partly stupefied with mere fatigue. If the bands had played very refined music for him—say the Priest's march from Mozart's Magic Flute, the overture to Gluck's Alceste, the Elysian Fields music from Gluck's Orpheus, or the entry to the Castle of the Grail from Wagner's Parsifal—he would have been fast asleep in three minutes. And when the Chalk Farm Band played a piece of empty but exciting circus music for him in the most violently spirited way, he woke up and was pleased, as most of the audience were. But it woke him up at the cost of switching off the current of religious enthusiasm and switching on

the current of circus excitement. It woke him up very much as a tablespoon of brandy would have woken him up. And with all its racket, which was powerfully reinforced by the low roof and the terrific clatter of the overtones set up by the instruments, it was not nearly as stirring as I'm climbing up the golden stairs to glory or When the roll is called up yonder. Music can be impetuous, triumphant, joyful, enrapturing, and very pretty into the bargain without being rowdy or empty. I know the difficulty of keeping up the necessary supply of good marches, and the danger of wearing out the best ones by too frequent repetition. But after making all allowances, I think it is a pity that the Salvation Army, which has produced a distinctive type of religious service and religious life, should not also produce a distinctive type of marching music.

Later Shaw wrote of a great Salvation Army meeting in memory of Mrs. Booth at the Albert Hall that "the massed Salvation bands played the Dead March from 'Saul' as I verily believe it has never been played in the world since Handel was alive to conduct it," and he resented publicly, in letters to the press, any suggestion that he was libeling Army bands in his play. General Booth himself had supplied Shaw with a seat "in the middle of the centre grand tier box, in the front row," from which he sang "When the roll-ll-ll is called up yonder," he wrote John Vedrenne (2 October 1905), "as it has never been sung before. The Times will announce my conversion tomorrow."[6] His relations with the Salvation Army had been good from the beginning, and he genuinely admired its work if not its theology.

"I took on myself," Shaw noted in a letter in the *Daily Citizen* (26 October 1912), "the duty of leading the singing in my box, being of opinion that hymn-singing, when the tune is a jolly one (and the Salvation Army has enough genuine religion in it to specialise in jolly hymn tunes), is a highly enjoyable, healthy, and recreative exercise. Now the art of leading a choir, or an orchestra, or anything else, consists, not in being 'carried away,' but in carrying other people away; and this I did with such success that a young lady in the Army bonnet took my hands as we left the box at the end of the meeting, and said, with moist eyes, '*We* know, don't we?' And really I think we did."[7]

But after the hymns, Booth expected a "sobriety of the soul," Shaw thought, which is why the General refused to take a high moral tone with sinners, a worldly realism found in few pulpits. That perspective may have had an impact on *Mrs Warren's Profession*, which Shaw wrote only two years after Booth's book. "Terrible as the fact is," Booth had observed without prudery or theological polemics, ". . . there is no industrial career in which for a short time a beautiful girl can make as much money with as little trouble as in the profession of courtesan." In industry a penny an hour was possible; in a brothel a woman might surpass the earnings of a cabinet minister. Recalling her girlhood to Vivie, Mrs Warren explains that one of her sisters "worked in a whitelead factory twelve hours a day for nine shillings a week until she died of lead poisoning. She only expected to get her hands a little paralyzed; but she died." Another sister, Liz, after watching Vivie's mother wear herself out as a barmaid, exploded, "What are you doing there, you little fool? wearing out your health and your appearance for other people's profit!" And Liz would give Kitty Warren her start as prostitute and procuress.

"Why shouldn't I have done it?" she challenges her daughter. And Vivie can only reply, in terms General Booth would have understood, "You were certainly quite justified—from the business point of view."

"What's the use in . . . hypocrisy?" Mrs Warren agrees. "If people arrange the world that way for women, theres no good pretending it's arranged the other way. No: I never was a bit ashamed really."

And "Unashamed" would be the working motto of the most Boothian character that Shaw would create in *Major Barbara*, a play that owes much to General Booth.

Very likely even before Shaw had completed his first play—the manuscript fragment has the appearance of the 1880s—he had sketched an encounter that has in it all the makings of Snobby Price, Bill Walker, Jenny Hill, and Barbara Undershaft. The setting is a Salvation Army shelter.

> The solitary rough is not brave. He is restless and shamefaced until he meets with other roughs to keep him in countenance. He especially dreads that strange social reformer, the Hallelujah lass. At first sight of her quaint bonnet, jersey, and upturned eyes, he rushes to the conclusion that chance has provided him with a rare lark. He hastens to the outskirts of her circle, and after a few inarticulate howls, attempts to disconcert her by profane and often obscene interjections. In vain. He may as easily disconcert a swallow in its flight. He presently hears himself alluded to as "that loving fellow creature," and he is stricken with an uncomfortable feeling akin to that which prompted Paul Pry's protest, "Don't call me a phoenix: I'm not used to it." But the Hallelujah lass is not done with him yet. In another minute she is praying, with infectious emotion, for "his dear, precious soul." This finishes him. He slinks away with a faint affectation of having no more time to waste on such effeminate sentimentality, and thenceforth never ventures within earshot of the Army ex-

cept when strongly reinforced by evil company or ardent spirits. A battalion of Hallelujah lasses is worth staying a minute to study. . . . As long as they speak strenuously, they consider themselves but little about lack of matter, which forces them to repetitions which, it must be confessed, soon become too tedious for anyone but a habitual Salvationist to endure."[8]

Later, when "the general" quoted some of Shaw's comments on the excellence of Salvation Army bands "again and again in public"— these are Shaw's recollections—Shaw "took advantage of the relations thus established to ask the Army staff why they did not develop the dramatic side of their ritual by performing plays." He "even offered to write a short play as a model of what might be done. The leaders of the Army . . . could not venture to offend the deep prejudices against the theatre that still form part of evangelism." Unless, Shaw was told, "I could assure them that all the incidents in the play had actually happened; otherwise the play would be considered a lie. To my mind, of course, a very curious misapprehension of the difference between truth and mere actuality." Finally, Booth's daughter-in-law, wife of his heir-apparent, Bramwell, told Shaw that the Army would prefer a large subscription rather than a model play.

The possibility "of using the wooing of a man's soul for his salvation as a substitute for the hackneyed wooing of a handsome young gentleman for the sake of marrying him," Shaw recalled, had occurred to him years before when, as a Radical lecturer in the 1890s, "he had often found himself on Sunday mornings addressing a Socialist meeting in the open air in London or in the provinces while the Salvation Army was at work on the same ground. He had frequently, at the conclusion of his own meeting, joined the crowd round the Salvation lasses and watched their work and studied their methods sympathetically." If the Army did not want to create its own model play, Shaw would write it himself, with the raw material which the Army had already provided him. Many of the Salvation lasses had sung, "with great effect," Shaw recalled,

> songs in which the drama of salvation was presented in the form of a series of scenes between a brutal and drunken husband and a saved wife, with a thrilling happy ending in which the audience, having been persuaded by the unconscious art of the singer to expect with horror a murderous attack on the woman as her husband's steps were heard on the stairs, were relieved and delighted to hear that when the villain entered the room and all seemed lost, his face was lighted with the light of Heaven; for he too had been saved. Bernard Shaw was not at

that time a playwright; but such scenes were not lost on him; the future dramatist was collecting his material everywhere.[9]

He was not merely collecting material; he would be using it all his life. After *Major Barbara* Shaw would dramatize another upper-middle-class daughter, Margaret Knox of posh and respectable Denmark Hill, in *Fanny's First Play* (1911), who is carried away by a prayer meeting which changes her life. One of the unforeseen results is that she assaults a policeman and lands in prison, but she finds her soul. "I can only say," Shaw observed in an interview in 1911, "that I myself have participated with enormous enjoyment in just such a prayer-meeting as that which carried Margaret off her feet, although my natural sphere of enjoyment is in the artistic world."[10] His Lavinia in *Androcles and the Lion* (1912) and his *Saint Joan* (1923) embody the power of faith and the struggle for reason when in the grip of religious ecstasy; and in *Too True to Be Good* (1931) Shaw creates a mesmerizing preacher (turned burglar) and evangelical army sergeant. Even as late as *Buoyant Billions,* completed in Shaw's ninetieth year, Shaw would depict a self-styled World Betterer, who in a pre-atomic world might have followed Booth's course.

Booth's remedies for the regeneration of England had long before captured Shaw's attention. He had already noted in his diary (19 July 1889) the purchase of the Army's official gazette, *War Cry.*[11] When Booth's *In Darkest England* was published, Shaw was first alerted to it by fellow Fabian Graham Wallas, who took him into the library at the National Liberal Club to read Thomas Huxley's letter to *The Times* "on General Booth's scheme," which was one of many responses skeptical not only about the Army's demands for conversion and obedience but also about its statistics and its social strategies. That combination of a militaristic religious organization and social engineering had already made the newly published book a lively focus of controversy. The utopian projects required start-up funds, and one letter writer to *The Times* had offered £1,000 if ninety-nine others would subscribe similar amounts. None publicly did, but Booth went ahead with pennies and shillings from his broadest constituency, the poor.

One of Booth's schemes was a model farm at Benfleet, which Shaw planned to visit. He also noted in his diary plans to attend a lecture by a Mr. Reed on Booth's book. Yet he missed the lecture, and—a chronic oversleeper—he missed the train from Fenchurch Street Station. But it is clear that he read *In Darkest England* and that not long after he saw the farm at Benfleet. It would take a dozen years more, but Shaw would eventually incorporate both Booth's social engineer-

ing ends and his own sweeping reservations about the means into
Major Barbara. Even the matching-funds idea went into the play when
Shaw's Salvation Army leader—a woman commissioner, perhaps to
deflect identification from Booth—asks for five wealthy businessmen
to match a £5,000 donation from Lord Saxmundham, formerly Hor-
ace Bodger, the millionaire distiller. Referring to Booth's ends and his
own skepticism about Booth's means, and the Thomas Huxley controversy in *The Times* when *In Darkest England* was first published, Shaw
observed to Beatrice Webb (30 July 1901), "Nothing is more unpopu-
lar in England than hauling down a flag, even if it has become a
flagrantly impossible flag. If General Booth were to declare tomorrow
that he had given up the Bible & adopted the views of Huxley, he
would obliterate himself from public life, because the Huxleyites
would give him no credit for coming to his senses, & would never
attach the least importance to a man who had compromised himself
by salvationism; the pious people would be horrified; & everybody
would regard him as an apostate." Conceding Booth the peg on which
to hang his program, and long attracted to paternalistic but efficiently
planned industrial communities, Shaw put into *Major Barbara,* as Undershaft's utopian Perivale St Andrews, Booth's scheme of "a series of
Industrial Settlements or Suburban Villages, lying out in the country,
within a reasonable distance of all our great cities," with cottages "of
the best material and workmanship," and cooperative stores "supplying everything that was really necessary at the most economic prices."
For, as Booth had explained, the gospel of thrift was of no consequence to a man who had nothing to eat nor threepence to pay for
lodging. But Booth did not add, as Shaw would in *Major Barbara,* that
the unemployed poor should not have to embrace any other kind of
gospel in order to join the queue for economic salvation.

When St. John Ervine approached Shaw about writing his biography, Shaw assured the biographer of Booth (29 October 1932), "I like
the little I heard from him (the story of Major Barbara will be the only
interesting chapter in your book) and . . . I really believe what his
Commissars said when I put it to them, that he would have fought just
as hard for the poor and their salvation if there had been no other
world for him than this." Booth, he felt, was a reformer who employed the tools of religion rather than a religious zealot who used the
language of social reform. It was more in fun than truth when Shaw
teased playwright Arthur Pinero (29 November 1909), "Nowadays
when I contemplate your remarkable nose, I think of that other remarkable nose, the nose of General Booth—both noses out for soul
saving."

When Shaw's Barbara vows a return to soul-saving on different premises than she had first assumed, her father tempts her to try her hand on his workmen, since their bellies were full and they could have no material motive. The fear of a this-world hell had been removed. As Andrew Undershaft would, Booth described the underside of England—"the submerged tenth" of the population—as living in "Dante's Hell." Shaw had already used Booth's metaphor in *John Bull's Other Island* (1904), in which the unfrocked priest Father Keegan describes "this world of . . . torment and penance" as hell. "For me there are only two countries: heaven and hell," he adds; "[and] but two conditions of men: salvation and damnation." Keegan may be Irish and Catholic, but the conception might have been Booth's. Darkest England is given life in the shelter scene of *Major Barbara*, and in other comments by his munitions-czar hero, and when the demands of the drama require that some aspects of the problem—and solution—be relegated to the play's long preface, they reappear as the sardonically titled "Gospel of St Andrew Undershaft." (Unseen but oft-mentioned in the play is Undershaft's gentle Jewish partner Lazarus, a reasonable name to suggest a Jew, and suggestive in other ways as well. It is no surprise, then, to find early in Booth's book a reference to the biblical Lazarus—but only to suggest the ragged and starved unemployed. Still, the name may have lodged in Shaw's subconscious.)

A striking link is Booth's reference to the seven deadly sins "which of late years . . . have contrived to pass themselves off as virtues," a description which Undershaft turns to the "seven deadly sins" of "Food, clothing, firing, rent, taxes, respectability and children"—burdens which only money can lighten. To the startled Barbara, Undershaft claims to have saved her own soul from them through his generous allowance for her upkeep. Drink, too, is a major theme of Booth's—his certainty that the craving for it sprang from the need to blot out the pain of living, and that the inevitable addiction was the root of most social evils. But he saw no likelihood that poverty would be abolished by a Socialist Millennium. Dismissing two of the books most influential on Shaw's thinking in the 1880s and 1890s, Henry George's *Progress and Poverty*, which relied on a redistribution of wealth through a tax on land values, and Edward Bellamy's utopian—and secular—socialism in *Looking Backward*, as "religious cant," Booth sought immediate relief. "When the sky falls we shall catch larks. No doubt. But in the meantime?"

The utopian schemes of Socialism, he warned, required "a bloody and violent overturn of all existing institutions." Those who had something to lose by that possibility would be more prudent, he suggested, in financing his spiritual revolution, for the religious discipline guaranteed social change within social order. Booth's recipe for the regeneration of man has the ring of a Shavian preface, and Shaw uses the same catalogue approach:

> *The first essential that must be borne in mind as governing every Scheme that may be put forward is that it must change the man when it is his character and conduct which constitute the reasons for his failure in the battle of life.* No change in circumstances, no revolution in social conditions, can possibly transform the nature of man. Some of the worst men and women in the world, whose names are chronicled by history with a shudder of horror, were those who had all the advantages that wealth, education and station could confer or ambition could attain.
>
> The supreme test of any scheme for benefiting humanity lies in the answer to the question, What does it make of the individual? . . . You may clothe the drunkard, fill his purse with gold, establish him in a well-furnished home, and in three, or six, or twelve months he will once more be on the Embankment, haunted by delirium tremens, dirty, squalid, and ragged. Hence, in all cases where a man's own character and defects constitute the reasons for his fall, that character must be changed and that conduct altered if any permanent beneficial results are to be attained. If he is a drunkard, he must be made sober; if idle, he must be made industrious; if criminal, he must be made honest; if impure, he must be made clean; and if he be so deep down in vice, and has been there so long that he has lost all heart, and hope, and power to help himself, and absolutely refuses to move, he must be inspired with hope and have created within him the ambition to rise. . . .
>
> Secondly: *The remedy, to be effectual, must change the circumstances of the individual when they are the cause of his wretched condition, and lie beyond his control.* Among those who have arrived at their present evil plight through faults of self-indulgence or some defect in their moral character, how many are there who would have been very differently placed to-day had their surroundings been otherwise? . . . Favourable circumstances will not change a man's heart or transform his nature, but unpropitious circumstances may render it absolutely impossible for him to escape no matter how he may desire to extricate himself. The first step with these helpless, sunken creatures is to create the desire to escape, and then provide the means for doing so. In other words, give the man another chance.
>
> Thirdly: *Any remedy worthy of consideration must be on a scale commensurate with the evil with which it proposes to deal.* It is no use trying to bail out the ocean with a pint pot. This evil is one whose victims are counted by the million. The army of the Lost in our midst exceeds the numbers of that multitudinous host which Xerxes led from Asia to attempt the

conquest of Greece. Pass in parade those who make up the submerged tenth, count the paupers indoor and outdoor, the homeless, the starving, the criminals, the lunatics, the drunkards, and the harlots—and yet do not give way to despair! Even to attempt to save a tithe of this host requires that we should put much more force and fire into our work than has hitherto been exhibited by anyone. There must be no more philanthropic tinkering, as if this vast sea of human misery were contained in the limits of a garden pond.

Fourthly: *Not only must the Scheme be large enough, but it must be permanent.* That is to say, it must not be merely a spasmodic effort coping with the misery of to-day; it must be established on a durable footing, so as to go on dealing with the misery of to-morrow and the day after, so long as there is misery left in the world with which to grapple.

Fifthly: *But while it must be permanent, it must also be immediately practicable.* Any Scheme, to be of use, must be capable of being brought into instant operation with beneficial results.

Sixthly: *The indirect features of the Scheme must not be such as to produce injury to the persons whom we seek to benefit.* Mere charity, for instance, while relieving the pinch of hunger, demoralises the recipient; and whatever the remedy is that we employ, it must be of such a nature as to do good without doing evil at the same time. It is no use conferring sixpennyworth of benefit on a man if, at the same time, we do him a shilling's worth of harm.

Seventhly: *While assisting one class of the community, it must not seriously interfere with the interests of another.* In raising one section of the fallen, we must not thereby endanger the safety of those who with difficulty are keeping on their feet.

What Shaw perceived was that Booth's Victorian idealism about hard work and human renewal was slipping away as the Army succeeded in winning converts. There were too many branches, too many inexperienced officers. Spirituality excited more innocent fervor than economics, and the emphasis in any case was becoming one endemic to charitable organizations. It became more vital to save souls and to count the collection, to stir and restir the faithful to pay the increasing costs of maintenance of the growing network of Army personnel and rented chapel space. Booth's goal of social regeneration to eliminate the causes of poverty was giving way to the goal of building and buttressing the charity bureaucracy of Salvation Army colonels and majors and captains. Its chapels where the poor received bread-and-scrape, and a hymn book, and the promise of some kind of job, usually unrealized, was substituting for the farms and factories and new towns that had been the models for tomorrow.

That realization gives added meaning, and even poignancy, to Undershaft's challenge to Major Barbara and her fiancé, Dolly Cusins, "Dare you make war on war? Here are the means!" Booth had almost ceased to make war on the sources of poverty; rather, he was accepting what amounted to unacknowledged bribes from the whiskey distillers and from other entrepreneurs whose commodities were counterproductive to social change, to keep the West Ham shelter in East London, and others like it, alive to dispense soup and salvationism. The reorganization of work and the workplace about which William Booth wrote in his *In Darkest England* was left to Shaw, who drew upon Booth and Barbara's other spiritual fathers to challenge charity to furnish more than a Band-Aid and thus eliminate the need for its own existence. That bureaucratic instinct to survive, and then to prosper on the pennies of the faithful, is seen now with a melodramatic glare in the soap-opera saga of the "electric church" of television evangelism.

"What is the use of preaching the Gospel," Booth asked in *In Darkest England*, "to men whose whole attention is concentrated upon a mad, desperate struggle to keep themselves alive? . . . The first thing to do is to get him at least a footing on firm ground, and to give him room to live. Then you may have a chance." More bluntly, but in the same terms, Shaw's Undershaft would challenge Barbara, "It is cheap work converting starving men with a Bible in one hand and a slice of bread in the other. . . . Try your hand on my men: their souls are hungry because their bellies are full."

Booth's description of a typical afternoon and evening at a Salvation Army shelter could be the scenario for Act 2 of *Major Barbara*. A wash and a meal are followed by "a rousing Salvation meeting," during which "there are addresses, some delivered by the leaders of the meeting, but most of them [are] the testimonies of those who have been saved at previous meetings, and who, rising in their seats, tell their companions of their experiences. Strange experiences they often are of those who have been down in the very bottomless depths of sin and misery." But Shaw remains skeptical about confessions for bread. As Rummy Mitchens complains to Snobby Price in Shaw's depiction of the shelter, "Thats whats so unfair to us women. Your confessions is just as big lies as ours; you dont tell what you really done no more than us; but you men can tell your lies right out at the meetins and be made much of for it; while the sort of confessions we az to make az to be whispered to one lady at a time. It aint right." But Barbara's true-believer reaction, in her ecstasy of worldly innocence, commends Snobby: "Ive hardly ever seen them so much moved as they were by your confession, Mr Price. . . . If you had given your mother just one more kick, we should have got the whole five shillings!" Undershaft offers to contribute the odd tuppence, but Barbara refuses her father's offer: his money is tainted, as she thinks her pitiful collection is not.

Undershaft's allegedly suspect millions are made in munitions manufacture, supplying one of the necessities of modern civilization. However tainted, and however threatening they seem to the very civilization which the jobs he creates sustain, their impact is much like that of Booth's ideal—utopian "self-sustaining communities, each a kind of co-operative society, or patriarchal family, governed and disciplined on the principles which have already proved so effective in the Salvation Army." Its motto, Undershaft has already explained, might be his own: "Blood and Fire."

"But not your sort of blood and fire, you know," counters his future son-in-law, Charles Lomax.

"My sort of blood cleanses: my sort of fire purifies," Undershaft explains; and Major Barbara says "So do ours." And in his preface to the play Shaw suggested "that when General Booth chose Blood and Fire for the emblem of Salvation instead of the Cross, he was perhaps better inspired than he knew; such knowledge, for the daughter of Andrew Undershaft, will clearly lead to something hopefuller than distributing bread and treacle."

Bread and treacle without an ideal left an emptiness of soul, something which Shaw had recognized years before he put down a word of *Major Barbara*. One of the positive elements of Booth's Army, he found, was the replacement of Christian gloom by Christian vitality:

> Joyousness, a sacred gift long dethroned by the hellish laughter of derision and obscenity, rises like a flood miraculously out of the fetid dust and mud of the slums; rousing marches and impetuous dithyrambs rise to the heavens from people among whom the depressing noise called "sacred music" is a standing joke; a flag with Blood and Fire on it is unfurled, not in murderous rancor, but because fire is beautiful and blood a vital and splendid red; Fear, which we flatter by calling Self, vanishes; and transfigured men and women carry their gospel through a transfigured world, calling their leader General, themselves captains and brigadiers, and their whole body an Army: praying, but praying only for refreshment, for strength to fight, and for needful MONEY (a notable sign, that); preaching, but not preaching submission; daring ill-usage and abuse, but not putting up with more of it than is inevitable; and practising what the world will let them practise, including soap and water, color and music. There is danger in such activity; and where there is danger there is hope.

The danger, he saw, was still money. The Salvation Army was

> building up a business organization which will compel it eventually to
> see that its present staff of enthusiast-commanders shall be succeeded
> by a bureaucracy of men of business who will be no better than bish-
> ops, and perhaps a good deal more unscrupulous. That has always
> happened sooner or later to great orders founded by saints; and the
> order founded by St William Booth is not exempt from the same
> danger. It is even more dependent than the Church on rich people
> who would cut off supplies at once if it began to preach that indispens-
> able revolt against poverty which must also be a revolt against riches.[12]

"Where does all the money go to?" Snobby Price charged in words
deleted in the manuscript of the play. "Why old Booth gets millions."
Shaw knew better than to suggest misappropriation of Army dona-
tions, even when spoken by the sly but ignorant Snobby Price, and
dropped the line.[13] Yet Shaw was concerned about the evangelical
distortion of Christ's "Blessed are the poor in spirit" into "Blessed are
the poor." One Salvationist who had seen the play in December 1905
came away shaken, and drafted a fourteen-page typewritten report to
an Army Commissioner, Alex M. Nicol. "You come away feeling not
very sure of yourself," the writer confessed. "Human nature is shewn
as such a rotten sort of thing, that you even wonder if you aren't a bit
of a humbug yourself."[14] Humbugging, one assumes, to extract
money from the poor as well as for the poor.

The *War Cry* of 4 November 1905 had been more cautious. "A leading dramatist," the official voice of the Army reported, "has written a
new play, 'Major Barbara,' which concerns the love affair of a Salvation
Army officer, and is woven more or less around the General's slum
work. The second act is laid in a Salvation 'doss-house,' and the dialogue is largely the expression of views on General Booth's religious
campaign. 'I greatly admire his rescue work,' said the dramatist."[15]
Not a mention of Bernard Shaw!

Notes

1. Entry for 30 April 1897 in *Burne-Jones Talking: His Conversations as Preserved by His Studio Assistant, Thomas Rooke*, ed. Mary Lago (Columbia: University of Missouri Press, 1981), p. 144.

2. Shaw, *Immaturity* (1878–79), published in the *Collected Edition* as vol. 1; the manuscript is in the National Library of Ireland.

3. Shaw, *Dramatic Review*, 26 September 1885, reprinted in *Shaw's Music*, ed. Dan H. Laurence (New York: Dodd, Mead, 1981), p. 364.

4. Shaw, *The Star*, 13 May 1889, reprinted in *Shaw's Music*, p. 627.

5. Report to the Salvation Army, 31 March 1906, published as "The Bands of the Salvation Army" in *Shaw's Music*, pp. 588–94.

6. *Collected Letters*. All extracts from Shaw's letters are from *CL* unless otherwise identified.

7. Letter to the *Daily Citizen*, 26 October 1912, reprinted in *Agitations*, ed. Dan H. Laurence and James Rambeau (New York: Frederick Ungar, 1985), p. 150.

8. "Open Air Meetings," autograph manuscript, p. 6, c. 1879–80, in the Harry Ransom Humanities Research Center, University of Texas at Austin. Reproduced with the permission of the HRHRC and published with the authorization of the Society of Authors on behalf of the Bernard Shaw Estate. Copyright © 1990 by the Estate of Bernard Shaw.

9. "Facts about Major Barbara," a press release drafted by Shaw for *The Sun*, New York, 26 December 1915, reprinted in the *Bodley Head Bernard Shaw*, III:193–97.

10. Press cutting from the Ivo Curral collection, Royal Academy of Dramatic Art, London, identified as from *The Standard* (London), September 1911.

11. Diary entry for 19 July 1889, in *Bernard Shaw: The Diaries*, ed. Stanley Weintraub (University Park: Penn State University Press, 1986), p. 523. Other diary references are from this edition.

12. Preface to *Major Barbara*, Bodley Head edition.

13. Garland facsimile edition of the *Major Barbara* manuscript, ed. Bernard F. Dukore (New York: Garland, 1981), leaf 69.

14. Alex M. Nicol, Commissioner of the Salvation Army, TLS, 18 December 1905, accompanying a fourteen-page typewritten criticism of the play by an unidentified Salvationist who had attended the 15 December 1905 matinee of *Major Barbara*. HRHRC Austin, #315 in the catalogue, *Shaw: An Exhibit*, ed. Dan H. Laurence (Austin: Humanities Research Center, The University of Texas, 1977).

15. Quoted from the *War Cry* in Arch R. Wiggins, *History of the Salvation Army* (London: Nelson, 1968), 4:251–52.

Leon H. Hugo

PUNCH: J. M. BARRIE'S GENTLE SWIPE AT "SUPERSHAW"

When the Lord Chamberlain refused to license *Press Cuttings* in 1909, Shaw responded with customary speed and acerbity. In a letter to *The Times* on 26 June, he inveighed against the objection to "personalities expressed or understood" in *Press Cuttings,* and mentioned that he had himself been "represented on the stage with the Lord Chamberlain's full approval, in a little fantasy by no less well-known an author than [his] friend Mr J.M.Barrie." He followed this up the next day with a self-drafted interview in the *Observer,* mentioning Barrie's "little fantasy" again: "You may remember, not long ago, the production of two plays by Mr J. M. Barrie. In the first, a very charming little sketch, *Punch and Judy,* there was a person called Superman, an unmistakable and confessedly humorous skit on myself."[1]

Shaw's memory was slightly at fault in two particulars: Barrie's skit was called *Punch,* without his Judy in the title, and "Superman" was really "Superpunch." *Punch* was produced at the Comedy Theatre on 5 April 1906 in a triple bill that included *Josephine,* also by Barrie, and *The Drums of Oude* by Austin Strong. Critical response was not enthusiastic. The *Observer* (8 April 1906), lumping *Josephine* and *Punch* together, said they "proved to be very poor stuff, alike in their puerile personalities and their infantile satire" and also a "breach of good manners" and "simply deplorable." Other critics, similarly afflicted with a sense of propriety, queried the "good taste" of *Punch* but reluctantly admitted that it had some "charm." Only A. B. Walkley (*The Times,* 6 April 1906) came out in favor of the evening's entertainment, going so far as to describe Barrie as "our spoiled child . . . allowed to do things which would bring stern reproof on other children . . . allowed to do what no one has been allowed to do in a long time—bring the contemporary political situation straight on to the stage." Of *Punch* itself Walkley said "This is not a new trick of our clever spoiled child's. It is an old one in a new guise: but here again he shows both his daring and the law he is allowed. . . . A quaint, very slight, sentimental, subtle, sharp-edged little sketch, full of the Barrie quips and cranks, the unexpectedness, the audacity, the touch here and there of something which in another setting would sound very like silliness." The Shavian presence on stage in the person of Superpunch earns little more than a passsing, dismissive word. In Walkley's eyes Barrie could do no wrong, and the playwright featured in the piece did not count.

He praised the acting, as did the other critics. The program identifies the cast:

"PUNCH"

A Toy Tragedy in One Act

By Mr J. M. Barrie

Punch	Mr Dion Boucicault
Judy	Miss Eva Moore
O'Caries	Mr Arthur Eldred
Superpunch	Mr A. E. Anson

The play ran for only fourteen performances. It is unlikely that either piece by Barrie was ever revived; what is certain is that neither has ever been published. They are listed in the Appendix of the Definitive Edition of *The Plays of J. M. Barrie* (London: Hodder and Stoughton, 1942) but are not printed even there. As the editor, A. E. Wilson, remarks of these and other pieces, Barrie would not have wished such items to be preserved. (Shavians might not have such scruples, however.)

The text given below is from the Lord Chamberlain's collection of plays, that is, the text that was licensed for performance (License No. 165; 26.3.1906), now housed in the British Library, Bloomsbury. It will be noted that the approved text and the program differ in certain respects: the "little Tragedy" became a "Toy Tragedy" and the "New Man" became "Superpunch." We cannot know whether similar changes crept into the dialogue during rehearsal, but it is tempting to imagine Barrie and the cast tinkering with the script. One notes in the text, for example, how carefully Barrie distances the "New Man" from a known "personality" by stipulating, for the Lord Chamberlain's benefit no doubt, that he has to be made up to look, "not like Mr Shaw, but like the man who played Superman."[2] But was this distancing maintained in peformance? Quite probably not.

The text of *Punch* is far from ready for the press. It is rather carelessly typed: punctuation is casual and occasional words are omitted; there is scant adherence to the finer conventions regarding the presentation of a play-text. Some restrained invisible editing has accordingly been done.

Two allusions are worth noting. "The drama's laws . . . ," spoken by O'Caries, quotes Samuel Johnson's *Prologue Spoken by Mr. Garrick at the Opening of the Theatre in Drury Lane* (1747). Punch's "Prunes and prisms . . ." is adapted from Dickens's *Little Dorrit:* "Papa, potatoes, poultry, prunes, and prisms are very good words for the lips: especially prunes and prisms."

Punch is published here for the first time through the courtesy of Samuel French Limited.

Notes

1. The other sketch, *Josephine,* depicted Asquith and Balfour in thinly veiled "disguise;" indeed, it was more the obvious representation of personalities, political personalities at that, in this piece that raised Shaw's ire and the comment: "I conclude that the Lord Chamberlain does not read my plays with the same impartiality—or the same partiality, perhaps—that he reads Mr Barrie's." *The Observer* (London) 27 June 1909.

2. Made up, that is, to look like Granville Barker, who was a Shaw-like Tanner in the original production at the Court Theater in 1905.

J. M. Barrie

PUNCH
A Little Tragedy in One Act

Characters: PUNCH, O'CARIES, THE NEW MAN, JUDY

It is a humble room, entrance stage L. Fireplace R. There is an oblong stout kitchen table R. There are several armchairs without seats to them. Pictures of murders on walls. At back is an ordinary sash window, but without any window frame, so that it is all open. This window is supposed to represent the window or stage from which Punch gives his immortal performances. We are seeing it from inside. PUNCH is performing here as curtain rises. He is performing to an unseen crowd outside, so that his back is to audience and his legs dangle outside unseen. He is in the middle of some well-known part of his performance with the figures, and is giving utterance to his popular cries. Any accompanying music comes from the familiar Punch musician who is unseen and is supposed to be somewhere outside below window. The figures PUNCH manipulates are marionettes and he holds them in the well-known way, and as we are looking from the inside we see how it is done. Several of the figures of the show are lying in readiness on the table, and JUDY, a quaint little old lady, naturally very prim, is attending to them and helping PUNCH. The opening would be in this manner. PUNCH is dancing gaily alone. JUDY is excitedly tidying a figure, runs to him with it and slips it into his hands; he manipulates it in the well-known way, finally knocks it into the room and dances gaily. JUDY now puts up herself (perhaps only head and shoulders) as a figure with quick change of headgear: they dodge each other till he knocks her into room; she immediately picks herself up, gets another figure and hands it to him. He manipulates it and knocks it into room. All this has been very quick: PUNCH uttering the well-known cries and JUDY rushing about as lively as a teetotum. PUNCH has now reached a point in the performance where he is accustomed to wait for applause, and, as this point draws nigh, JUDY awaits the public verdict very nervously. PUNCH bows to audience outside and then, instead of applauding, this unseen audience outside bursts into a storm of hissing, hooting and booing. Things are flung at him, and he comes tottering down the steps in an agony of mortification. The chief oddity about his appearance besides his general Punch get-up is that he has silly legs, i.e. he has got into the way of using them like the legs of a marionette, as limp things. Thus he flings them over what he is to sit on instead of using them in the usual way. Sometimes also they cross and get stuck. JUDY, though at present so excited that she rushes and whirls about like a thing on wires, is naturally a very staid and prim little lady. She is cheaply but very neatly dressed in a plain little black merino with white cuffs and collar. To perform she has flung over this the conventional head-dress, but removed it at once when knocked down. As PUNCH comes down stage in distress, JUDY in sympathy with him rotates furiously shaking fist at unseen crowd &c. They should be as odd a pair as two birds.

JUDY. Bear up Punch dear—don't you take it so much to heart now—don't you, my deary.

PUNCH. I'm done for, Ju, hooted, hissed! *My* show booed. (*Sits on table.*) I'll never come above this—never. It's the end of me. Here lies Punch. (*Lies forlornly on table.*)

JUDY (*flinging up arms and speaking very quickly in one cry*) What's to be done, what's to be done! (*Looking at him.*) Oh, it's terrible to see a strong man in tears.

PUNCH (*sitting up*) Let them flow, Ju, let them flow. (*He is taking a certain pride in being abject.*)

JUDY (*a whirlwind again*) Drat the public, drat 'em, drat 'em, drat 'em. My own, they'll come to their senses to-morrow—they'll be cheering you again to-morrow.

PUNCH. No, my pretty, no—we got to look it in the face. This is no sudden thing. I've seen it coming for weeks and weeks. They're dog-sick o' me and my show, Ju. Woe's me, they say we're crude.

JUDY. Crude? What's that?

PUNCH. I don't know, wifey. I never had a dictionary and I'm too old to have one now. But they say I've fallen behind the times, and my show is out of date! Here lies Punch. (*Lies back again.*)

JUDY (*rocking her arms*) O wa wa wa wa wa wa wa! (*Diffidently.*) Punchy, can it be that they don't like the murders?

PUNCH (*sitting up indignantly*) Not like murders! Not like murders! (*In a screech of scorn.*) Hoity toity, hoity toity, hoity toity! Not like murders! What's the world coming to!

JUDY. Don't be angry wi' me, deary. I just mean—I've sometimes thought myself that maybe the murdering was cruel.

PUNCH (*hissing through teeth at her*) Sentimentalist! Sentimentalist! Pro-Boer! Little Englander!

JUDY. But as a lesson to the young? If there was a moral in it, Punch?

PUNCH. I used to snick in a moral, if desired, at superior parties. (*Sniggers a little.*) I ended up wi' a speech saying "Dear little boys and girls, Punch was a naughty man for murdering so much, and he will suffer terrible, terrible remorse." And then I couldn't help larfing, and the little boys and girls larfed too, and it all ended as pleasantly as though there had been no moral at all! (*Pulling himself together.*) But that's no good now. They just don't love me the same.

JUDY (*stringing herself up to do something great—holding up arms*) Let the blow fall! (*With self-abnegation.*) Punch, I'm willing to offer myself up for the good of the show. Here I stand offering myself up.

PUNCH. What is it, Ju?

JUDY (*tragically*) My marriage lines that I've been so proud of this many a year—I'm willing to let them go. (*Takes from bodice and gives them to him.*)

PUNCH. Is this my Judy speaking?

JUDY. Punch, I know what's wrong. I've been loath to tell you, but now, let it out. Our show is not serious drama, my love. I've been reading all about it in the papers, and it's never serious drama if they are really man and wife. For the show's sake, Punch, I am willing to pretend that we're not married.

(*She sinks to the floor in woe. He goes to her much moved.*)

PUNCH. Noble Judy!

JUDY. For the love I bear you, dear.

PUNCH. Can Punch accept this sacrifice? Oh, never! If by this only can my show be saved, let it perish. (*Rather grandly.*) Judy once my wife, always my wife. Take back your marriage lines. (*He insists and she thrusts them back into her bodice with passionate pride in them—he moves away—his legs get stuck.*) My love, I'm tangled. (*She puts his legs right for him.*) Little Ju! (*He looks at window longingly.*) They're quiet now. (*Shows he is eager to give them another chance.*) They're fond o' me still—do you think? (*She has no hope—he is fierce.*) They are fond o' me, woman?

JUDY (*faintly*) Yes—oh, yes.

PUNCH (*imploringly*) Yes, I'm an institution?

JUDY (*quick*) Yes, you are, yes, you are.

PUNCH (*making himself sanguine*) That's what I am, an institution! (*Goes boldly to window and is about to fling his legs over sill—falters, looks round anxiously at Judy, peeps at crowd round side of window—is afraid— hoots and boos break out again—it breaks him up, he whispers.*) Down wi' the blind, Ju, or they'll wreck the house. (*She from side so as not to show herself pulls down blind. In the meantime he sits on table.*)

JUDY. It's down.

PUNCH. Here lies Punch. (*Lies down on table, a door below is heard opening and shutting. JUDY looks at door.*)

JUDY. I think it's some o' the audience. (*PUNCH jumps up, gets his stick, and carrying it in the well-known way looks very pugnacious.*)

PUNCH. I'm ready for them—one at a time, two at a time, three at a time! (*Jumping about in the Punch way, and evidently prepared to deal death all round.*)

JUDY. No, no. Speak them fair, Punch—kow-tow to them, my own, kow-tow.

> (*Enter O'CARIES; he is the butcher's errand boy and is carrying a basket on his arm.*)

O'CARIES (*coming down to footlights and addressing audience*) I am O'Caries. It's a Greek word and means the public.

PUNCH. The public! I do hope you're bobbish, sir.

O'CARIES. I'm always bobbish. (*He is cavalier in manner.*)

JUDY. You'll sit down, honoured sir. Dear, dear, there's no seat to any o' the chairs. You see, I took all the seats out o' them because Punch and me, we've sat so long on the window ledge, we don't feel comfy on anything broader, we prefer to sit on the arms o' the chairs and dangle.

O'CARIES. The dyer's hand, ma'am, the dyer's hand!* (*Sitting on table.*) But I'll be all right here. (*She signs to PUNCH to be affable.*)

PUNCH. Make yourself at home, Mr Caries.

O'CARIES. Course I will, I *am* at home.

PUNCH. Eh? (*He and Judy are standing.*)

---

*My nature is subdu'd
To what it works in, like the dyer's hand.

(Shakespeare, Sonnet 111)

JUDY (*warningly*) Punch!

O'CARIES. Ain't it *my* house? I'm the public and I let it to you for so long as you amoose me. (*PUNCH looks for his stick. JUDY puts it further away.*)

JUDY. And *how* P. has amused you! A thousand times I have seen you in front roaring and slapping your knees.

PUNCH. Caries, that's gospel, I've seen you myself. (*Anxious.*)

O'CARIES. All true. You've amoosed me tremenjous for many a day.

PUNCH (*relieved and rushing at him and seizing his hand*) Bless you, Caries, bless you, old patron. Out with the jug, Ju, and we'll make a night of it, me and Caries.

O'CARIES. Stop! You did amoose me, Punch, but that's ended. I'm tired o' you.

PUNCH (*faintly*) You'll take back those words, Mr Caries?

O'CARIES. I wish I could. I have a weak side for old favourites. But I can stand it no longer, Punch.

PUNCH. It's as bad as that? (*He is humble.*) What is it that is wrong in my show, Mr Caries?

O'CARIES. I dunno.

JUDY (*in excited fit*) Canaille, canaille, canaille!

O'CARIES. The drama's laws, ma'am, the drama's patrons give. For those who live to please must please to live.

JUDY. Rubbidge, rubbidge, rubbidge!

PUNCH (*nobly quiet*) Quiet, wife. It's quite true, Mr Caries, and very well expressed.

O'CARIES. There's another performance I prefer now.

PUNCH. You mean—the noo man?

O'CARIES. That's who I mean. (*Lovingly.*) There was a time I couldn't stomach him, but now!

JUDY. That man you spoke about, Punch? (*He nods.*)

PUNCH. What is it that's so remarkable about him, Mr Caries?

O'CARIES. I dunno. I'm not one as troubles about reasons. The cognoscenti chaps have liked him—with reasons for a long time—but that was nothing. Then *I* took to liking him without reasons, and from that moment all was well wi' the noo man.

JUDY. To leave our house! To give up our calling!

O'CARIES. That's so. I've let to the noo man.

JUDY (*on knees*) Punch, join me on my knees to him.

PUNCH (*with dignity*) No, Judy, no. Never shall it be said of Punch that he begged from them whom he has so often bashed! Rise, wife. (*Raises her grandly.*)

O'CARIES. I like your spirit, Punch. Die game.

PUNCH. And you—die game too.

> (*He has got on other end of table with stick. He travels along this table à la Punch in the show. O'CARIES dodges him, they bob back and forwards with the familiar cries. At last PUNCH gives him a terrific whack on the back of the head, another on face and a third on back of head which makes O'CARIES fall on floor. PUNCH jumps down and furiously bangs him till life is extinct. JUDY has been standing nearby; her manner is that of one who fears the neighbours will talk. Having completed murder, PUNCH glances at her to see how she takes it.*)

JUDY (*shaking her head*) It's not the thing, Punch.

PUNCH (*sneering fiercely*) Prunes and prisms, prunes and prisms!

> (*She looks down disapprovingly—he goes to her trying to wheedle her—he makes little giggling sounds implying that the murder was a very funny incident. She resists for a time, but soon his giggles are infectious and they are hilarious together. They take to looking at the door a little apprehensively. JUDY gets on the arm of chair near fire, picks up her knitting and knits demurely. PUNCH gets on table, carrying himself like a naughty boy. Both are awaiting something from the door and are self-conscious. ENTER at door the two theatre FOOTMEN, carrying a stretcher. They are impassive, they put body on stretcher and carry it off, expressing no surprise or feeling whatever, as if this were their regular job. While they are on, PUNCH on table whistles consciously and defiantly like a boy who knows he has done wrong; also takes side glances at the footmen. When they are gone he gets down.*)

PUNCH (*with feeling*) I daresay that's my last murder!

JUDY. Don't say it, Punch.

PUNCH. Oh, the happy days before the noo man came!

> (*PUNCH sits on opposite arm of same chair—they dangle facing each other and should look a quaint couple.*)

PUNCH. To think *I* have brought you to misery, Ju—you that was born so genteel.

JUDY (*chirping*) Don't you dare say such a thing. Oh, you naughty fellow. Such a long happy married life we've had—Darby dear! (*She puts her hand on his.*)

PUNCH. You won't be so proud o' me no more!

JUDY. Will I ever fail my Punch? (*Quickly.*) Never, never, never.

PUNCH. Better for you in your old age, Ju, if you had married the curate.

JUDY. Curate! Curate indeed! (*like an owl*) Hoo hoo hoo hoo.

PUNCH. He was desperate fond o' you.

JUDY (*with a toss of her head*) Oh, I daresay.

PUNCH. I think your heart would have turned to him, Ju, if I hadn't come bounding into your sight.

JUDY. A man without a nose—never.

PUNCH. Your father wanted you to take him.

JUDY. Because father was a vicar himself.

PUNCH. As a clergyman's wife, Ju, your life would have been very different from what it has been wi' me. I've sometimes thought o' that when you were handing me up the figures. I suppose it was the glamour of me that took your heart by storm.

JUDY. It was your dash and masterfulness. You mind I wanted you to run away wi' me, and you said so grandly you would do nothing clandestine, and you mind how father got you to pretend you were a bad man, so that my love for you might go.

PUNCH. It nearly broke me up.

JUDY. And then he saw you were a son-in-law any vicar could be proud of, and he asked for the honour of an alliance.

PUNCH. He called me Davy—I never could understand why. Do you mind, Ju, when he was arguing once wi' me about immortality, and I gave him such a whack wi' my stick on his shiny bald head.

JUDY (*reproving*) You were naughty.

PUNCH. But he had *such* a shiny bald head. (*He tries to make her laugh; she resists for a time.*)

JUDY (*yielding*) It *was* shiny.

(*They laugh together like people trying in vain to restrain their mirth.*)

JUDY. Forty years ago! Even our children are all grown up now.

PUNCH. Some of them have done well, and some I flung out o' the window. (*Pause.*) You have no regrets, Ju?

JUDY (*fondly*) My prince! And you?

PUNCH. Forty years! You have no sense of humour, Ju, and yet like a true and loving wife you have laughed at my jokes for forty years. What more could a husband ask?

(*A strong knock is heard at door below. PUNCH and JUDY rise.*)

JUDY. Will that be—him? The noo man?

PUNCH. Yes. See wi' what confidence he knocks. Get your shawl, Ju—it's time for you and me to go.

JUDY. What's he like, Punch?

PUNCH. He has a beard. Everything in drama has changed, Ju, since the coming of the beard. It came originally, I've heard tell, from Norway, and had a roughish time, but quickly it spread all over the drama—like the first rabbit in Australia.

JUDY. I'll lock him out. (*Locks door.*)

PUNCH. It's no use—there's no lock the noo man can't force. Our only chance is for me to lure him on to the table, and then—(*Signifies that he would then murder him with stick.*) I hear him on the stair—he's singing!

(*The NEW MAN is heard outside humming "The Wearing of the Green." He has an Irish accent. He shakes the door, then bursts it open with masterful ease and enters. He is made up, not like Mr Shaw, but like the man who played Superman. His trousers are straight from the press. His manner is jaunty but not offensive. He has a cane which he twirls like a shillelagh.*)

NEW MAN (*advancing to footlight and addressing audience*) I am the noo man. I am the people's idol. I am the commercial theatre. Observe the line down my trousers. Afternoon, Punch, Ma'am. (*Bows to JUDY.*)

PUNCH. Afternoon. Have you come to take possession?

NEW MAN. That's it. They're waiting for me.

(*PUNCH peeps out at side of blind. A low hostile murmur greets him.*)

I'm uncommon sorry for you, Punch, but—it's *me* they want.

PUNCH (*sadly*) It used to be me.

NEW MAN. And by and by it will be some other body, but just at present, it's me.

JUDY. Punchy, is he Ibsen?

NEW MAN (*smiling*) Ibsen! Queer now to think that Ibsen was once considered advanced. Strange to think that he was once looked upon as a pioneer. I don't want to hurry you, Punch, but—(*Looks at window.*)

PUNCH. We're going, sir, we're going. Judy—

JUDY. If you would sit down a minute first, Mr Noo Man—the chairs are wanting, but—the table's very comfortable.

NEW MAN. Thank you, ma'am—though I never was one to talk. (*Sits on table.*)

> (*JUDY slips the stick into PUNCH's hands. He understands her meaning, and gets with affected carelessness on to the other end of the table while following dialogue goes on.*)

JUDY (*who is merely making conversation to give PUNCH time to do his work*) Let me see now—we'll leave you the figures, sir—we'll need them no more.

NEW MAN. Thanks, but I have no use for mechanical figures.

PUNCH (*amazed and angry*) No use for mechanical figures!

JUDY (*dazed*) What *is* this bearded drama? Is it not action, action, action?

NEW MAN. No, it's ideas, ideas, ideas. See here, madam (*puts his finger through his beard*)—and every hair with an idea in it.

PUNCH. Here's the only good idea I ever had!

> (*PUNCH has worked himself along the table and now gives NEW MAN terrific whacks on the head with his stick. They have no effect on NEW MAN. At the third whack the stick breaks. NEW MAN looks round genially, as one who only now sees what has been happening.*)

NEW MAN. It's no good, Punch. The public tried that on me at first, in the days when I merely maddened him, and if sticks or stones could have done it, I should have been dead long ago. I've fought him with my back to the wall, and he's had his teeth in me—but I have him in my pocket now.

PUNCH (*vanquished*) Let's go, Ju. He has earned his place fair and square, I bear no malice, sir. I've had a long innings. (*Shakes hands.*) It's time to give the young 'uns a chance. (*Hesitates.*) I don't know—it's usual—what do you think—about giving a farewell performance, wi' everybody crying?

NEW MAN. Better not, I think.

PUNCH. The old window ledge—*my* old window ledge—do you think they would mind if Judy and me was to sit there for the last time and sing Auld Lang Syne—very brightly?

(NEW MAN shakes his head. PUNCH yields the point, goes to his figures and addresses them in the old squeaking words, hitting them with his stick, but evidently with passionate love. Then he lays down on the table what is left of his stick.)

PUNCH. Come on, Ju.

(She has her shawl and he has his hat, but she gets the stick lovingly, kisses it and puts it beneath her shawl. They look at the NEW MAN who goes quietly to window, pulls up blind, sits on ledge and flings his legs over in the PUNCH manner. He is received by the crowd with a storm of applause. He keeps on bowing to them, amid which PUNCH and JUDY EXEUNT arm in arm.)

CURTAIN

NOTE. If Author is called for, NEW MAN and O'CARIES eventually appear together and shake hands as Manager and Author sometimes do on first night.

James Gindin

THE BELATED SHAVIAN INFLUENCE: WARTIME DISILLUSION AND GALSWORTHY'S *THE FOUNDATIONS*

Critics and historians of the "new" drama that emerged in England in the first years of the twentieth century often classified Shaw and Galsworthy together, as if consciously united in a movement to transform the drama. Those who saw their work as representing a new realism in opposition to the sterilities of stage convention, a simplification that neither dramatist ever endorsed, tended to make few distinctions between them. The most penetrating critic of the age, William Archer, linked Shaw and Galsworthy as his two principal "pioneers" in the "almost miraculous renascence" of an art "incalculably more faithful, more subtle and more highly developed than that of late seventeenth century comedy . . . more observation, more invention, more thought in it—a higher and more complex order of intellectual effort."[1] Galsworthy and Shaw did acknowledge similar intentions to use the stage as a forum for contemporary social issues, but the two did not, as dramatists, think themselves at all alike.

They first met in 1906 when Galsworthy, encouraged by Edward Garnett, submitted *The Silver Box* to the stage company at the Court Theatre that had already produced Shaw's *Candida*. Granville Barker and Shaw read the play over a weekend and decided to stage eight matinees. Shaw valued *The Silver Box* and the later *Justice* because they theatrically "smite our consciences."[2] But he recognized the dramatic and tonal differences from his own work. In a 1907 letter to the

classicist and translator Gilbert Murray, Shaw complained of Granville
Barker's direction of *The Devil's Disciple:* "the play revolts Barker's
soul: he strives earnestly to crush the cast and get a delicate galsworthy
[*sic*] result."[3] Galsworthy suspended his reservations about Shaw's
plays in his admiration for their social and pedagogical utility. In
1906, he wrote his young friend Ralph Mottram: "We've been to see
two Bernard Shaw plays. *John Bull,* etc., and *Man and Superman.* The
beggar riles me with his out-Williaming of William, but he's a witty
dog and his work (ephemeral enough) is serving a good contemporary
purpose. He is only irritating in his pretensions and personality."[4]
Galsworthy was edgy about suggestions that he was a tamer Shavian:
he commented in his diary on a 1911 burlesque skit about the apostles
of the new drama, "why try and lump me into that galère—me who
have no affinity at all with Ibsen or Shaw."[5] In later years, Galsworthy
stated the contrast between himself and Shaw in terms that, while
somewhat self-serving, suggest something of the difference between
the two writers' characteristic handling of dramatic form: "It might be
said of Shaw's plays that he creates characters who express feelings
which they have not got. It might be said of mine, that I create characters who have feelings which they cannot express."[6]

The issue of expression, of the dramatic function of talk, begins to
define one of the principal differences between these two dramatists,
who shared a sense of the theater's possibilities as an instrument of
social reform. In the beginning of the century, Shaw shaped a remarkably witty, theatrical, sometimes outrageous, far-ranging rhetoric of
assault against social simplicities. Galsworthy, in contrast, in his best
plays, such as *The Silver Box, Strife,* and *Justice,* used the stage to depict a
social contrast in a moment of locked stasis, a moment of irresolvable
silence. As in *Strife,* which centers on an industrial conflict in which
neither side is seen as right, the whole play builds to the overwhelming
irony of a moment of silent recognition and mutual defeat for the two
most honest, articulate, and extreme antagonists, the "two best men
broken." Shaw appreciated *Strife* as important in stage history, "solid
and absorbing," but he rightly complained that the meeting of the
striking workmen had been done entirely "without knowledge of mob
oratory."[7] Shaw's talk could spin beyond his ostensible themes, could
swell, turn, or undercut itself, as in the final injunction in *Man and
Superman* to "go on talking." Galsworthy's plays, in contrast, seem to
measure speech carefully and stringently to the requirements of plot
and theme. They lock in the silence of a final dramatic statement that
keeps the unresolved problem within the structure of existent society.
Shaw's talk enabled his social commentary to reach for the intellectual

excitement of the affinities he called the third stage of genius in his Epistle Dedicatory to *Man and Superman,* the stage of Goethe, Mozart, Bunyan, Blake, Ibsen, and Tolstoy. Galsworthy's commentary could, in Shaw's terms, pass the first "Dickens-Macaulay-Dumas-Guizot stage," but remained mired in what Shaw called the intermediate second, "the Stendhal-Meredith-Turgenieff stage."[8] Galsworthy would have accepted both the more restricted intellectual aims and the particular models. Other ways of stating the contrast carry no such implication of hierarchical judgment. Rebecca West, in acknowledging her debts to her literary progenitors, her four uncles—Wells, Bennett, Shaw, and Galsworthy—saw the drama of the latter two in terms of the health of the public body. She valued highly both the red-blooded energy of Shaw's wit, necessary to save the soul of the state, and the more pallid ministrations of "Uncle Phagocyte," Galsworthy, necessary to repel the infections of upper-middle-class smugness.[9]

Personally, and as public figures, Shaw and Galsworthy were close in the years between 1907 and 1911, when they both helped lead the campaign to persuade Parliament to change or demolish the system under which the Lord Chamberlain, through his Examiner of Plays, could censor drama (a system that Archer had begun opposing as early as 1892). Yet their methods and styles in political controversy were entirely different, just as they differed on some specific social and economic issues. Shaw later generalized about their different approaches: "Galsworthy always pictured the poor as forlorn and helpless. He pitied where I hated."[10] Before the 1909 Parliamentary Committee, Shaw was openly combative, proposing to read his printed book-length statement into the record and writing two iconoclastic short plays, *The Shewing-up of Blanco Posnet,* a play with blasphemous language about a horse thief's religious conversion, and *Press Cuttings,* a topical satire about suffragettes, just in order to have them denied licenses, which they were. Galsworthy was more terse and conciliatory. He wrote to Edward Garnett (whose banned play *The Breaking Point* had begun the protest) that, although he strongly opposed the system, he was unable to propose any plausible alternative: "My convictions are always negative or destructive, never constructive; I have a horror of construction, which implies the beginnings of tyranny."[11] The difference in tactics between Shaw's positive defiance and Galsworthy's negative moderation seemed rather amusing to both of them, as well as irrelevant to a Parliament that substantially changed nothing.

A difference both writers took more seriously, as their mutual fear of European war began, emerged in 1911. In the midst of the Balkan crisis, Galsworthy wrote a petition to ban the use of aeroplanes in time of war, trying to prevent bombing. He explained it and circulated it among writers, academics, and prelates. A good many signed, including Hardy, Archer, Granville Barker, Pinero, and Wells. Some, like Edward Elgar and Arnold Bennett, signed but doubted that the protest would do much good. Shaw, however, writing three serial postcards from Austria, absolutely declined, calling the protest an "absurdity" and wondering how Galsworthy could involve himself in such "pious piffle."[12] Galsworthy felt affronted, as if badgered into taking the underside of *Major Barbara* literally. Shaw consistently defended his position in later refusals to sign statements he thought sanctimonious and in articles proclaiming that modern war required unsentimental skill in both bombing and avoiding enemy bombs. Despite the fact that by 1917 they lived close to each other in Adelphi Terrace, only a few hundred yards from a theater actually bombed, they saw much less of each other than they had before the war. Shaw later told Stephen Winsten that Galsworthy was "by far the shyest man I had ever met" and "I liked him but I don't think he cared for me. He has never forgiven me for not backing his proposal that aircraft should not be used in war. I called it pious piffle."[13]

This difference in means or method, in sentiment or sentimentality, was, however, less than the stammering silence and depression they shared when confronted with the actual horror and jingoism of a war that neither of them had ever wanted. Neither had the slightest touch of the shallow, insular Du Maurier xenophobia, represented in the popular success of *An Englishman's Home,* or of the 1914 confidence that the troops would be home by Christmas. Shaw had advocated a pan-European pact in which all nations were to come to the aid of any nation attacked. He feared barbaric, "inexhaustible," despotic, czarist Russia, the uncivilized, unenlightened populations of the East. He assumed that Russia still owned Alaska.[14] Galsworthy better understood the facts and ambivalences of imperialism and racial xenophobia, as Shaw better understood those of technology. In mid-1913, Galsworthy had finished a play called *The Mob,* in which a young member of Parliament becomes a martyr in his refusal to yield to those pressures, represented within his own family, of convention, church, military establishment, and state that have promulgated an unspecified colonial war. In a partial inversion of the *Lysistrata* theme, his separated wife even offers herself only if he will stop speaking against the war, and then feels guilty about her potentially political use of sexuality. The play, produced in the spring of 1914, failed to register with critics or public, Desmond MacCarthy acutely commenting that its definition of conflicts was already outdated, more appropriate in wise, retrospective opposition to the Boer War than for any of the conditions of 1914.[15] *The Mob* soon embarrassed Galsworthy; he never permitted a revival. In the summer of 1914, both writers seemed shocked into uncertainty and extreme statement, each trying first to work his way out in the form of the public essay explaining why he was not a pacifist yet could not endorse the jingoistic version of England manifest in the popular press. Shaw, after a number of hesitant starts, finally wrote *Common Sense About the War*, in which, among other suggestions, he advocated that the soldiers on both sides shoot their brutal, aggressive, aristocratic officers and go home.[16] His target was what he, and many others, called the spirit of Junkerism. When Shaw insisted that England had more members of the Junker class than did Germany, and suggested that being conquered might do England some good, Galsworthy thought the statement showed a "lack of taste because it threw salt on open wounds."[17] Galsworthy's diffuse focus for all the current evil and horror was Christianity. In both his diary entry of 4 August 1914 and in essays he wrote for American periodicals in order to explain the war from the point of view of a nonmilitant, nonjingoistic Briton, he thought that "if this war is not the death of Christianity, it will be odd. We need a creed that really applies to life instead of talking of it."[18] He wanted to separate the humanity and forgiving qualities he found in the New Testament's depiction of Jesus Christ from any of the cosmological or judgmental associations, the representations of God as authoritarian or vengeful, he found in the Old. Wiser about the ambivalence and complexities in all creeds and talk, Shaw's skepticism was more likely to lead him to extrabiblical sources for the religious imagination other than those transmitted by conventional institutional Christianity, to mixtures of Testaments and reinventions of classical or medieval voices. Yet, by 1917, at least in their continuing essayistic prose for public audiences, Galsworthy and Shaw had both moved to strong support of the position represented politically by Lloyd George, the absolute necessity of winning the war.[19] Defeating Junkerism, more militant and oppressive in imperial Germany than in the far-from-perfect Britain, required technology, imperialism, and abandoning some of the central principles of Liberal, turn-of-the-century England, principles like opposition to conscription or to coercive industrial organization. Personally, as always, they responded in different ways. Shaw rather enjoyed the excitement of his visit to the front, the applications of technology and the intelligent energy of the men, despite his recognition of all the unjustifiable horrors, whereas Galsworthy enjoyed the classless cameraderie in cellars during bombing raids.

Without ever losing their centrally humane commitment or abandoning their aversions to xenophobic nationalism, they found both trivial and cultural meanings for the war through the experience of the war itself.

Essayistic positions, however, even for dramatists who regarded the stage as a public forum, could not suggest the complexity of artistic response to the almost overwhelming shock and disillusion of the war. For both Shaw and Galsworthy, by the time they could work themselves back to writing plays, the compelling issues of the time seemed to demand new forms, new ways of representing the experience on stage. Shaw moved to the creation of Chekhovian metaphor, *Heartbreak House*, which he called a "Fantasia in the Russian Manner," a play he began on 4 March 1916, although it was not staged until after the war. In his preface, Shaw calls *Heartbreak House* "cultured, leisured Europe before the war," and he depicts the house shaped as a ship, its timbers' bookshelves lined with the works of Galsworthy and other agents of social responsibility. Among the characters in *Heartbreak House*, only the women and the eighty-eight-year-old captain can operate effectually, can propel the plot or understand what others are doing, reflecting a world in which young men are away, lost in a senseless war. Yet enough happens within the house to create "the sort of pain that mercifully goes beyond our powers of feeling. When your heart is broken, your boats are burned: nothing matters any more. It is the end of happiness and the beginning of peace." The talk of the play suggests something of Shaw's usual commentary on contemporary social, political, economic, and sexual issues, a commentary that implicitly satirizes the earlier English society of "Horseback Hall," a world in which inconvenience is regarded as the greatest sin. But *Heartbreak House* has learned that soul and body are inextricably connected, that human beings can relate to each other without requiring the sublimation of riding horses, and that England has greater range than just the "equestrian classes and the neurotic classes" of "Horseback Hall." Yet, despite all the lively philanderings and politics, all the mistaken identities, *Heartbreak House* is still paralyzed, the ship that is "this soul's prison we call England." At times, the old·captain, poring over his charts, assumes that knowledgeable navigation can still save England. But the lights go out, and the play ends with falling bombs. That the only characters killed in the raid are the two made least attractive, the predatory capitalist and the pious burglar, two "practical men of business" who had sought to hide, is only a gesture in a world in which talk glides senselessly on the surface of experience and apocalypse seems imminent. Yet most of the characters survive, at least for the moment, and full apocalypse is far from certain. The structure and the texture of Shaw's play suspend the ship in its pain, disillusion, and unresolved trivial talk, confronting violent destruction with no sense, articulate or otherwise, of what the end might be. The shadow of ambivalence, implicit in some of the earlier plays, about the function of talk, books, and rational navigation deepens, darkens, and overwhelms consciousness.

For Galsworthy, the Great War, out of its pains and deprivations, also helped to propel new forms. If discussing the major achievements of each, critical justice would require contrasting Shaw's plays with Galsworthy's novels—and the war helped move Galsworthy away from years of writing heavily thematic and schematic fiction, static and polarized treatments describing specific social problems and classes, the rich and the poor, the aristocrats and the middle class, town life and rural life. During the war, particularly in 1918, he returned to his family of Forsytes, his chronicle, his attempt to shape the diverse and multiple details of experience with greater complexity and less dependence on theme, creating his finest work. Before finding his more capacious and appropriate form, however, in 1916, during his period of deepest depression about the war, just before going to southeastern France to work at a hospital for the shell-shocked and disabled for five months, Galsworthy wrote a play called *The Foundations*, that sounds significantly like the voice of the earlier Shaw.

The Foundations, alone among all Galsworthy's plays, is set in the future, in the economically uncertain postwar world to which Lord William Dromondy, an unusual hero who cared for and protected his men during the war, has returned. One of his footmen recalls, "Why he didn't even hate the Huns, not as he ought. I tell you he's no Christian."[20] But his Park Lane mansion, despite all his efforts and concern, rests on the foundation of rotting beams that dig deep into the earth—a society that, for once, is not entirely contained by Galsworthy's metaphor of architectural structure, his country houses, for example. The house is more permeable, subject to outside influences; and a parallel to Shaw's house of "heartbreak." On the evening on which Lord William and his wife are to give their annual "Anti-Sweating" dinner (an organization opposed to the exploitation of sweated labor), the footmen discover what is apparently a bomb placed deep in the foundations of the house. Although Lord William and his family attempt to handle the episode with admirable coolness, having always recognized the tenuous foundations on which their apparent superiority rests, the press discovers the bomb and, looking for the "heart-beat," sensationalizes: "Guy Fawkes is nothing to it. The

foundations of society reeling! By George, it's a second Bethlehem."[21]
The bomb, which turns out not to be a bomb, has been left by mistake
by a lively, articulate, radical worker for the gas company, Lemmy.
Both Lemmy and his mother, a forceful woman who has brought up a
large and variously indigent and amoral family by sewing the button-
holes, flies, and linings of stiff corduroy trousers for pennies, represent what may be the coming revolution to redress the inequities of
English society. Galsworthy's Shavian poor, in this instance, are far
from "forlorn" or "helpless."

The play opens with comedy about the changing biblical names of
footmen and concern for what is or is not "safe" within the house. Yet
spirited and unsafe talk, reminiscent of the Shaw of *Major Barbara* or
Man and Superman, carries the play: a long dialogue between the press
and Lord William on the differences between jingoistic, pious Christianity and the latter's idea of accidental brotherhood derived from
the Sermon on the Mount; the antiphonally shaped conversation of
two little girls, one upper-class and one lower-class, that relies on the
hymnal verse of William Blake; the satire, through the impercipient
butler, of early twentieth-century theories of eugenic purity, as well as
that of high-minded Liberals at boring meetings who drink only cocoa
or who talk of a "spiffing crowd" and things "really going Bolshy."[22]
The most provocative talk is Lemmy's rhetoric of revolution, the ex-
plosive voice from the gas pipes and the world of cooking kippers that
inveighs against the world of "pork wine" and some "butler broad as
an observytion balloon" watching the future "conflygrytion in the
sky."[23] Lemmy shifts the ideal of "liberty, equality, fraternity" to a
"new religion" of "Blood an' Kindness"[24] in a rhetoric that both echoes
and mutes the more extensively developed "Blood and Fire" in *Major
Barbara* (both may well be semiparodic adaptations of Bismarck's slogan for unifying Germany with "Blood and Iron"). Lemmy and Lord
William engage in dialogue on the dangers of censorship, as well as on
the virtues of shared blood, social theory, and attention to French
history. In addition, Lemmy as a character seems almost derived from
Shaw in his resemblances to Henry Straker, the "new" man of lower-
class origins who is skillful in understanding technology, both as process and as metaphor, deliberately and defiantly drops his aitches, and
intelligently and wittily insists on his individual dignity while assault-
ing class judgments. Lord William is as full of theory and as accommo-
dating as Jack Tanner, each realizing and respecting both the conditions and the technological knowledge of the "new" man. Finally, too,
as is increasingly evident in the Shaw of *Heartbreak House*, the admirable talk in *The Foundations* resolves nothing. Lord William's silence

before the crowd is seen as ineptitude, not as the ironic eloquence of the final irresolvability in the earlier Galsworthy plays; Lemmy's words to the crowd keep the house momentarily safe, but they are depicted as gas, the technologically modern substance his pipes control amidst crumbling foundations. The only achievable change Lemmy and Lord William both advocate is to label a scapegoat, the Press, whose "gas" ought to be "cut 'orf at the meter."[25]

Despite the interest and vitality of its Shavian elements, Galsworthy's *The Foundations* is finally somewhat less involving a play than are many of Shaw's. Galsworthy attenuates his social commentary: his bomb, unlike Shaw's, is a mistake and never goes off. Galsworthy can be, at moments, too schematic or sentimental, as in his contrast of the rich and poor children. His symbols for a coming futuristic revolution are worn and dated. The off-stage crowds, audible at least five times during the play, can only cry for "Bread" or sing the *Marseillaise*, the notes of which Lemmy plays on the violin to rouse his mother. Galsworthy's historical and revolutionary imagination is tamer, more pedestrian, and lacking something of the historical range and hyperbolic comic ingenuity of Shaw's. Nevertheless, this one Galsworthy drama genuinely echoes Shaw, develops a rhetoric central to the whole play that is a comically expressed articulation of new social and technological perspectives designed to educate, provoke, and implicitly perhaps even reform the audience, while acknowledging that social reform at the level of the problem is unlikely. It is as if, during the stress and pain of the war, Galsworthy's art acknowledged that the Shaw he thought unfeeling about armaments, comically outrageous, and sometimes pretentious, had been right all along. *The Foundations* ran on the London stage less than three weeks in the summer of 1917, when wartime conditions ensured long and successful runs for many plays. Galsworthy expressed disappointment, as he never did about any response his fiction engendered.[26]

After the war, Shaw and Galsworthy were less close, both personally and professionally, than they had been before. They remained in somewhat distant contact, Shaw still sending his derisively jocular postcards. When Galsworthy edited a periodical called *Reveille*, supported by the Ministry of Pensions for wounded and maimed returning servicemen, publishing stories and poems contributed by his friends as well as articles on new methods of prosthesis or legal rights for the disabled, he asked Shaw for a contribution. Shaw said he had nothing currently suitable and suggested that, instead, Galsworthy reprint "Poe's story of the man who married his grandmother under the impression that she was under thirty. She was all artificial. Nothing like a little comic relief."[27] When, in 1924, Galsworthy, then the president of the international PEN, recruited Shaw, he was somewhat surprised that Shaw succumbed. Shaw replied, "WHITEMAILER! Very well, I will go quietly. It's your doing, though. But I will not face the recurrent irritation of a guinea a year. Here is twenty guineas for a life subscription (I am 68). If they won't accept that they can make me an honorary member, and be d——d to them."[28] As usual, Shaw won the economic gamble. Such exchanges were funny and distant, not the sort of issue over which Galsworthy would experience the resentment he had over the petition to ban bombing. The one close personal friend of both, Granville Barker, after the war, having abandoned both the contemporary theater and his first wife, the actress Lillah McCarthy, was Galsworthy's friend much more than Shaw's. Shaw was preeminently a man of the theater, and when others, like Bennett and Galsworthy, said publicly that they tried to present their more obvious or immediately recognizable ideas on stage, keeping the more difficult and internal for their fiction, Shaw replied publicly in *The Nation:* "I will simply take one of the shortest, most intense, and most famous scenes in English literature and rewrite it as a chapter in a novel in the style of my friends Bennett and Galsworthy when they are too lazy to write plays."[29]

Although most of his creative energy in the 1920s did go into the private and complex world of his fiction, Galsworthy continued to write plays. His best and most successful plays of the 1920s, *The Skin Game* and *Loyalties,* returned to the dramatic structure of *The Silver Box* and *Strife,* the shaped social conflict, presenting both sides with ironies both against each other and within themselves, crystallized statically and theatrically in the silence of recognition. Shaw demonstrated less explicit interest in the social condition of England than he had and extended his fantasias further into legend, history, myth, and inventing new religions as in *Back to Methuselah* or *Saint Joan.* Personally, they saw little of each other, and their social, political, and communal ideas, somewhat proximate during the days at the Court when they both thought that the "new" drama might help reform complacent England, had diverged sharply. Galsworthy experienced none of Shaw's wavering and ambivalent attraction to the new, highly ordered, and controlling systems of the 1920s and 1930s, like Italian Fascism and Soviet Communism. Yet, from the point of view of the importance of trying to solve human problems through political change, Galsworthy could be seen as too complacently and superficially the outdated or sentimental benevolent liberal. Shaw always had the more fertile and extravagant intellectual imagination, as well as the greater wit and the willingness to risk the misunderstanding and simplification with which an audience can respond to wit. He made more public intellectual mistakes than Galsworthy did, although, within the public forum of the theater, Shaw's contribution reaches further both historically and aesthetically. Both the intellectual and personal differences between the two are visible in a statement Shaw was reported to have made to Stephen Winsten in the late 1920s, at a time when Shaw was increasingly interested in the universal implications of various religious myths: "Epstein [Joseph Epstein, the sculptor] told me that he remembers visiting the Leicester Galleries when the Christ was on exhibition and noticed a man just emerging from the room with clenched fist and furious face. It was John Galsworthy. Have you noticed how men often typify the very things they attack?"[30] For Shaw, Galsworthy, in part, was still caught speechlessly within the culture he rebelled against. Shaw kept reaching out as Galsworthy (with effectively complex resonance in his fiction) burrowed ever more deeply into himself. But, for a short time, both socially and dramatically, in shaping a theatrical rhetoric of lively political talk, Galsworthy seemed to absorb Shaw's style and focus, to demonstrate a more fundamental connection with Shaw than he ever explicitly acknowledged.

Notes

1. William Archer, *The Old Drama and the New: An Essay in Re-Valuation* (New York: Dodd, Mead, 1926), pp. 24–25.

2. Bernard Shaw, *An Autobiography, 1898–1950: The Playwright Years,* selected from his writings by Stanley Weintraub (New York: Weybright and Talley, 1970), p. 128.

3. Bernard Shaw, *Collected Letters II, 1898–1910,* ed. Dan H. Laurence (New York: Dodd, Mead, 1972), p. 715.

4. R. H. Mottram, *For Some We Loved: An Intimate Portrait of Ada and John Galsworthy* (London: Hutchinson, 1956), p. 67.

5. John Galsworthy, *Diary,* 7 September 1911. Galsworthy's diaries, 1910–1918, have not been published. They were included in the Galsworthy Memorial Collection at the University of Birmingham Library from 1962 to 1979 and have since been sold to *Forbes Magazine,* 60 Fifth Avenue, New York.

6. John Galsworthy, *Plays,* Manaton edition (London: Heinemann, 1923), pp. vii–viii.

7. *Bernard Shaw's Letters to Granville Barker,* ed. C. B. Purdom (New York: Theatre Arts Books, 1957), p. 150. The letter was written to Granville Barker on 9 March 1909.

8. Bernard Shaw, *Man and Superman* (Harmondsworth, Middlesex: Penguin Books, 1952), pp. xii–xiii.

9. Rebecca West, *The Strange Necessity* (Garden City, N.Y.: Doubleday, Doran, 1928), pp. 219–20.

10. Stephen Winsten, *Shaw's Corner* (London: Hutchinson, 1952), p. 118.

11. Edward Garnett, ed., *Letters from John Galsworthy, 1900–1932* (London: Jonathan Cape, 1934), p. 154. The letter is dated 19 August 1907.

12. Bernard Shaw, three serial postcards to John Galsworthy, 22 August 1911, in the Galsworthy Memorial Collection. See note 5.

13. Stephen Winsten, *Days with Bernard Shaw* (London: Hutchinson, 1949), p. 98.

14. Stanley Weintraub, *Journey to Heartbreak: The Crucible Years of Bernard Shaw, 1914–1918* (New York: Weybright and Talley, 1971), p. 103.

15. Desmond MacCarthy, "John Galsworthy: The Mob," *New Statesman* (London), 2 May 1914.

16. Stanley Weintraub, *Journey to Heartbreak*, p. 57.

17. Stephen Winsten, *Jesting Apostle: The Life of Bernard Shaw* (London: Hutchinson, 1956), p. 158.

18. John Galsworthy, *Diary*, 4 August 1914. See note 5.

19. Stanley Weintraub, *Journey to Heartbreak*, p. 239.

20. John Galsworthy, *The Foundations*, in *The Plays of John Galsworthy* (London: Duckworth, 1929), p. 498.

21. Ibid., p. 468.

22. Ibid., p. 493.

23. Ibid., pp. 480–81.

24. Ibid., p. 486.

25. Ibid., p. 506.

26. John Galsworthy, *Diary*, 14 July 1917. See note 5.

27. Bernard Shaw, letter to John Galsworthy, 29 September 1918, Galsworthy Memorial Collection. See note 5.

28. Bernard Shaw, letter to John Galsworthy, 9 June 1924. Quoted in H. V. Marrot, *The Life and Letters of John Galsworthy* (London: Heinemann, 1935), p. 544.

29. Stanley Weintraub, *Journey to Heartbreak*, pp. 141–42.

30. Stephen Winsten, *Days with Bernard Shaw*, p. 64.

Thomas R. Whitaker

GRANVILLE BARKER'S ANSWER TO *HEARTBREAK*

When Granville Barker's *Waste* was revived by the Royal Shakespeare Company in 1985, the production received high praise and later transferred with success to the West End. Indeed, some London reviewers were surprised to find in that play a theatrical skill, a political intelligence, and an articulate compassion that they could not expect from even the best of more recent British playwrights. For much of this century the very existence of Granville Barker as a master of the theater seems to have been a secret rather well kept from reviewers and producers alike. It is a sad fact that what may be his finest play has not yet received a professional production. As Eric Salmon has said, "there is everything about the text of *The Secret Life* to suggest that it would live triumphantly in the theatre, given the right handling."[1] Its difficulties, which have led theater folk and academics to regard it as a closet drama, are really those of a subtle score for performance. And surely there are a number of national and regional theaters in Britain and the United States that could give it the "right handling": ensemble acting, a style of evocative realism, and a delight in both wit and passion. In such a theater the world premiere of *The Secret Life* would be an occasion of historic importance. If that premiere followed soon after a production of Shaw's *Heartbreak House*, audiences would be able for the first time to share in one of the most notable dialogues in modern British drama.

The Secret Life looks back on the first two decades of the century through a panorama of lives that have been touched by romantic, political, and philosophical disillusionment. For Barker himself the play was clearly a midlife assessment. He began it in 1919, the year after he divorced Lillah McCarthy, married Helen Huntington, distanced himself from Bernard Shaw, and virtually ended his active life in the theater. He began it, moreover, in the year that finally saw the publication of *Heartbreak House*, a play on which Shaw had been working during the period in which Barker seems to have treated Shaw's house as his own. Barker finished *The Secret Life* in 1922, soon after what to Shaw was the heartbreaking failure of his own play on the London stage. Once *The Secret Life* had been drafted, Barker addressed his theatrical father as some prophetic Jacob might address his youngest son: "Confound you, Benjamin," he said, "your Heartbreak House. In *matter* for the theatre it may be 50 years before its time. But the actors of 50 years hence may equally find its *manner* abhorrent to them. It sets them no artistic problem."[2] *The Secret Life* clearly proposes to do just that. Taking up the issues and motifs of Shaw's comedy of negation, it translates them into what Barker called "a tragedy of negation." And its appropriately "negative technique"[3] also provides an answer to Shavian dramaturgy. Barker's play is therefore able to undertake a subtler and more realistic analysis of romantic idealism, postwar disillusionment, parliamentary democracy, the relations between *eros* and *polis*, and the deep anxiety of a social order that has lost its bearings. "The life of the mind is a prison in which we go melancholy mad. Better turn dangerous . . . and be done away with" (78).[4] If Captain Shotover had made that remark, we would laugh uneasily. When we hear it from the politician and historian Evan Strowde in the context of Barker's social panorama, we register a more chilling despair.

That despair, however, is not the play's last word, nor is realistic pathos its only response to the desperate verve of Shaw's most problematic comedy. In order to understand the complex nature of Barker's answer to heartbreak, we need to look closely at its dramatic mode and its orchestration of details. William Archer complained in 1923 that the play lacks "outward & visible" drama. "Perhaps thirty years hence," he said, "audiences may be purged of all lust for the event, & may have their faculties sharpened & speeded up to the sort of salmon-spearing by torchlight which the apprehension of your dialogue demands. But the theatre of thirty years hence leaves, & will leave, me strangely cold."[5] But that same objection could have been made to much of Chekhov. Barker's retort was firm: "I protest I never have—I *cannot*—write an unactable play: it would be against nature, against second nature anyhow. I act it as I write it. But"—he acknowledged—"there is no English company of actors so trained to interpret thought and the less crude emotions, nor, as a consequence, any selected audience interested in watching and listening to such things."[6] That hint of professional heartbreak should remind us that Barker's directorial work had often paralleled that of Stanislavsky, whom he visited in Moscow in 1914.[7] Indeed, just as he was finishing *The Secret Life*, he also published *The Exemplary Theatre*, a call for a national theater and school that would take the British some distance toward the Russian achievement. In 1937 he would write to John Gielgud: "I pinned my faith to the *theatre* solution; and finding it—with a war and a 'peace' on—no go, I got out." He urged Gielgud to establish, if not a "National" Theater, "such a one as Stanislavsky's or even Rheinhardt's of 30 years back."[8] Today, thanks in part to the work of Stanislavsky and Barker, and thanks also to the Chekhovian tradition of exploring the subtextual life beneath speech, we are surely ready for *The Secret Life*. Barker was no doubt wrong in suggesting that late twentieth-century actors would find the "manner" of *Heartbreak House* "abhorrent": its self-consciously theatrical techniques, though harking back to nineteenth-century opera and playing styles, more than hold their own on the stage. But we are now also schooled in other possibilities. In an essay first intended as a preface to *The Secret Life*, Barker declared that "the natural speech of the people" often contains "that power of expression and concentration of meaning which is the essence of poetry, even though the form be prose."[9] That language of the theater should not seem strange in the age of Beckett and Pinter.

The script of *The Secret Life* therefore asks for an attentive rereading. When St. John Ervine complained of bafflement after two readings, Barker retorted: "I am mischievously tempted to tell you to read it *twice* more and to read it as you would read—if you could—an orchestral symphony."[10] Shaw would have grasped that point. "A first-rate play," he had said in 1906, pointing to *The Voysey Inheritance* and to plays by Ibsen and Galsworthy, "seems nowadays to have no situation, just as Wagner's music seemed to our grandfathers to have no melody, because it was all melody from beginning to end."[11] Such a play is all situation, and it therefore requires, as Shaw said in 1910, the repeated reading or hearing that we would give to a Wagner opera or a Beethoven symphony in order to possess its themes. "Familiar as I am with Mr Granville Barker's methods and ideas," he added, "I find that until I have been through his plays at least six times I have not fairly got hold of them."[12] But as musicians of the theater, Shaw and Barker were in many respects antithetical. Barker's style and taste, said Shaw in his memorial tribute of 1946, "were as different from mine as Debussy's from Verdi's."[13]

Although *The Secret Life* is no *Pelléas et Mélisande* in answer to a Shavian *Rigoletto*, the musical comparison is apt. Its opening moments, as they sound Shavian leitmotifs by way of Wagner (whom Shaw had praised to Barker in 1918 as the model of motivic development),[14] are already translating the ironic agitation of *Heartbreak House* into a more Chekhovian music. Before us is a house that faces the sea. A piano has been moved out onto its loggia. From behind the parapet of the loggia we hear a male voice, punctuated by ironic remarks from others, "*coming to the end of a curious, half-sung, half-spoken performance of 'Tristan and Isolde'*"(3). The group has been evoking with wry nostalgia an operatic passion of their student life more than two decades ago. Indeed, a bit later this performer, the politician Stephen Serocold, will recall an occasion when an Italian with a guitar "offered to pass the time for us by singing 'Rigoletto' right through for three lire" (24). But in these opening moments we have also seen on the moonlit steps of the house a solitary figure in white—not a young girl like Ellie Dunn but the mature Joan Westbury. Her stillness hides a bitter exhaustion. Eighteen years ago she had rejected the proposal of her Tristan, Evan Strowde, and had settled for marriage with a diplomat appropriately named Mark. Since then she has lost two sons to the war, and lost her house to a fire. These opening moments should recall to us Act 2 of *Heartbreak House,* where Hesione Hushabye draws Mangan to the garden door saying, "There is a moon: it's like the night in Tristan and Isolde" (123)[15]—and also Act 3, in which Shaw's company gathers in the now moonless garden to assess its shared heartbreak. "It is a curious sensation," Ellie has said: "the sort of pain that goes mercifully beyond our powers of feeling. When your heart is broken, your boats are burned: nothing matters any more" (123). Both Joan Westbury and Evan Strowde have experienced just that sense of heartbreak. When he compares the moon to a ship on fire, she answers: "Burnt out" (6). And she prays to the moon "as one burnt-out lady to another" (10). Strowde soon begins to suggest the larger meanings of Shavian heartbreak: "When the war came," he says, "my beliefs about men and things were an enemy the more. I fought against them and beat them . . . and they're dead" (35). And he says later to Oliver, his unacknowledged son by the Countess of Peckham, "You cease to suffer . . . you cease to hope. You have no will to be other than you are" (124).

Neither play suggests an easy transcendence of this self-conscious apathy. "Heartbreak?" asks Shotover. "Are you one of those who are so sufficient to themselves that they are only happy when they are stripped of everything, even of hope?" And Ellie answers: "I feel now as if there were nothing I could not do, because I want nothing" (131). Strowde, too, says that one who ceases "to hope" becomes "extraordinarily efficient" and can therefore "ruthlessly" be something (125).

But both plays recognize that such acceptance of heartbreak leaves the heart open to the devils of destruction. Shaw's Ellie calls for the return of the zeppelin that has blown Mangan and the burglar to bits. Barker's Oliver, having lost an arm in the war, flirts with anarchism, although it is characteristic of Barker's quieter wit that Oliver abjures bombs because he does not see enough difference between a dead Prime Minister and a live one (48). But Barker concludes his panorama of botched statecraft and maimed lives by disclosing that Joan Westbury—whose desire that love remain unattainable has shielded her secret self from intimacy (140)—suffers a fatal tumor of the brain. In both plays the chief philosophic spokesmen also find it hard to transcend heartbreak. Shotover rails through his nonsense at those who will not learn to navigate the ship of state. Mr. Kittredge, the elderly American who shares Joan Westbury's last moments, says that "we're all driven to talk nonsense at times . . . when no other weapon is left us against the masters of the world . . . who have made language and logic, you see, to suit their own purposes" (72). But Shotover seeks through the seventh degree of concentration a weapon that will explode all the explosives of the world, while Kittredge, aware that "Doing defeats itself" (72) and poised between a necessary ignorance and a difficult faith, follows a very different course. He moves through a somewhat Shavian confidence in an experimental life force (79) and a gentle acceptance of the Buddhist prayer for release from "the need to know by name or form" (143) toward an affirmed distinction between "flesh" and "spirit" (144) that recalls St. Paul's letter to the Romans (8:9). In *Heartbreak House* action turns against itself in comic negation. In *The Secret Life* a tragic negation of action leads toward a difficult detachment.

That difference says much about Barker's answer to heartbreak. But before turning to its implications, we may usefully glance at two ways in which *The Secret Life* is a yet broader retort to Shaw. As early as *Candida*, Eugene Marchbanks had turned his back upon happiness because he had "a better secret than that" in his heart, and had walked out into what Shaw later told James Huneker was "Tristan's holy night."[16] No doubt Shaw told the same thing to the young actor who played Marchbanks for him in 1900—Granville Barker. Nearly twenty years later (just the span of time that has elapsed since Joan Westbury's rejection of Evan Strowde), Barker began to explore the ironies that might lurk in Candida's rejection of Marchbanks and Marchbanks's rejection of love, in "Tristan's holy night," and in that "secret" in the poet's heart. "I feel," says Strowde when Joan again rejects him, "like a boy crossed in his first love affair" (111). But *The Secret Life* was also, in effect, a response to a play that Shaw had not yet written. Joan Westbury, who is "of a very still habit" (24), makes her presence felt at first mainly through her silence. When in 1924 Barker wrote to Shaw about *Saint Joan*, he objected to what he called its characters' habit of always beginning at *A* and speaking straight on to *Z*. That Shavian obsession seemed to him "hardest" on Joan herself. "Because it must have been what she quite silently *was* which impressed people—oh, far more than anything she said."[17] Shaw's Joan had already been answered by his own as he set new problems for the post-Stanislavskian actor and director.

Heartbreak House articulates its critique of romantic idealism, self-deceptive poses, and political incompetence mainly through set dialogues that display the Shavian genius for rhetorical dialectic and demolition. The only real political force, Hastings Utterword, is called a numskull (60) but is kept safely offstage. We see the ineffective idealist Mazzini Dunn, the hollow businessman Mangan, the lapdog Hector, the rotter Randall Utterword, and an array of charming and touching but rather useless women. *The Secret Life*, however, orchestrates in more genuinely Chekhovian fashion a world in which the poetry, pathos, and intellectual brilliance seem attributable less to some playwright-puppetmaster than to its real and complex people. (John Galsworthy once said that Shaw "creates characters who express feelings which they have not got," whereas he created "characters who have feelings which they cannot express." Granville Barker here follows a middle road of highly articulate yet realistic feeling.) Barker's politicians and men of affairs—Strowde, Serocold, Sir Geoffrey Salomons, Sir Leslie Heriot, Lord Clumbermere—have undeniable talents that have been compromised, deflected, or wasted in the process of parliamentary government. Heriot, who thrives in this milieu, has become a vulgarized and ragbag image of the electorate. He has accommodated himself to political heartbreak: statesmanship, he says, "is the act of dealing with men as they most illogically are, and with the time as it nearly always most unfortunately is" (104, 97). Clumbermere, who is partly based on the soap manufacturer William Hesketh Lever, first Viscount Leverhulme,[18] is a self-made man of the old school, nourishing his soul on such inspirational verse as John Burroughs's "My Own Shall Come to Me" (151)—a much shrewder, solider, and more genuinely touching figure than Shaw's Mangan. And Barker's women, although less scintillating than Shaw's, have more ethical, emotional, and even intellectual substance. Joan Westbury can rightly say of her secret self, "I could never flatter it into being a heart-breaker" (140). So much for the vanity of both Hesione and Ariadne. The Countess of Peckham combines their worldly passions with sound judgment and maternal solicitude. Strowde's sister Eleanor has been helping him with the multivolume history project that he now abandons for an attempted return to politics, and has also been soliciting funds for social action. And Kittredge's granddaughter Susan—the Ellie-like image with which Barker's play finally leaves us—is a New England girl of grave simplicity who can ask, "What's to happen to this world if people won't choose their duty and stick to it though their hearts break?" (156). It is Susan who earns the right, in the play's motivic development, to become the healing Isolde to Oliver's wounded Tristan.

That realistic complexity deepens what Barker called "the tragedy of the barrenness of idealism" and also lets it pose what he called the "larger" and "very dreadful" question, "How to propagate spiritual goodness?"[19] We see the evasions, the acceptances of the second-best, that have led Joan Westbury and Evan Strowde to such barrenness. We also see the limitations of Salomons's cynicism, Heriot's pragmatism, Clumbermere's equating of righteousness with profit, and Susan's simplicity. The play confronts us with a poignant spectacle of death and judgment, redeemed only by a few highly qualified gestures toward new life. That is why, after the penultimate scene has shown us Joan's approach to death, attended by the sympathetic Kittredge, the play finally brings together Susan and Oliver. Here *The Secret Life* moves beyond the spiritual marriage of Ellie and Shotover, and beyond the ironically sketched romance of Anna and Trofimov at the end of *The Cherry Orchard*, toward a realistic rethinking of Ibsen's *When We Dead Awaken*. Susan has commonsensically said that if Joan loved Strowde, she should have married him. "Love isn't all of that sort," responds Oliver. "Sometimes it brings Judgment Day." "But that's when the dead awake . . . isn't it?" asks Susan. "Yes . . . ," says Oliver, "to find this world's done with." Susan persists in her optimism, declaring that Strowde, because he has loved Joan to the last, will "be born again . . . in a way." And a moment later, after Oliver has teased her for believing in miracles, she challenges him: "Wouldn't you want to be raised from the dead?" "No, indeed," he says. To which she responds, "You'll have to be . . . somehow." Oliver, who is on the point of leaving, stops at the door and considers her—his willful despair threatened by her confidence in what Barker calls "*an honest mind and her unclouded youth.*" Then he says, "Do you wonder I'm afraid of you, Susan?"—and goes out (158–60).

In leaving us with that question, and with that image of tacit spiritual power, the play suggests why, despite its Chekhovian texture of

analogous and contrapuntal situations, Barker could say to William
Archer, "The later Ibsen is my master." He added at once, however, a
circuitous qualification: "I don't name Tchekov. But (or 'for' or
'though') it was when I saw the Moscow people interpreting Tchekov
that I fully realised what I had been struggling toward—and that I saw
how much actors *could* add to a play."[20] Barker's emphasis on performance has important relations to the play's psychological and ethical
substance. What finally *is* "the secret life"? Eric Salmon, who sees here
an unreconciled conflict between the "ultimate unreality" of Doing
and the "ultimate reality" of Being, says that in the story of Joan
Westbury and Evan Strowde, "Being merges in loving and loving in
death, the perfect un-activity."[21] But surely the play looks with a
rather cool irony on any such Wagnerian *Liebestod,* and surely it also
transcends the duality of Doing and Being. It offers us a range of
meanings for "the secret life." One, of course, is Susan's simplicity.
Others are expressed by Strowde, by Joan, by Kittredge, and by the
full spectrum of the performance event. Strowde, who first uses the
phrase, says that men's strength "must spring from the secret life . . .
and what is it, as a rule, but the old ignorant savagery?" (32). For Joan,
however, the secret life has been a "sacred self that cannot yield to
life," an empty and agonizing freedom of questionable worth (143).
Kittredge, speaking of neither the savagery that may impel action nor
the aloof freedom that refuses action, offers yet another understanding of the secret life. He tells Joan that "the generation of the spirit"
produces a "virtue" that is "diffused like light, generously, unpriced"
(144). That virtue asks that we "keep nothing of our own" and "aban-
don everything but hope" (78). Barker himself told Archer that he
inclined toward Kittredge's answer, which is manifest in his continuing physical and psychological presence to the dying Joan.[22] That
answer transcends the duality of Doing and Being by understanding
"spirit" as a selfless and nonacting action that moves through us.

As Barker clearly understood, that answer inheres also in the "secret life" of any convincing performance of the script. This is evident
from Barker's comments on the Moscow Art Theatre and on modern
theater generally. When the people in Moscow showed him "how
much actors *could* add to a play," they were not adding the arbitrary or
adventitious but were finding the subtext that is implicit in Chekhov's
lines. And they were doing so, as Barker emphasizes in *The Exemplary
Theatre,* through a collaboration that brings unity of understanding
out of a diversity of viewpoints. When this process occurs in the
theater, the substance of the play becomes for the audience a sharing
in the actors' discovery in themselves of the characters—and their

discovery in the characters of aspects of themselves.[23] During a performance of the kind that Barker endorses, we would refine and clarify a sharable secret life by attending to the actions of the characters, to the implicit actions of the actors who are exploring the characters for us, and to our own necessarily Kittredge-like witnessing of this double action.

Awareness of that shared life in the theater tends to resolve here and now on the level of performance exactly those problems of idealism, self-definition, and social and political life with which the world *in* the play is so urgently and often pessimistically concerned. Barker was quite certain of that, as is plain from the contemporaneous account of drama that he offered in *The Exemplary Theatre*. "Acting," he said, is "the art of sympathy," and the theater is "the epitome of social life itself." The "key to government," he also said, is "self-understanding, which . . . must mean, in terms of a community, mutual understanding"—and in that mutual understanding we find "the knowledge of our souls." Implicitly, Barker was bringing us back by this route to the symbolic import of the role of Kittredge. In sum, dramatic art is the "working out" of "the self-realization . . . of society itself." The diverse talents and points of view that have been brought to the script join in a "genuine reconciliation" in which the audience can participate. Barker summed up this doctrine in sentences that must have been written with *The Secret Life* at least in the back of his mind: "Unity in diversity must be our social ideal, and it is this that the drama in its very nature does expound and, through the sympathetic power of impersonation, interpret. This is the drama's secret."[24]

And this, finally, is Barker's answer to heartbreak. In responding to *Heartbreak House*, he pointed toward the "secret life" of drama itself. "A play is material for acting," he said in what he planned as an introduction to *The Secret Life*. "It may be far more, but it must be that to begin with."[25] *The Secret Life* is indeed far more—one of the most intricately and beautifully *written* plays to come out of England in this century. It is possible, no doubt, for an intelligent reader of the play to conclude that its manner is rather cold and that it might leave an audience uninvolved. But precisely because this script is "material for acting" to begin with, and because it understands that phrase in a far more Chekhovian way than does Shaw's "Fantasia," it demands that readers themselves begin by searching for the subtexts that actors would realize together on stage. *The Secret Life* should lead us in the theater toward a sympathetic identification with each of its remarkably various characters. *Heartbreak House*, in its brillantly and self-consciously histrionic mode, throws us back upon ourselves with an unaswered challenge: How, beneath all our poses, are we to live our lives? *The Secret Life,* picking up that challenge and exploring it more deeply, draws us into the sympathetic role-playing of the theater itself where we may find an answer. Or rather, where we *should* find an answer if only some ensemble company would give us the opportunity.

Notes

1. Eric Salmon, *Granville Barker: A Secret Life* (London: Heinemann, 1983), p. 308.

2. *Granville Barker and His Correspondents*, ed. Eric Salmon (Detroit: Wayne State University Press, 1986), pp. 158–59.

3. Ibid., p. 102.

4. References in the text to this play are to Harley Granville-Barker, *The Secret Life* (London: Chatto and Windus, 1923).

5. *Granville Barker and His Correspondents*, p. 86.

6. Ibid., p. 96.

7. Salmon, *Granville Barker*, p. 109.

8. *Granville Barker and His Correspondents*, p. 410.

9. Harley Granville-Barker, "The Heritage of the Actor," *The Quarterly Review* 240 (July 1923): 71.

10. *Granville Barker and His Correspondents*, p. 500.

11. *Shaw on Theatre*, ed. E. J. West (New York: Hill and Wang, 1958), p. 110.

12. Ibid., p. 114.

13. Ibid., p. 266.

14. *Bernard Shaw's Letters to Granville Barker*, ed. C. B. Purdom (London: Phoenix House, 1956), p. 198.

15. All references in the text to this play are to Bernard Shaw, *Heartbreak House* (Baltimore: Penguin Books, 1964).

16. Bernard Shaw, *Candida* (Baltimore: Penguin Books, 1956), p. 75; James Huneker, "The Truth about *Candida*," *Metropolitan Magazine* 20 (August 1904): 635.

17. *Granville Barker and His Correspondents*, p. 160.

18. Ibid., p. 104n.

19. *Granville Barker and His Correspondents*, pp. 102–3.

20. Ibid., p. 102.

21. Salmon, *Granville Barker*, pp. 303–4.

22. *Granville Barker and His Correspondents*, p. 103.

23. I have shown in *Fields of Play in Modern Drama* (Princeton: Princeton University Press, 1977) how this process may enable the "action of performance" to transcend and effectively reverse the ostensible meaning of the "performed action." For comments on Chekhov's *Three Sisters* that are at least roughly in harmony with my reading of *The Secret Life,* see pp. 79–89. For a phenomenological analysis of the meaning of performance as involving the actors' "standing in" for the audience as role-playing explorers

of the world of the play, see Bruce Wilshire, *Role Playing and Identity* (Bloomington: Indiana University Press, 1982).

24. Harley Granville-Barker, *The Exemplary Theatre* (1922) (Freeport, N.Y.: Books for Libraries Press, 1970), pp. 248, 284, 53, 49, 128.

25. Granville-Barker, "The Heritage of the Actor," p. 53.

David Huckvale

MUSIC AND THE MAN: BERNARD SHAW AND THE MUSIC COLLECTION AT SHAW'S CORNER

Shaw's personal collection of musical scores and gramophone records remains intact at Shaw's Corner, now preserved by the National Trust, in Ayot St. Lawrence. This material not only complements Shaw's musical writings but also reveals much about his other musical interests. The collection contains musical manuscripts and tributes sent to Shaw for approval or as accolades.[1] There are also several works by mainstream European composers such as Bach, Haydn, Mozart, Beethoven, Wagner, and Richard Strauss, as well as a large body of music by English composers from the turn of the century until as late as the 1930s.

In conjunction with his large collection of 78-rpm gramophone records, Shaw relied on piano transcriptions to learn and understand various musical works. Piano reductions, which presented operatic and symphonic works in a form suitable for the piano, provided the only way for many people to listen to music before the advent of recordings. If the sound quality of the piano limited the audience's initial response to orchestrated symphonic and operatic works, at least people could become familiar with music they would not otherwise know. Authenticity of performance was not so fashionable then as it is now, so changes in instrumentation did not necessarily bother a turn-of-the-century audience. In one of Shaw's gramophone recordings of *Don Giovanni*, with Fritz Busch conducting Salvatore Baccaloni and the Glyndbourne Opera House Orchestra, a grand piano accompanies the recitative passages instead of the harpsichord that we would now expect. This was not regarded as an occasion for pedantic intolerance.

Shaw's intense irritation with academic musicians did not determine what he included in his collection. In his 10 May 1893 review of Charles Villiers Stanford's *Irish Symphony*, Shaw indicated his stance on unimaginative musical pedants:

> The success of Professor Stanford's Irish Symphony last Thursday was, from the Philharmonic point of view, somewhat scandalous. The spectacle of a university professor "going Fantee" is indecorous, though to me it is delightful. When Professor Stanford is genteel, cultured, classic, pious and experimentally mixolydian, he is dull beyond belief.[2]

However, Shaw's library contains a considerable amount of music by Stanford—*A Sheaf of Songs from Leinster, Four Irish Dances, A Fire of Turf* (*A Cycle of Irish Songs*), and *The Revenge* (a choral work). Shaw's opinions come not from prejudice, but from study.

Shaw's exchanges with music critic Ernest Newman (1868–1959) about their differing opinions of Strauss's *Josephslegende* ballet score also reveal Shaw's highly practical approach to music. Newman preferred to read Wagner's scores rather than to hear them in performance, believing that the true grandeur and spectacle of Wagner's vision could be found only in the imagination. Such an approach to music infuriated Shaw, as he emphasized in his letter of 10 August 1917:

> By all means put Mozart in his place; but don't be led into thinking that it was not a very high place. And don't *read* his scores; sing and hear them. If you *look* at his blessed old dominant sevenths, they will never be anything but dominant sevenths to you. If you listen to them only, you will sometimes find yourself going to the score to find what a strange chord it is you have heard, and being astonished and infuriated to find that it is as plain and platitudinous a seventh on paper as anything in "When Other Lips."[3]

This defense of Mozart, whom Wagnerians of the period disparaged as being somewhat superficial, is typical of Shaw's broad and catholic outlook.

Shaw's collection offers further proof of his broad-minded approach to music, for his piano reductions include works by Wagner, Meyerbeer, and Verdi (notorious for dividing their followers into often bitterly opposed camps) as well as a well-thumbed and often-repaired copy of Beethoven's *Ninth Symphony* in Liszt's piano transcription. Judging from the battered appearance of the Liszt transcription, Shaw spent many hours trying to master it.

Between 1873, when the departure of Shaw's mother brought an end to music in his Dublin home, and 1876, when Shaw moved to London, he attempted to fill the musical vacuum by playing various pieces on the piano. He joked about the maddening annoyance that this inflicted on anyone within earshot. At Shaw's Corner, he often sang and played to Charlotte while she lay in her bed upstairs, performing on a very unusual *Jugenstil* Bechstein piano which he had owned since as early as 1905. How effectively Shaw played we do not know, but he provided his own assessment in a letter to Molly Tompkins, who had decided to take up painting: "You paint now as I sing and play (when nobody but Charlotte is listening), and as no doubt you dance, for the fun of it . . . but you couldn't make your living by it."[4] Shaw's collection of piano transcriptions nevertheless reveals an extensive range of difficulty. His copies of Karl Schmalz's reductions of Strauss's *Symphonic Poems* are much easier to play than those by Otto Singer, whose reduction of Strauss's *Alpine Symphony* is physically impossible to perform. Shaw must have struggled manfully with those versions that challenge even the best of pianists.

Shaw's collection includes two pieces by Nicholas Slonimsky (b. 1894) which pose such a challenge: a song to words by Paul S. Nickerson entitled *My Little Pool* and a suite of piano pieces, the *Studies in Black and White*, dating from 1929. The latter bears this inscription: "To G. Bernard Shaw in appreciation of his charitable attitude towards the vagaries of modern music. Nicholas Slonimsky. Boston, Sept. 15, 1936."[5] *Studies in Black and White* would have required Shaw to master a composition in which the left hand plays only the black keys and the right hand only the white. *My Little Pool* requires not only this ability but also the capacity to sing in a different key. How successfully Shaw performed these pieces, or whether he even attempted them, remains unknown.

The collection includes several works sent to Shaw for his approval. In his letter of 10 August 1917, after advising Ernest Newman to hear rather than read Mozart, Shaw commented that he was corresponding about music partly as a relief from Fabians and politics. In part of the music collection, however, music and politics overlap. After Shaw had made it known that he disliked the tune of the socialist song *The Red Flag*, several people sent alternative versions. One came from the first bassoonist in the Municipal Symphony Orchestra at Cape Town,

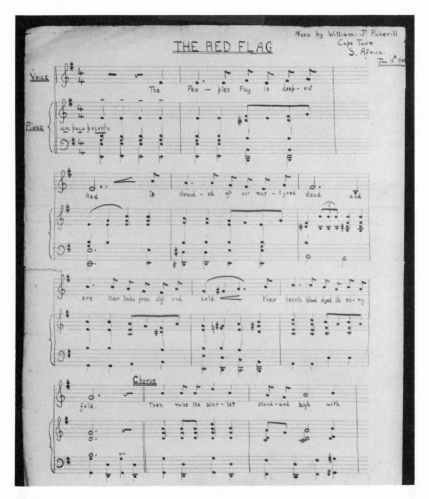

Fig. 1.

South Africa, on 1 May 1920 (Fig. 1). The composer, (Sir) William Pickerill (1892–1955), wrote in his covering letter,

> The pitiful figure cut by the Labour procession in South Africa on May Day last year and this, attempting to march to the unsuitable tune it is at present clothed in, persuaded me to make the attempt to write a new one. I have attempted to make it simple without being commonplace and "cheap" and at the same time not "R. Strauss" or "Debussy."
>
> I want no pecuniary reward for my work and hope it will be suitable to the Socialist movement. If not, I have done no harm.

I am 1st Bassoon of the Municipal Symphony Orchestra in Cape
Town and a socialist to boot.[6]

Pickerill's tune sounds more like a funeral march than a revolutionary
song.

Another entry came on 24 April 1923 from the Reverend Francis
Wood, who wished to dedicate his version to G.B.S. Unsurprisingly,
given Wood's clerical background, this setting bears a strong resem-
blance to a Bach chorale (Fig. 2).

Fig. 2.

More valuable from a purely musical perspective is the collection's
manuscript of *Utopian Hymn* by (Sir) William Walton (1902–1982),
which was written for the film version of *Major Barbara*. Walton's
score, which did not become part of the finished film due to cost

overruns, sets words especially written for the film and exploits a large chorus. Only a piano reduction of what was presumably intended as an orchestral work remains in the music collection (Fig. 3).

Fig. 3.

Less serious, although not from the perspective of the hopeful composer who submitted it to Shaw for his approval, is a piano piece entitled *Pastorale*. This is very poorly written out in pencil and is explained by a covering letter dated 7 June 1925:

Very many thanks for your r.e. [received] of 3rd inst. Acting upon
your kind advice I have a copy of Hull's "Modern Harmony" on order.

I believe the enclosed scribbled copy of a "Pastorale" is somewhat
more modern in style than "The Mighty Sea" but have hesitated to
forward it lest you should consider me too intrusive. My excuse is that
I am anxious for you to see that *all* my compositions are not written in
the "John Leach" vein, for your r.e. shows I have led you to think they
are.

Though I should be highly delighted to learn your opinion of this
piece, I would rather you ignore it than inconvenience yourself looking through it. You have already treated me very kindly and I have
really no right to trouble you further.

With many thanks

I am yours faithfully

Wallace H Salter.[7]

Accolades in Shaw's collection include a *Hebraic Hymn* (Fig. 4) to "Sir
Bernard Shaw" from a Hungarian journalist, Jerichem Leibermann,
"as a token of my admiration to You whose efforts of saving the world
and civilization from a destructive catastrophe I so greatly admire and
appreciate."[8] Written in 1939, the tribute strikes one as somewhat
premature.

Theo Dejoncker (1894–1964) scored *Le Portrait Musical de Bernard
Shaw* (Fig. 5), another accolade, for a small orchestra. Dejoncker sent
not only a copy of the full score but also a complete set of orchestral
parts. In his covering letter, of which only the first page survives,
Dejoncker commented, "Your musical criticism too I have found convincingly sound. But you irritate me intensely when you discuss the
formulary side of music in terms of 'textbook jargon.' "[9]

Another piece (Fig. 6) came from an obscure German composer,
Rudolf Neidermayer, who constructed his musical tribute to G.B.S. by
means of a musical cipher. This uses the German nomenclature for
the notes G, B (i.e., B flat), S (i.e., E flat), and Ch (H being the
designation for B natural), forming a musical motto in the tradition of
Schumann's *Abegg Variations* and *Carnaval*. (Presumably the *Ch* refers
to Charlotte.) The canon carries the dedication, "*Dem grossen Denker
und Philosophen Bernard Shaw*" ("For the great thinker and philosopher
Bernard Shaw"), beautifully handwritten in Gothic script, and sets
Neidermayer's own text: "*Alle-zeit geist-reich frisch und froh ist Bernard
Shaw*" ("Always witty, fresh, and joyful is Bernard Shaw").[10]

Shaw's collection includes several mainstream composers. He had
copies of virtually every Strauss opera and reductions of the *Symphonic
Poem* which he sumptuously rebound. He met Strauss in January 1922

Fig. 4.

at a luncheon party where Edward Elgar (1857–1934) was also present: "To my great surprise," he wrote to Charlotte, "both he and Elgar
denied having any sense of absolute pitch. As I've always regarded my
own want of it as a sign of musical deficiency I was rather gratified."
Shaw added that "Elgar made endless puns; a quaint anachronism,"

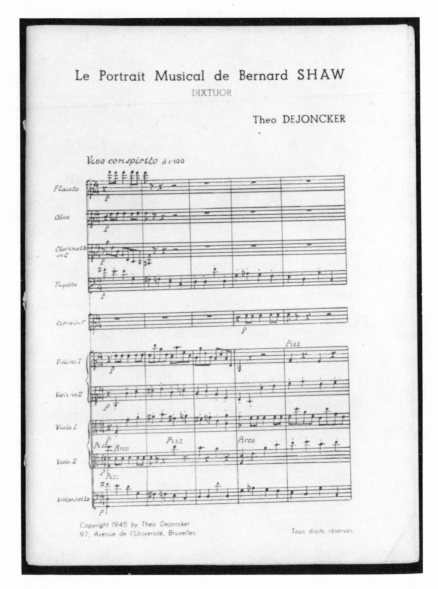

Fig. 5.

and that Strauss wanted Shaw "to go to Salzburg in August to hear him conduct Don Giovanni and Cosi fan Tutti."[11]

However, more interesting is the array of English modern composers represented in the collection. There are many songs by Elgar,

Fig. 6.

including one he composed for the "Fight for Right" movement in 1916 (Fig. 7), setting a text by William Morris: "Then loosen the sword in the scabbard / And settle the helm on thine head / For men betrayed are mighty / And great are the wrongfully dead."

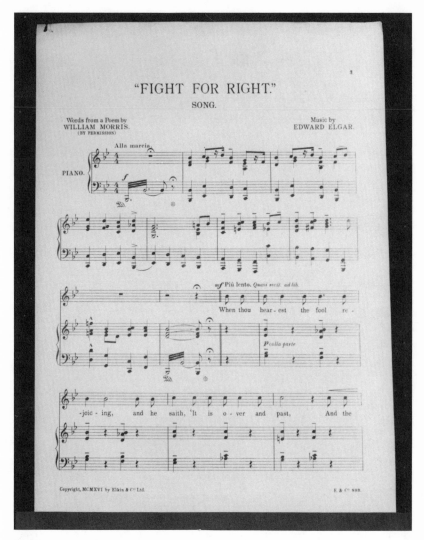

Fig. 7.

Shaw wrote to Elgar on 26 September 1921 that "All the other geniuses whom I venture to admire let me down one time or another; but you never fail."[12] (This was long before Elgar borrowed £800 from Shaw, pleading a family emergency, only to spend it on an automobile for Elgar's comely secretary.)

Another musical acquaintance of Shaw represented in the collection was Rutland Boughton (1878-1960), who also set texts by William

Morris. One song in the collection is *In Prison,* with the inspiring socialist dedication, "To all imprisoned in the mines, jails, factories and shops of the British Empire." Another song, *The Love of Comrades* (Fig. 8), which sets a text by Walt Whitman, has the dedication "To the Comrades everywhere."

At first, since he suffered a stream of hopefuls who sent him their

Fig. 8.

manuscripts, Shaw was suspicious of yet another composer asking him
to listen to his work. In 1908 Shaw complained about Boughton's
unsolicited requests: "Why do you want to come and play your *King
Arthur* to me? I do not insist on reading my plays to you. Do you
suppose that I am an impresario, or that I have influence at the Opera
or with music publishers? If so, I assure you you are mistaken. I can
do absolutely nothing for you. . . ."[13] In his letter of 2 January 1912,
which ended with the plea "Send me no more, Rutland, send me no
more," Shaw provided a graphic evaluation: "This note represents my
opinion of you as a composer" (Fig. 9).[14]

Fig. 9.

However, Boughton won Shaw over in time. In 1934, Shaw wrote,
"Now that Elgar has gone you have the only original style on the
market. . . . I find that I have acquired a strong taste for it." Shaw
possessed piano reductions of Boughton's stage and choral work,[15]
and he included a tribute to Boughton at the end of the fourth edition
(1923) of *The Perfect Wagnerite:* "He selected Glastonbury as his
Bayreuth; and has established an annual festival there which can already show a remarkable record of work done." According to Shaw, it
is in Boughton's festival "that the Wagnerist dream has been best
realised in England."[16]

Perhaps Boughton's most explicitly socialist work was his published
but unperformed ballet *May Day* (Fig. 10), the piano reduction of
which is in Shaw's collection. This percussive and modernist piece
depicts, in stylized terms, a communist revolution with a "Heaving
background" symbolic of the masses, a "Feeble dance for Black Legs,"
tableaux such as "Britannia rules the rusty machines" and "The Revolt
that Failed," a "Pas de Deux for a Red Bogy and a Black Shadow," and
a finale on "The Joy of Work." In fact, the ballet, written in 1929, is
somewhat in the style of Soviet realism then much in vogue in the
U.S.S.R. and would have appealed to Shaw's Soviet sympathies.

Fig. 10.

Frank Bridge (1879–1941) also features largely in Shaw's collection. The first editions of many of Bridge's pieces, published by Winthrop Rodgers, are still to be found at Shaw's Corner, ranging from the romantic and lyrical pieces from before World War I to the more experimental work which emerged both during and after the conflict that thoroughly outraged the pacifist Bridge. A particularly striking

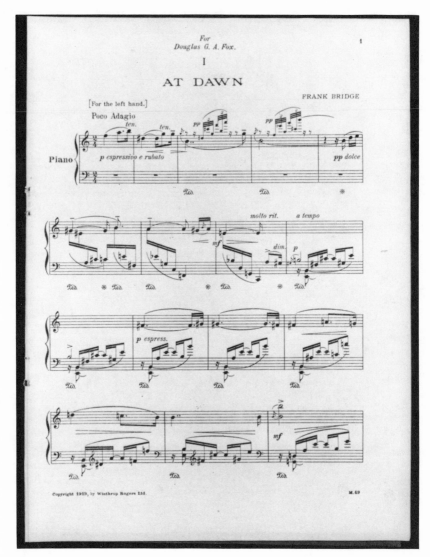

Fig. 11.

example of Bridge's experimental harmony is in this excerpt from a
1919 study for the left hand called *At Dawn* (Fig. 11).

Shaw's collection reveals a surprising taste for the experimental.
Several songs and piano pieces by Cyril Scott (1879–1970) remain at
Shaw's Corner. With the exception of Lord Berners (1883–1950),
Scott, rather misleadingly labeled "The English Debussy," was the

most avant-garde composer in England at this time. Scott and Shaw corresponded, and it is revealing that Shaw's musical tastes would enable him to appreciate Scott's advanced efforts.

Shaw also acquired an almost complete collection of compositions by Lord Berners in all their original editions, including piano reductions of the ballets *A Wedding Bouquet* and *Luna Park* and the opera *La Carosse du Saint Sacrement*. Originally Gerald Hugh Tyrwhitt-Wilson, Lord Berners, like Shaw, was a self-taught musician and a flamboyant polymath. His music is ironic and parodies romantic conventions in a manner that suggests he was a romantic at heart. So bewildering were his many artistic achievements that *The New Statesman* satirized him in 1939:

> Lord Berners
> Told a crowd of learners
> That if they wished to compose
> They should paint or write prose.[17]

Also represented in the music collection at Shaw's Corner are the less well-known and by now very obscure songs by Ada Galsworthy (setting poems by her husband John) in printed and manuscript versions, work by the prolific Else Headlam Morely, songs by Henry Festing Jones (1851–1928), and musical character sketches of Bette Davis and Toscanini by Arthur T. Cremin. The huge collection represents more than Shaw's continued interest in the musical life of his time. It reveals the immense importance of music in Shaw's life and the public perception of that interest, and stands as a tribute to his tireless enthusiasm, remarkably broad-minded approach, and eclectic taste for this branch of the arts.

Notes

1. Musical score reproductions from Shaw's Corner are reproduced with the permission of the National Trust.

2. Bernard Shaw, *Music in London* (London: Constable, 1932), II:303.

3. Bernard Shaw, *Collected Letters, 1911–1925*, ed. Dan H. Laurence (London: Max Reinhardt, 1985), p. 499.

4. Peter Tompkins, *Shaw and Molly Tompkins* (New York: Clarkson Potter, 1960), p. 165.

5. Music collection at Shaw's Corner, Ayot St. Lawrence.

6. Ibid.

7. Ibid.

8. Ibid.

9. Ibid.

10. Ibid.

11. *Collected Letters, 1911–1925,* pp. 761–62.

12. Ibid., p. 733.

13. Michael Hurd, *Immortal Hour* (London: Routledge & Kegan Paul, 1962), p. 38.

14. Music collection at Shaw's Corner.

15. Hurd, *Immortal Hour,* p. 28.

16. Bernard Shaw, *The Perfect Wagnerite* (London: Constable, 1932), p. 277.

17. Peter Dickinson, "The Most Professional Amateur," *3: The Radio Three Magazine* 2 (September 1983), p. 26.

Howard Ira Einsohn

THE BIOPHILE: FROMMIAN AND ARISTOTELIAN PERSPECTIVES ON SHAVIAN ETHICS

Over the years commentators have associated Shaw with a universe of luminaries in a continuing effort to grasp the full significance of his thought. Blake, Bunyan, Shelley, Butler, Lamarck, Schopenhauer, Hegel, Nietzsche, Marx, Bergson, and Teilhard de Chardin are among the brightest stars in whose galaxies Shaw is said to have orbited. No one has linked Shaw with the distinguished psychoanalyst and social philosopher, Erich Fromm (1900–1980). The Frommian corpus illuminates key aspects of Shavian ethics in ways that bestow upon them a cogency and currency some may find surprising. Although neither knew the other's work, their views converge on so many points that they fashion a finely wrought symphony in which Frommian harmonies orchestrate Shavian melodies.[1]

Where Shaw accurately identifies the disease afflicting contemporary capitalist civilization and outlines its roots, Fromm confirms the diagnosis and supplies a detailed etiology. In addition, both prescribe the same remedy: a free society, along socialist lines, that gives collective well-being the highest priority. Put simply, Fromm's theories substantially support Shaw's insights; they flesh out what is skeletal in the latter. Fromm provides a fully developed and intellectually respectable framework that elucidates the psychological dynamics underlying the unwholesome behavior Shaw depicts in his plays and prose. Fromm also uses this framework to argue compellingly for a humanistic ethic firmly grounded in *biophilia*—the love of life—whose emphasis on the autonomous self and sane living parallels Shavian notions in critical respects. Ultimately, however, the ethics of Shaw and Fromm merit close attention because they are in the tradition of Aristotle, which has the potential to provide an objective and universal basis for morality.

The fundamental principles of Shavian ethics appear in the *Quintessence*. They are the primacy of "private judgment in questions of conduct as against all institutions," and the insistence that "conduct must justify itself by its effect upon life and not by its conformity to any rule or ideal."[2] Strictly speaking, Shaw attributes these views to Ibsen, but they represent his own moral outlook on the world. Fromm holds essentially the same position. In *Man for Himself*, Fromm states that humanistic ethics, the creed to which he is devoutly committed, is based on two basic tenets: "only man himself can determine the criterion for virtue and sin, and not an authority transcending man," and " 'good' is what is good for man and 'evil' what is detrimental to man; the sole criterion of ethical value being man's welfare."[3]

Clearly, both thinkers posit the self as the conclusive source and final arbiter of all that is morally binding in human relations.[4] So does Aristotle. The *Nicomachean Ethics* maintains that we alone, in exercising our freedom and judgment, establish the goodness and badness of things. Furthermore, the moral standards of Shaw and Fromm— "life" and "man's welfare," respectively—are, for all practical purposes, identical: By "life," Shaw intends what Fromm means by "man's welfare," the full realization of human potential in a humane state. They both envision a society in which autonomous individuals, asserting their untrammeled wills, will promote the flourishing of humanity rather than its deformation. This notion of a flourishing humanity, of a universal blessedness, is what Aristotle understands by *eudaimonia*, the teleological end toward which, he says, all human activity is naturally directed.

In line with emphasizing the self, Fromm and Shaw see a close connection between passion, will, character, behavior, and ethics. Following Freud, Fromm defines character as a dynamic system of forces that motivates behavior.[5] Fromm further conceives these motivational forces as a *"relatively permanent structure of passions."*[6] Among the passions that constitute character, he includes the will. "The will," Fromm says, "is not an abstract power of man which he possesses apart from his character. On the contrary, the will is nothing but the expression of character" (*MFH* 233). The last link in the chain also derives from Freud, who implicitly connects character and ethics by equating virtue with a productive (genital) character and vice with a nonproductive (pregenital) character. Fromm accepts this basic dichotomy and elaborates it extensively, particularly with respect to the productive character which, he says, Freud leaves undeveloped because of his focus on neurotic behavior.

In brief, Fromm argues that the productive character is ethically superior to the nonproductive character because the former fosters self-realization (which is synonymous with well-being, the supreme virtue in humanistic ethics), while the latter fosters self-mutilation (which is synonymous with sickness, the supreme vice in humanistic ethics). Thus, the morally commendable act virtuously because their behavior flows from a virtuous (productive) character, and the morally culpable act wickedly because their behavior flows from a wicked (nonproductive) character. For Fromm, the crucial factor in the moral equation is character, the self's actualization of will in behavior. Accordingly, Fromm asserts that "the subject matter of ethics is *character,* and only in reference to the character structure as a whole can value statements be made about single traits or actions" (*MFH* 33; Fromm's emphasis). "*The true subject matter of ethics,*" he adds, is "*the virtuous or the vicious character, rather than the single virtues or vices*" (*MFH* 33; Fromm's emphasis).

Shaw, too, stresses the centrality of character in any ethical evaluation of behavior. He also makes the will, understood as one among many passions, the prime mover in human action. Shaw and Fromm are strikingly similar in this regard. Like Schopenhauer, Shaw maintains "that reason is no motive power; that the true motive power in the world is will (otherwise Life)."[7] At the same time, Shaw declares that "no action, taken apart from the will behind it, has any moral character" (*Quint* 113). Moreover, says Shaw, when we are no "longer afraid to look life straight in the face," we will "see in it, not the fulfilment of a moral law or the deductions of reason, but the satisfaction of a passion in us of which we can give no rational account whatever" (*Sanity* 323–24). That passion, he tells us, is the "will to live" (*Quint* 23). In the end, contends Shaw, after all our excuses have been exhausted, we at last must acknowledge the real mainspring of our behavior: "I did it because I am built that way" (*Sanity* 324). That is to say, "I did it because my character made me the way I am." Like Fromm, Shaw holds that behavior is a manifestation of character and that character expresses itself through a self that wills.

In the Shavian view, as for Fromm, the difference between the moral and the immoral is not so much a question of whether one follows traditional morality. It is rather a matter of the kinds of passions that comprise character, since it is character that issues in action (*Sanity,* 315–17). At bottom, what distinguishes the wicked from the upright is not that the upright have "killed passion" in themselves, but that they are "mastered by holier passions"—including those of "kindness," "truth," and "justice" (*Sanity* 317). In other words, the upright are governed by a virtuous character: their behavior produces well-being in the self and' is therefore virtuous; hence, they are self-realized and worthy of moral approbation. The wicked, in turn, are governed by a vicious character: their behavior produces sickness in the self and is therefore unvirtuous; hence, they are self-mutilated and deserve moral condemnation. Thus, Shaw links will, passion, character, behavior, and ethics exactly as Fromm does.

For Fromm and Shaw, as is unquestionably the case for Aristotle, ethics is primarily a question of virtue, a question of practice, of habituated modes of behavior, in which character, not duty or principle, is the focal concern. Thus, it follows that both reject all forms of authoritarian ethics which, Fromm tells us, make "obedience . . . the main virtue and disobedience . . . the main sin" (*MFH* 12).[8] The paramount question for Shaw, as for Fromm, is not which rules did you obey, but "did you prevent any happiness that you might have caused, or cause any suffering that you might have prevented?" (*CL* 278). Or, to use Fromm's language, have you acted so as to further or retard "the growth and development of man?" (*MFH* 248). Clearly, human welfare is the moral measure here. Unquestioning obedience is ethically irresponsible. "The most important element" in recognizing "the truth," says Fromm, "is the courage to say *no,* to disobey the commands of power and of public opinion" (*BTC* 180; Fromm's emphasis). Shaw seconds this point by likewise noting that the truly moral must "always be prepared to act immorally," that is, to act against convention and the ruling authorities (*Quint* 130).[9]

Thus, Fromm and Shaw endorse Aristotle's contention that absolute, substantive rules prescribing how we should act do not exist.[10] Both are explicit on the matter. Fromm denies that "ethical propositions are unquestionably and eternally true and neither permit nor warrant revision" (*MFH* 238). Following Ibsen, Shaw holds "that you cannot be moral by rule of thumb, that the search for golden rules of conduct and fixed modes of duty is as chimerical as the search for the philosopher's stone, and that we must always act under the full responsibility put upon us by the knowledge that if our 'morality' causes evil, it is no more to be excused for its own sake than 'immorality' " (*CL* 278). Ethics for Shaw and Fromm, as for Aristotle, is an imprecise field of inquiry, a domain in which it is impossible to formulate infallible rules of conduct.

This is not to say that Shaw and Fromm advocate a normless society.

While anarchists in the intellectual realm, both acknowledge that the existing scale of human social organization is far too complex to be managed without rules of some kind. What they do insist on, however, is that our moral and legal norms are not inviolable ends in themselves but rather amendable means for maximizing the opportunities people have to live rich and fulfilling lives. Although not immutable, norms can nonetheless be objective and universal, Fromm claims, because they follow logically from a scientific study of an invariant human nature. The argument proceeds by analogy: people everywhere have the same mental apparatus, as they have the same physiological apparatus; and as they will perish if they are denied food, clothing, or shelter, so too will they find life unbearable if they are denied the satisfaction of psychological needs. Such species-specific needs, which must be sharply distinguished from mere wants, include, among others, a sense of belonging, a sense of dignity, and a sense of meaning and purpose for existence.[11] Thus, the psychoanalyst, one kind of scientist who studies human nature empirically, can specify the conditions that nourish the full flowering of what is uniquely human. These are the goods we ought to pursue because they are at once conducive to and constitutive of an all-inclusive good that we desire for its own sake: well-being. The psychoanalyst can also specify what dehumanizes us. These are the evils we ought to shun because they are deleterious to well-being.

For Fromm, ethics reduces to applied psychology. This is a position congenial to Shaw since he argues that we need "to found our institutions . . . on a genuine scientific natural history"[12]—that is, on the knowledge of the way people and the world really are instead of on a distorted picture of what we imagine them to be. This is also Aristotle's position. Aristotle frames his famous treatise on ethics with the question "What is good for man?" and, much like a biologist who explores the universe of living organisms, bases his answer on a thorough examination of the race's distinctive characteristics. What emerges from this investigation provides a secure, although not certain, foundation for generalizations about morality. Hence, for all three, ethical norms can be valid without being absolute. Like the statements of science, they are tentative, subject to revision in the light of new evidence, but hold sway until more fully validated norms displace them. In the absence of ethical certainty, we must depend on the virtuous character and good sense—practical wisdom in Aristotle's language—to guide us through the moral minefields that lie beneath our feet.

But here a potential problem arises. If people are encouraged to decide right and wrong for themselves, will they not destroy themselves and society in a paroxysm of egotism? No, say Shaw and Fromm, because people naturally strive for the good. Unless exceptional circumstances supervene, they explain, an inner drive, what Aristotle calls a teleological force, impels us all toward self-realization.[13] For Shaw, moral evil is an accidental state of affairs that, in principle, can be evolved out of the world through effort and education. It is a product of ignorance, not malice. It arises most often because people, with the best intentions, mistake the good or the means to it and are unwilling to compromise. In the Shavian worldview, human limitation, remediable in time, rather than inborn depravity, is the cause of society's ills.[14] Fromm, too, sees moral evil as a second-order phenomenon that need not inevitably occur. For him, it is a pathological rather than a healthy condition that stems not from inherent disposition but from the frustration of people's primary tendency toward the good. According to Fromm, "Man is not necessarily evil but becomes evil only if the proper conditions for his growth and development are lacking" (*MFH* 218).[15]

Ideally, then, we need not fear an epidemic of immorality if ethics is anchored in character as opposed to inflexible rules. At issue here is human freedom, without which self-realization is impossible. If we maintain with Marx, who influenced Fromm and Shaw considerably, that the essence of human nature is spontaneous free activity, then any ethic that compels blind obedience negates human freedom and thereby alienates people from themselves and others. Authoritarianism is one such ethic: it forces people to conform to standards of behavior that they do not freely choose but that are imposed on them from outside. Under such conditions, some, usually a small minority, dominate, and others, usually a large majority, are dominated; and wherever societal relations are constituted by power relationships based on domination rather than fraternity, alienation exists.

Thus, it is no wonder that both Shaw and Fromm disparage conformity, since it is symptomatic of the alienation that has poisoned life in the contemporary era, even in nonauthoritarian countries where brute force is not state-sanctioned policy. In fact, although never offered as a rigorous scientific analysis, Shaw's portraits of the philistine, idealist, and realist in the *Quintessence* are remarkably suggestive intuitively. For when these profiles are viewed not simply as moral types or psychological types but as Frommian character types that possess a dynamic sociocultural dimension as well as a moral and psychological component, Shaw's distinctions provide a perceptive picture of the extent to which the alienation engendered by industrial capitalism has deformed the human psyche.

Fromm maintains that character is largely a product of cultural processes, so much so that we can speak meaningfully of a "social character," a constellation of traits shared by the majority of a group.[16] This reflects the Marxian notion that the material basis of society, its specific mode of economic organization, determines the ideological consciousness of its members. Fromm, however, supplements Marx by postulating a psychosocial construct that mediates between base and superstructure: the social character. In this view, each society produces the kind of citizen it requires to function smoothly and persist through time. Each society manipulates its citizens into wanting to do what they have to do in order to perpetuate social solidarity. As hypnotists implant posthypnotic suggestions into susceptible subjects who later erroneously think they are acting freely, so societies control behavior from without while simultaneously providing their people with subjective feelings of freedom that are false in reality.

Thus, although individual variations will exist, the character structure of entire groups can comprise an "essential nucleus" of characteristics that derive from "the basic experience and mode of life common" to a particular society (*EFF* 277). Two such types—the automatous conformist and the authoritarian—are particularly relevant to an exploration of Shavian ethics: they correspond, respectively, to the philistine and the idealist. At the same time, Fromm understands that, as there are some persons who cannot be hypnotized, there will always be some who can stand on their own two feet, some whose behavior springs from a true character rather than from a manufactured one. These are individuals with productive characters, and they correspond to Shaw's realists. The significance of these correspondences becomes clear in the connection Fromm makes between freedom and character.[17]

For Fromm, freedom is a phenomenon with two aspects: negative and positive. Negative freedom is freedom *from* external restraints that block human growth and development. Positive freedom is freedom *to* achieve the full realization of self. The one signifies a passive state, the absence of barriers, and the other an active state, the pursuit of fulfillment. With the waning of the Middle Ages, when people felt secure and knew their place in the scheme of things, the bonds that shackled personal expression dissolved. This breakup of medieval society, Fromm says, left man with "no choice but to unite himself with the world in the spontaneity of love and productive work or else to seek a kind of security by such ties with the world as destroy his freedom and the integrity of his individual self" (*EFF* 23). Only a few, those with a productive character, take the first path. They successfully make the transition from negative to positive freedom. The vast majority, those with automatous or authoritarian characters, take the second path. They fail to make the transition. What accounts for this massive failure of spirit?

In the modern age, argues Fromm, the prospect of positive freedom is an anxiety-ridden potential most are afraid to realize because it arouses almost unbearable feelings of loneliness, insignificance, and powerlessness. With the disintegration of Christendom and the passing of feudalism, Western civilization experienced an existential crisis in which the masses were cut adrift from the traditional moorings that had structured their lives for centuries. In the resultant ethical vacuum, many felt isolated and impotent in the vastness of a hostile and indifferent universe: they lacked the inner resources to deal productively with the exigencies of the human condition on their own. Consequently, instead of actualizing their freedom, the terrified majority tried to escape from it by unconsciously turning to conformist or authoritarian behavior. These unconscious escape mechanisms, while offering some comfort and assurance against a paralyzing dread, ultimately vitiate human freedom and cripple the self. However, some with productive characters have the courage to embrace their freedom, to confront the world as it really is, without a need for comforting illusions that cloak threatening realities. Only they can achieve well-being. They alone can become what they potentially are: healthy, autonomous, humane, and fulfilled selves.

The relationship between freedom and character brings the full significance of the parallelism between Fromm and Shavian character types into sharp focus. In order to cope with the immensity of the outside world, the automatous conformist, Fromm says, "ceases to be himself; he adopts entirely the kind of personality offered to him by cultural patterns; and he therefore becomes exactly as all others are and as they expect him to be" (*EFF* 185–86). This description applies equally to the philistine, the Shavian automaton who routinely conforms to society's norms without ever questioning their validity. Comprising 70 percent, or 700 persons, of Shaw's hypothetical British community of 1,000, the philistines blithely accept the given institutions of society, marriage, and the family as "quite good enough for them" (*Quint* 29), even if they are, in Shaw's view, based on illusions that create unhealthy and unjust exploitative situations. That so many should forsake positive freedom by unthinkingly conforming to conventional standards accords well with Fromm's belief that this "mechanism of escape [i.e., automatous conformity] is the solution that the majority of normal individuals find in modern society" (*EFF* 185).

A second culturally significant escape mechanism is authoritarian

behavior. The authoritarian, in Fromm's words, may be "characterized by his attitude toward authority. He admires authority and tends
to submit to it, but at the same time, he wants to be an authority
himself and have others submit to him" (*EFF* 164). In this respect,
authoritarians are essentially sadomasochists, and how they act in a
particular situation depends on which trait dominates the character
structure.[18] If the masochistic tendency prevails, the authoritarian will
try to overcome feelings of inadequacy by "giv[ing] up the independence of one's individual self and . . . fusing oneself with somebody or
something outside oneself in order to acquire the strength which the
individual self is lacking" (*EFF* 141). If the sadistic tendency prevails,
the authoritarian will try to overcome these same feelings by dominating others—by making "another being part of [him]self" (*EFF* 158)—
so that, again, "the strength which the individual self is lacking" is
increased proportionately. In each instance, the authoritarian sacrifices the self's integrity in a self-defeating attempt to come to terms
with "the overwhelming power of the world outside" (*EFF* 185). Here
the real although unconscious object of behavior is to rid oneself of
positive freedom's heavy burden, to disavow responsibility for living
an authentic life true to self, by either merging with or absorbing
other selves. We can observe both kinds of behavior in the Shavian
idealist.

Representing 29.9 percent, or 299 persons, of Shaw's hypothetical
community, the idealists know that marriage, emblematic of societal
norms in general, is a deeply flawed institution. Still they feel power-
less to speak out because "they cannot prevent the 700 satisfied ones
[i.e., the philistines] from coercing them into conformity with the
marriage law" (*Quint* 30). Therefore, instead of lobbying for change,
they capitulate—they submit to the will of the thoughtless majority.
Moreover, afraid to admit their failure to find satisfaction in marriage, the idealists make a virtue of necessity: they idealize the family
"as a beautiful and holy natural institution" (*Quint* 30) to which everyone, they insist, must yield. Thus, in following the marriage convention out of weakness, out of fear of expressing their true selves, the
idealists exhibit the masochistic side of the authoritarian character. At
the same time, the idealists exhibit the sadistic side of the authoritarian character by turning marriage into an ideal, a "fancy picture" that
does not correspond to anything in the real world, which they then
force others to accept as "standard moral conduct, absolutely valid
under all circumstances, contrary conduct or any advocacy of it being
discountenanced and punished as immoral" (*Quint* 30).

In contrast, the productive character, says Fromm, is characteristic of the spontaneous person, the person who uses positive freedom "to realize the potentialities inherent in him" (*MFH* 84). The productive person, moreover, is unalienated, "experiencing himself as the embodiment of his powers" (*MFH* 84). He is also guided by reason, which enables him to use those powers intelligently in various ways: to devise the appropriate means to valued ends, to separate the essential from the accidental, and to grasp the universal in the particular (*MFH* 102–3). "Not dependent on someone who controls his powers," the productive person is independent, the architect of his own actions (*MFH* 84). Instead of harkening to an authoritarian conscience, "the voice of an internalized external authority" that "we are eager to please and afraid of disappointing" (*MFH* 143, 158), the productive person heeds a humanistic conscience, the inner voice of the total self that "judges our functioning as human beings" without regard to "external sanctions and rewards" (*MFH* 158). Hence, the behavior of the productive person is governed by a virtuous character and is the willed expression of a real self rather than the reflexive echo of a socially conditioned pseudoself.

Thus, for Fromm, the productive person "is the aim of human development and simultaneously the ideal of humanistic ethics" (*MFH* 83). Fully developed, the productive person becomes what Fromm calls the "*biophile*," the person who loves life and makes its enhancement the standard of ethical conduct. Under a different name, the *biophile* is also the mature, morally passionate Shavian realist, the Don Juan character who acts on the understanding that his welfare and that of the species are inextricably tied.

Representing the remaining .1 percent of Shaw's imaginary community, the lone realist affirms "the validity of his own will" against the conventional views of a spent majority (*Quint* 34). He sees in society's reactionary ideals[19] "only something to blind us, something to numb us, something to murder self in us" (*Quint* 34). Not only do they oblige "self-denying conformity" (*Quint* 34), which thwarts self-realization, but in time they demand "human sacrifices" as well (*Quint* 131). Every manner of atrocity is committed in their name, often with good intentions, and that is precisely why hell is the home of the seven deadly virtues.[20] In the realist's view, he who "abnegates the will to live and be free in a world of the living and free, seeking only to conform to ideals for the sake of being, not himself, but a 'good man,' [is] morally dead and rotten" (*Quint* 34). For the realist, the truly moral are those who assert their wills, their selves, and their characters in defiance of stultifying social norms.

While positing self-assertion as a critically necessary factor in personal growth and moral progress, the realist also acknowledges that it is not sufficient: reason is required as well. "Ability to reason accurately," the *Quintessence* tells us, "is as desirable as ever; for by accurate reasoning only can we calculate our actions so as to do what we intend to do: that is, to fulfill our will" (*Quint* 24). "It is one thing," says Shaw the realist, "to ascertain what you want to secure and quite another to ascertain the right method of securing it" (*Illusions* 413). Ascertaining the right method in any endeavor requires reason, not blind emotion.[21] The difference between socialism and democracy, a matter of the utmost concern for Shaw, is not one of ends: both aim at "making the people livelier, freer, and happier than they can be without [them]" (*Illusions* 414). The difference, rather, lies in the means. For Shaw, as for Fromm, socialism "offers a better means of reaching" the stated goal than capitalism, the *modus operandi* of Western democracies.[22]

This conclusion follows a reasoned investigation into social dynamics which discloses that "the dominant factor in human society is not political organization, but industrial organization" (*Illusions* 413). Hence, reasons Shaw, "unless the Government controls industry, it is useless for the people to control the Government": achieving the latter without the former would simply "intensify slavery under the political forms and pretensions of freedom and equality" (*Illusions* 414). Thus, reason reveals that "industrial Collectivism [i.e., socialism] is the true political science of Democracy" (*Illusions* 414). In other words, reason shows that the best means of achieving the flourishing of humanity is through socialism, a conclusion shared by Fromm. In turn, reason demonstrates that the best means of attaining socialism is through incremental legislative reform rather than violent revolution. Razing capitalism to the ground in a violent orgy of pent-up anger and frustration will not make socialism a reality. Reason counsels a different, more prudent course: patience, permeation, and peaceful, piecemeal constitutional change (*Illusions* 418).[23] In the end, according to Shaw, it is reason, assisted by "self-control," that safeguards "the moral evolution of the social individual . . . from submission and obedience . . . to wilfulness and self-assertion" (*Sanity* 321). "Without high gifts of reason and self-control," he says, "no man dares yet trust himself out of the school of authority" (*Sanity* 321).

Presumably, it is also reason, in concert with a "realistic imagination,"[24] that enables the realist to perceive, correctly in Shaw's estimation, traditional ideals for what they are *in essence*: contingent states of affairs, that is, nonpermanent features of reality—the products of historical forces specific to a given place and time—that are alterable through human agency. Although once necessary in humanity's infancy, to secure stable societies, they are nevertheless transient, mere "swaddling clothes which man has outgrown" (*Quint* 34). As such, they are impediments to constructive social change and therefore, the realist concludes, ought to be scrapped or appropriately modified. An analogous argument holds for social institutions. They too are not eternal, they too have genealogies, and they too are subject to rational restructuring by a will that reason has helped find the right way, when they become obsolete.

The realist, then, must rouse the "ordinary respectable man" from his complacent moral slumbers, must rock "the moral ground beneath him by denying the validity of a convention."[25] "Every step in morals," Shaw says, "is made by challenging the validity of the existing conception of perfect propriety of conduct" (*Sanity* 314). Thus it is understandable that the realist, "in repudiating that on which his neighbors are relying for their sense of security," inspires "dread" and "fear" (*Brieux* 209). Nevertheless, no improvements to the general welfare are possible otherwise, and societies that do not keep pace with social evolution's relatively rapid rate will stagnate and eventually die. For this reason, Shaw says, realists should be granted the widest possible latitude in thought and deed. Their questioning of the status quo, their puncturing of society's most cherished illusions, signifies health and vitality, not disease and torpor.[26]

By following their own inclinations rather than ceding autonomy to external authorities, realists demonstrate that they possess humanistic consciences. Neither intimidated by the fear of sanctions nor bribed by the promise of blissful afterlives, realists strive for the good because they want to, because they have virtuous characters. They are doubtless the individuals Shaw has in mind when he writes that "a really good man is one who is good because he likes being good. His good life is a life of self-gratification, not of self-denial. He is made that way."[27] Moreover, realists well understand, rationally, that the quest for self-realization, through the satisfaction of individual will, may express two different kinds of character, one productive and the other not. Shaw associates the former with the "saint," the latter with the "demigod" (*Quint* 48). The demigod is deluded, believing mistakenly that his will is "indomitable," a "force that can overcome all other forces," even "destiny" (*Quint* 48). This is a dangerous fantasy for obvious reasons, sustainable "only by plunging into illusions to which every fact gives the lie" (*Quint* 48). The realist rejects this reckless idea "of unconditional self-realization" as "idiotic" (*Quint* 52).

Instead, the realist emulates the saint, who opposes the would-be tyrant on the ground that "godhead" is not only in "himself" but also in "others" (*Quint* 62). Consciously aware of the universal in the particular, the realist seeks "the empire of Man," not an empire of a privileged individual or group but of the species, "asserting the universal validity of his own will" (*Quint* 59). The realist, unlike the demigod, knows that his will is only one among many, each partaking of the divine, and each, therefore, worthy of consideration. Thus, in terms of will, reason, character, and self-realization, the Shavian realist and the Frommian productive person have the same qualities. What makes them both in their full psychological development *biophiles* is a common underlying ethic that at once informs their moral outlook and motivates their conduct.

The person with a productive character, according to Fromm, is also characterized by *biophilia*. *Biophiles*, Fromm says, have a distinctive ethic: "good is all that serves life; evil all that serves death. Good is reverence for life, all that enhances life, growth, unfolding. Evil is all that stifles life, narrows it down, cuts it into pieces. Joy is virtue and sadness is sinful" (*HOM* 47). This ethic is likewise the ethic of Shavian realists, individuals with productive characters who experience the true joy of living in working for a universal purpose—Shaw's *Life* Force—that transcends the satisfaction of selfish desires.[28] Such persons make the advancement of life their overarching concern. They are driven by a "will-to-live, and to live, as Christ said long before, more abundantly."[29] That is to say, they know that the race can avoid extinction and flourish "only if we give everybody the best possible chance in life"; only "if we begin to worship life . . . instead of merely worshipping mammon . . . and wanting to make money"; only "if we begin to try to get a community life in which life is given every possible chance, and in which development of life is the one thing that is everybody's religion."[30] Realists, in short, act on the understanding that they are "working for the purpose of the universe, working for the good of the whole of society and the whole world, instead of looking after [their] personal ends" (*RS* 19). They are guided by an inner conviction that they must strive "to make the world better and wiser, whether the change will benefit themselves or not" (*RS* 48). Thus, the realist and the *biophile* have the same character structure. Each is oriented productively toward the world. Each spurns "sadness and self-loathing" and "turns quickly to life and attempts to do good" (*HOM* 47).

The Frommian perspective shows that some potentially troubling Shavian pronouncements that bear directly on ethics are considerably less idiosyncratic or hyperbolic than might appear at first glance. For example, Shaw's assertion that "a man cannot believe in others until he believes in himself; for his conviction of the equal worth of his fellows must be filled by the overflow of his conviction of his own worth" (*Quint* 145) is understandable in the context of Fromm's notion that "self-love, not the negation of the individual but the affirmation of his truly human self, are the supreme values of humanistic ethics" (*MFH* 7). Before we can value others, we must value ourselves. Similarly, Shaw's statement that "the idealist hates himself and is ashamed of himself" (*Quint* 34) makes good sense when conjoined with Fromm's declaration that, contrary to popular opinion, the selfish person does not love himself inordinately but "in fact hates himself" (*MFH* 131). Because idealists efface themselves by initially submitting to external authority and subsequently rationalizing their servile behavior by appealing to the requirements of goodness, they are secretly filled with self-loathing. Far from ungrounded or excessive, these Shavian sentiments are in perfect keeping with "the principle of humanistic ethics" which, in Fromm's words, holds "that virtue is the same as the pursuit of man's obligation toward himself and vice the same as self-mutilation" (*MFH* 118).[31]

Shaw's remark that the way to social reform "lies through the most resolute and uncompromising Individualism" (*Quint* 109) can also be focused profitably through the Frommian perspective. This comment is intelligible in the light of Fromm's contention that self-interest is incompatible with selfishness. Elaborating his statement, Shaw writes that

> there is no hope in Individualism for egotism. When a man is at last brought face to face with himself by a brave Individualism, he finds himself face to face, not with an individual, but with a species, and knows that to save himself, he must save the race. He can have no life except a share in the life of the community; and if that life is unhappy and squalid, nothing that he can do to paint and paper and upholster and shut off his little corner of it can really rescue him from it. (*Quint* 110)

This elaboration is identical in sense to Fromm's argument that the humanistic ethic "does not imply that man's nature is such that egotism or isolation is good for him. It does not mean that man's purpose can be fulfilled in a state of unrelatedness to the world outside. In fact . . . it is one of the characteristics of human nature that man finds his fulfillment and happiness only in relatedness to and solidarity with his fellow man" (*MFH* 14).[32] At work in consciousness, for Shaw and Fromm, are feelings of empathy that create powerful bonds of human connectedness.[33] Furthermore, in citing the social nature of human-kind, both affirm Aristotle's claim that humans are creatures of the *polis*. That is to say, all three maintain that the species can flourish only within civil societies that optimize the opportunity each individual has to live the good life.

Thus, the Frommian perspective makes it possible for us to situate Shaw squarely in a tradition of humanistic ethics that looks back to Aristotle for its inspiration. However, as with many constructions of the human mind, between the ideal and the reality falls a darkening shadow. Both Shaw and Fromm knew that, for the most part, the productive, autonomous self which occupied so prominent a place in their ethical thought did not exist. Only a healthy self, in their eyes, could include all humanity within its compass, yet everywhere they looked, they saw only impoverished selves, the forlorn detritus bred of a voracious capitalism that reduced the living throng to a thanatotic servitude.[34] The conscious activity of such people could hardly be described as free, inasmuch as capitalist and laborer alike were slaves to an economic system that was inherently exploitative and dehuman-izing. In so forbidding an environment, the kind of self required by Shaw and Fromm could never thrive.

Nonetheless, both maintained that such a self was a real possibility for humankind, provided certain conditions obtained. Surely this is entailed by Shaw's evolutionary view of life. The future, for Shaw, was open; no eventuality, including salvation, was foreclosed. The species might someday achieve autonomy and productiveness, if only it would give up the genocidal pursuit of private gain and, in the manner of the realist, unite wisdom and potency in the service of humanity. Fully evolved, the realist would become the "Superman," "the Just Man made Perfect!,"[35] the Frommian *biophile*. In the Shavian universe, however, which is defined by its tragic optimism,[36] there are no guar-antees. Humanity might very well go the way of the dinosaur and the dodo, if—to borrow Juan's metaphor—it chooses to drift rather than steer.

Fromm, too, believed in "the perfectibility of man" (*BTC* 177), in the race's innate capacity to achieve positive freedom: "the freedom to become independent; the freedom to *be* much, rather than to *have* much, or to *use* things and people" (*BTC* 180; Fromm's emphasis). Like Shaw, he cautioned that "this perfectibility means that man *can* reach his goal, but it does not mean that he *must* reach it" (*BTC* 177; Fromm's emphasis).[37] Provide the proper nourishment, and as the acorn grows into an oak, the human seed will grow into an autonomous, productive self. So Shaw and Fromm supposed. However, if we starve that fragile kernel by depriving it of the necessary sustenance, we will leave behind an empty husk. For Fromm and Shaw, only one nutrient could sustain the self in its growth toward realization: socialism.

Shaw champions Fabian socialism; Fromm favors "communitarian Socialism" (*SS* 248ff.). Both strategies of reform are alike in many respects. Each seeks to de-alienate society by humanizing the relationship between individuals and the means of production. Under capitalism, the productive apparatus tyrannizes people; under socialism, people control the productive apparatus. Such a reversal, Shaw says, would emancipate humanity by substituting "the law of fellowship for the law of competition."[36] By fellowship Shaw understands the notion that we are all brothers and sisters under the skin, that we cannot injure others or allow another to suffer without diminishing ourselves. As Shaw sees it, fellow feeling would inspire not only reciprocity in the social sphere but also genuine aristocratic behavior in which individuals happily contribute more to the commonweal than they take.[39] Fromm also believes in "the unity of mankind" (*MFH* 4) in that "every human being is the bearer of all human potentialities" and that "human solidarity is the necessary condition for the unfolding of any one individual" (*MFH* 42, 101). Like Shaw, Fromm looks forward with anticipation to the advent of socialism, to the implementation of a mode of economic organization in which "every working person would be an active and responsible participant, where work would be attractive and meaningful, where capital would not employ labor, but labor would employ capital" (*SS* 248).

As a corollary, each variety of socialism seeks an equitable distribution of national wealth so that wide disparities of income, which appear inevitable in a capitalist society, do not embitter social relations and waste lives. "There are imperative needs," according to Fromm, "which *have* to be satisfied before anything else. Only when man has time and energy left beyond the satisfaction of primary needs, can culture develop and with it those strivings that attend to phenomena of abundance" (*EFF* 295; Fromm's emphasis). Positive freedom, productiveness, and self-realization are phenomena of abundance; they cannot be attained if people are mired in poverty and squalor. Shaw concurs[40] and therefore argues vigorously that we must distribute sufficient income to every person to ensure that, after basic survival needs have been met, there is a "surplus for education and culture: in short, for civilization."[41] "Without cultured homes," Shaw maintains, "civilization is impossible."[42] Where degradation and exploitation prevail, as they do under the worst excesses of capitalism, humanity cannot flourish.

As envisioned by Fromm and Shaw, socialism would also revamp a morally bankrupt system of education that is little more than a propaganda tool of the state. "In our culture," writes Fromm, "education too often results in the elimination of spontaneity and in the substitution of original psychic acts by superimposed feelings, thoughts, and wishes" (*EFF* 242). Instead of promoting independence in children, schools enforce conformity, and do so shamelessly in the name of enlightened learning. Shaw too is highly critical of his country's educational system, especially in regard to its treatment of the young. It achieves nothing, in his view, save to "inculcate submission" and to "break [the child's] will."[43] As a result, the British never achieve selfhood: they remain "a mass of people living in a submissive routine to which [they] have been drilled from [their] childhood."[44] Thus, England is rife with automatous and authoritarian character types. In the main, her citizens have all been miseducated—"they have been educated, not into manhood and freedom, but into blindness and slavery by their parents and schoolmasters, themselves the victims of a similar misdirection."[45] Until this vicious chain of ignorance is broken, England, or any nation with similar educational practices, will never attain a healthy society.

Both Frommian and Shavian socialism respond effectively to a deep human need for psychic wholeness. They facilitate the concrete realization of a coherent worldview that is intellectually and emotionally satisfying. To the external question about the meaning and purpose of existence, they both reply: we are here to serve life as autonomous moral agents, not to serve our selfish desires. This response to an age-old query gives structure and direction to individual lives which, in a time that has witnessed increasing fragmentation and despair, might otherwise be lacking. Fromm may speak of "frames of reference and devotion"[46] and Shaw of "Creative Evolution," but they have congruent notions in mind: a social gospel that is essentially religious, in a sense uncharacteristic of Western thought. Neither believes in the Judeo-Christian God or in an afterlife, yet both maintain that humanity can achieve unity and transcendence if people join together in a collective effort to secure universal well-being. In the worship of life and in ever-greater abundance, but not in riches or fame, lies our redemption. Although Shaw believes in a Life Force and Fromm does not, both deify life in the same way and both derive the same humanistic ethic therefrom. Summing up his thoughts on *biophilia*, Fromm writes that "love for life will develop most in a society where there is: *security* in the sense that the basic material conditions for a dignified life are not threatened, *justice* in the sense that nobody can be an end for the purpose of another, and *freedom* in the sense that each man has the possibility to be an active and responsible member of society" (*HOM* 52–53; Fromm's emphasis). This is exactly the kind of society he and Shaw labored indefatigably to realize through the building of a socialist state.

The ethics of Shaw and Fromm are clearly in the Aristotelian tradition. The mutual emphasis on character, virtue, autonomy, wisdom, *eudaimonia*, teleology, and human nature bespeak an intellectual kinship that spans the ages. This kinship, moreover, is the ultimate source of the enduring value of the Shavian and Frommian point of view, for it has been argued, most recently by Alasdair MacIntyre, that Aristotelianism is the only approach to ethics capable of providing a shared, rationally justifiable basis for morality.[47] Here the formidable adversary is Nietzsche, as MacIntyre points out.[48] Perhaps more forcefully than anyone, Nietzsche argues that all so-called appeals to objectivity in ethics are, in fact, subjective expressions of personal preferences and the will to power. Universal rational standards of conduct are, in principle, impossible under the Nietzschean perspective. For Nietzsche, each individual is destined to an inescapable moral solipsism. Each individual must, of necessity, fashion a code of conduct from scratch, in an ethical void, without the mediation of an informing social context. The notion of common goods inherent in the practice of communal living is foreign to Nietzsche.

Against this thoroughgoing skepticism, which so potently articulates the failure of contemporary, predominantly rule-centered ethical theories to justify themselves, stands Aristotle. For him, as for Shaw and Fromm, the primary ethical question is not "Which rules did you obey?" but "What is the good life for humankind?"; not "What is good for you or me?" but "What is good for *everyone*?" To this leading question the three give essentially the same answer: the ethical life within a flourishing social community. The goal or *telos* of human action, in their eyes, is well-being, which Aristotle conceives in terms of *eudaimonia*, and Shaw and Fromm in cognate terms of self-realization. Central to this vision are the autonomous self, virtuous character, and sound judgment, for one cannot live the good life by following an inflexible set of rules: there is no infallible set to be followed. All attempts to ground ethics on rules, whether of a utilitarian, Kantian, or divine kind, are widely acknowledged to have failed. Instead, the content of morality is to be determined, as Aristotle suggests, from a conception of what is good for the species, given its unique characteristics. It is precisely this conception, says Fromm, that the modern scientific study of human nature can *objectively* specify with, we may add, a degree of precision that validates Shaw's insights and augments Aristotle's achievement.

This is not to say that Aristotle and those who follow in his footsteps are immune to criticism. Several objections might be raised. Exactly what constitutes *the good for humankind* is debatable, perhaps even unresolvable; and even if we could identify such a good, the means to achieving it would also be open to (endless?) debate. The notion of self has been under heavy attack ever since Hume, who could find no empirical evidence for believing in it. The gulf between "is" and "ought," another Humean legacy, is still unbridged. Human nature is a notoriously fuzzy concept, and so is virtue. The question of freedom versus determinism remains a philosophical quagmire from which we may never extricate ourselves. The scientific community has largely rejected biological and universal teleology, turning from holism and finalism to reductionism and mechanism. To be sure, some of these issues do not arise for Aristotle since his worldview differs radically from ours. For us, however, they are all acutely problematic. In time, perhaps these matters can be resolved. Perhaps not. Still, one thing seems certain: if there is to be an adequate response to Nietzsche, it will be along Aristotelian lines or not at all.[49] For this reason, the ethics of Shaw and Fromm, who are both worthy heirs to Aristotle and *biophiles* of the first rank, may very well comprise an ethics of both ultimate concern and ultimate commitment.

Notes

1. I know of only one reference in Fromm to Shaw (*The Heart of Man: Its Genius for Good and Evil* [New York: Harper & Row, 1964], p. 125) and of no references in Shaw to Fromm. It is fair to say that, despite their affinities, neither man exerted a formative influence on the other. Fromm's one reference to Shaw occurs in a discussion of freedom and determinism—specifically in regard to punishment.

2. Bernard Shaw, *The Quintessence of Ibsenism*, in *Major Critical Essays, The Collected Works of Bernard Shaw*, vol. 19, The Ayot St. Lawrence Edition (New York: William H. Wise, 1931), pp. 133–34. Hereafter cited as *Quint* in the text.

3. Erich Fromm, *Man for Himself: An Inquiry into the Psychology of Ethics* (New York: Rinehart, 1947), pp. 12–13. Hereafter cited as *MFH* in the text.

4. See also Alfred Turco, Jr., *Shaw's Moral Vision: The Self and Salvation* (Ithaca: Cornell University Press, 1976). Turco has demonstrated more convincingly than anyone the preeminence of the self in Shaw's ethical thought.

5. Erich Fromm, "The Applications of Humanist Psychoanalysis to Marx's Theory,"

Socialist Humanism: An International Symposium, ed. Erich Fromm (1965; Garden City, NY: Anchor Books, 1966), p. 229.

6. Erich Fromm, *Greatness and Limitations of Freud's Thought* (New York: Harper & Row, 1980), p. 54; Fromm's emphasis.

7. Bernard Shaw, *The Sanity of Art, Major Critical Essays,* p. 323; hereafter cited as *Sanity* in the text. Cf. Shaw: "The strongest, fiercest force in human nature is human will" (Preface to *Misalliance, Prefaces by Bernard Shaw* [London: Constable, 1934], p. 80; hereafter cited as *Prefaces*).

8. See Shaw's letter to Jules Magny, *Bernard Shaw: Collected Letters 1874–1897,* ed. Dan H. Laurence (New York: Dodd, Mead, 1968), pp. 277–79 (hereafter cited as *CL* in the text); *The Sanity of Art,* p. 320; and *Everybody's Political What's What?* (New York: Dodd, Mead, 1944), p. 172. Cf. Fromm, *Beyond the Chains of Illusion: My Encounter with Marx and Freud* (New York: Simon and Schuster, 1962), p. 176; hereafter cited as *BTC* in the text.

9. See also Bernard Shaw, "Fragments of a Fabian Lecture 1890," *Shaw and Ibsen: Bernard Shaw's* The Quintessence of Ibsenism *and Related Writings,* ed. J. L. Wisenthal (Toronto: University of Toronto Press, 1979), pp. 81–84.

10. See, for example, Jonathan Lear, *Aristotle: The Desire to Understand* (Cambridge: Cambridge University Press, 1988), pp. 157–58, 166, and 171.

11. For a nontechnical discussion of the difference between needs and wants, see Mortimer J. Adler, *Ten Philosophical Mistakes* (New York: Macmillan, 1985), pp. 124–26.

12. Bernard Shaw, Preface to *Plays Pleasant, Prefaces,* p. 703.

13. Shaw's teleology is nowhere more evident than in the Preface to *Back to Methuselah,* where the dramatist, in the role of metabiologist, rejects Darwinian evolution in favor of Lamarckian evolution (*Prefaces,* pp. 484, 486–87; see also Shaw's *Sixteen Self Sketches* [New York: Dodd, Mead, 1949], p. 125). Both theories, Shaw says, equally account for the facts and cannot be refuted; but, in his estimation, one has a decisive advantage over the other: the latter entails the view that human mind—will, intention, purpose, and intellect—are efficacious in the world, whereas the former, with its emphasis on accident and blind chance, does not, and consequently leads to a fatalistic pessimism. For Shaw, the old adage "where there is a will there is a way" is more than a platitude. It is a way of life, an inspirational credo, an orientation to living that spurs us on to energetic pursuit of our goals.

14. Wickedness *per se* does not preoccupy Shaw. What "concerns" him is the harm done by "normally innocent people" (Preface to *Saint Joan, Prefaces,* p. 609). Fromm shares this concern: "*The ordinary man with extraordinary power,*" he says, "is the chief danger for mankind—not the fiend or the sadist" (*The Heart of Man,* p. 22, Fromm's emphasis; hereafter cited as *HOM* in the text).

15. It is noteworthy that Fromm attributes our inability to nurture the self to lack of knowledge: we deceive ourselves about our real needs and how to satisfy them. That is, because we are prone to self-deception, we do not know how to foster self-realization and the full unfolding of human potential. We are, then, as Shaw maintains and Fromm reiterates, "ignorant" of what is good for us as human beings (*Man for Himself,* p. 125).

16. Erich Fromm, *Escape from Freedom* (1941; New York: Holt, Rinehart and Winston, 1972), pp. 277–99; hereafter cited as *EFF* in the text. For comparable discussions, see, for example, Fromm, *The Sane Society* (1955; New York: Fawcett Premier, 1985), pp. 76–184 (hereafter cited as *SS* in the text); *Beyond the Chains of Illusion,* pp. 71–87; and *Greatness and Limitations of Freud's Thought,* pp. 61–62.

17. For a view that parallels mine in some respects, see Richard F. Dietrich's "Shavian

Psychology," *SHAW: The Annual of Bernard Shaw Studies* 4 (1984), pp. 149–71. Dietrich argues, among other things, that "Shaw's Realists, Idealists and Philistines are primarily psychological categories" (149). However, without a Frommian perspective, Dietrich is in danger of underestimating the impact of sociocultural forces on the development of human character and its expression in action. While he acknowledges that Shaw's distinctions "fall under the rubric of 'social psychology' " (152, 155), Dietrich claims that "the balance between sociology and psychology is tipped to the latter" (152). This contention takes no notice of Fromm's notions that the will is a manifestation of character, that character is shaped by external factors that become internalized, and that these internalized contents, which are often repressed, may therefore generate the very "warring psychic principles" by which, Dietrich says, Shavian protagonists are "torn" (154).

18. For both Fromm and Shaw, character is not an either-or phenomenon. "In reality," says Fromm, "we always deal with blends, for a character never represents one of the nonproductive or productive orientations exclusively" (*Man for Himself*, p. 112). Shaw, too, believes that our virtues and vices come mixed, that we "all have sinned, and fallen short of the glory of God" (Preface to *Imprisonment*, *Prefaces*, p. 302; original emphasis omitted). "We must get out of the habit," he writes, "of painting human character in soot and whitewash" (ibid.). In the domain of ethics, as is the case elsewhere, it is not true "that whatever is not white is black" ("The Illusions of Socialism," *Selected Non-Dramatic Writings of Bernard Shaw*, ed. Dan H. Laurence [Boston: Houghton Mifflin, 1965], p. 418; hereafter cited as *Illusions* in the text). Character comes in many shades of gray, and where behavior is the issue, it is always a question of which mixture of traits comes to the fore.

19. The language is Alfred Turco, Jr.'s; see his "Ibsen, Wagner, and Shaw's Changing Views of 'Idealism,' " *The Shaw Review* 17 (May, 1974), pp. 82–85, and *Shaw's Moral Vision*, pp. 151–53, 276, and 284–85.

20. Cf. Fromm: "There is no kind of cruelty and viciousness which has not been rationalized individually or in history as being motivated by good intentions" (*Greatness and Limitations of Freud's Thought*, p. 24).

21. Cf. Shaw: ". . . before a good man can carry out his good intentions he must not only ascertain the facts but reason on them" (*Everybody's Political What's What?*, p. 2). See also Robert F. Whitman, *Shaw and the Play of Ideas* (Ithaca: Cornell University Press, 1977), pp. 45–47.

22. In this and similar contexts, "better" and related terms have both a practical and an *ethical* sense. Although Shaw values efficiency, he understands the limitations of pragmatism. "The weakness of Pragmatism," he writes, "is that most theories will work if you put your back into making them work" (Preface to *Androcles and the Lion*, *Prefaces*, p. 567). Hence, Shaw insists that "even perfectly rational solutions of our problems must be humane as well if they are to be accepted by good men" (Preface to *Imprisonment*, *Prefaces*, p. 299). For Shaw, solutions to pressing social problems, such as the distribution of a nation's income, must be "righteous and practicable" (*The Intelligent Woman's Guide to Socialism and Capitalism* [New York: Brentano's, 1928], p. 30). In socialism, he believed he had found the desired solution.

23. See also *The Intelligent Woman's Guide to Socialism and Capitalism*, sections 27 and 75–76.

24. Bernard Shaw, Preface to *Misalliance*, *Prefaces*, p. 103.

25. Bernard Shaw, "Three Plays by Brieux," *Prefaces*, p. 210. Hereafter cited as *Brieux* in the text.

26. Cf. Fromm: "All that the human race has achieved, spiritually and materially, it

owes to the destroyers of illusions and to the seekers of reality" (*Beyond the Chains of Illusion*, p. 160).

27. *Everybody's Political What's What?*, p. 326.

28. The relevant passage is from the Epistle Dedicatory to *Man and Superman* (*Prefaces*, pp. 163–64).

29. Bernard Shaw, Preface to *Back to Methuselah, Prefaces*, p. 492; cf. Preface to *Androcles and the Lion, Prefaces*, pp. 546–47 and 579ff.

30. Bernard Shaw, *The Religious Speeches of Bernard Shaw*, ed. Warren S. Smith (University Park: Pennsylvania State University Press, 1963), p. 78. Hereafter cited as *RS* in the text.

31. For the all-important distinction between self-love and self-interest, on the one hand, and selfishness, on the other, which is crucial to a vindication of Shavian ethics, see Fromm, *Man for Himself*, pp. 119–41.

32. Fromm says essentially the same thing when he states that "a man's task in life is precisely the paradoxical one of realizing his individuality and at the same time transcending it and arriving at the experience of universality. Only the fully developed individual self can drop the ego" (*Beyond the Chains of Illusion*, p. 178).

33. Shaw, following Jesus, puts the matter this way: "we are members one of another" (Preface to *Androcles and the Lion, Prefaces*, p. 552); Fromm, using the language of psychology, puts it differently: "as long as any fellow being is experienced as fundamentally different from myself, as long as he remains a stranger, I remain a stranger to myself too. When I experience myself fully, then I recognize that I am the same as any other human being . . . [then] I discover that I am everybody, and that I discover myself in discovering my fellow man, and vice versa" (*Beyond the Chains of Illusion*, pp. 171–72).

34. According to Fromm, capitalism intensifies people's feelings of impotence by reducing them to "cog[s] in the vast economic machine" (*Escape from Freedom*, pp. 110, 276). Shaw notes the same effect when he writes that in a capitalist system, "wealth accumulates and men decay" (*The Intelligent Woman's Guide to Socialism and Capitalism*, section 42).

35. Bernard Shaw, Preface to *Man and Superman, Prefaces*, p. 167.

36. The oxymoron is Alfred Turco, Jr.'s; see his *Shaw's Moral Vision*, pp. 274–86.

37. Fromm writes that humanity faces two choices, life and death, and that "life and death . . . are not biological states, but states of being, of relating to the world" (*Beyond the Chains of Illusion*, p. 175). This recalls Shaw's distinction between the "angelic and diabolic temperament," which lies at the heart of the Hell Scene in *Man and Superman*. If we drift with the Devil, if we forgo *biophilious* ethics by manifesting a diabolic temperament, we will surely perish, perhaps not immediately, but eventually; if we steer with Juan, if we embrace the ethics of the *biophile* by manifesting an angelic temperament, we may yet endure and someday reach new evolutionary heights. The choice, say Shaw and Fromm, is ours—and ours alone. See also J. L. Wisenthal, *Shaw's Sense of History* (Oxford: Clarendon Press, 1988), pp. 123–34, especially pp. 124 and 132.

38. Bernard Shaw, Preface to *Back to Methuselah, Prefaces*, p. 304. ⋅

39. On the importance of the aristocratic ethic to Shaw, see my "The Intelligent Reader's Guide to *The Apple Cart*," *SHAW: The Annual of Bernard Shaw Studies* 9 (1989), pp. 145–60, especially pp. 149–50 and 155–56.

40. Shaw makes the same point in *The Intelligent Woman's Guide* when he anchors the case for an equitable—specifically, equal—distribution of a nation's wealth on the "rule . . . as old as Aristotle" which holds that "subsistence comes first and virtue afterwards" (p. 94). Andrew Undershaft puts the matter more poetically: "the spirit cannot soar until the millstones are lifted" (*Bernard Shaw: Complete Plays With Prefaces*, [New

York: Dodd, Mead, 1962], I: 434). That is, as Undershaft and the Preface to *Major Barbara* contend, until poverty and the iniquities it spawns are eradicated, civilization itself, including the prospect for an ethical society, will remain in grave jeopardy (see also the Preface to *Androcles and the Lion, Prefaces,* p. 556).

41. Bernard Shaw, Preface to *Farfetched Fables, Bernard Shaw: Complete Plays With Prefaces,* 6:459.

42. Ibid.

43. Bernard Shaw, Preface to *Misalliance, Prefaces,* p. 74.

44. Ibid., p. 104.

45. Ibid., p. 102.

46. Erich Fromm, *The Revolution of Hope: Toward a Humanized Technology* (1968; New York: Harper and Row, 1970), pp. 62ff.; see also *Man for Himself,* pp. 46–50.

47. Alasdair MacIntyre, *After Virtue* (Notre Dame, Ind.: University of Notre Dame Press, 1981).

48. Ibid., especially Chapters 9 and 18.

49. For an intriguing effort to reconcile Nietzsche and Aristotle, see Robert C. Solomon, "A More Severe Morality: Nietzsche's Affirmative Ethics," *Nietzsche As Affirmative Thinker,* ed. Y. Yovel (Dordrecht: Martinus Nijhoff, 1986), pp. 69–89, especially pp. 82–89.

Bernard Shaw

REVIEWER OF FORGOTTEN NOVELISTS: TWO EARLY UNSIGNED SHAW NOTICES FROM THE *PALL MALL GAZETTE*

Shaw began writing anonymous reviews for the Pall Mall Gazette, *in the custom of contemporary journalism, in May 1885. Later he would complain to his editor about the garbage he was given to review, but at the start, when he needed the money, he concealed most of his negative impressions under kindly ambiguity. Two late-1885 examples below illustrate his moderation: too much carping might have cost him the assignments. When he gave up such work on becoming a regular—and more honest—critic of music, the literary world lost very little; and when all his* Pall Mall Gazette *reviews are collected and edited, many of the authors about whom he wrote will have their first resurrection outside of rare footnotes.*

Julian Hawthorne, son of a famous father, could not live up to his name. Much of his third and fourth decades was spent in London, which he loved, and in which he produced literary journalism and subliterary fiction. In 1888, on his way out as a literary critic, Shaw reviewed a Julian Hawthorne novel in passing in a grab-bag notice entitled "A Batch of Books" (C471). A few years earlier he was more generous, giving an entire column on 30 December 1885 (C182) to Love—or a Name, *published by the dignified firm of Chatto and Windus, who claimed Mark Twain in England. Although Shaw brought in the name of Henry James early in the notice largely to compare Julian Hawthorne's handling unfavorably to that of his compatriot, James could not have been pleased. Reviewing two novels by young Hawthorne in the later 1870s, the best that James could say was that Hawthorne was "not commonplace" and sometimes reminded one of "his illustrious father," although he was "strangely sophomorical," guilty of "a certain incurable immaturity and crudity."*

Clark Russell, whose A Strange Voyage *Shaw had reviewed on 5 December 1885 (C177), came off slightly better because Shaw, who had begun writing art criticism, could throw in art references as well as his characteristic allusions to Dickens. Like Hawthorne, Russell was considered respectable, especially his sea melodrama* The Wreck of the "Grosvenor." *When, however, Joseph Conrad's early fiction was compared by critics, in innocent praise, to Russell's, Conrad expostulated to Edward Garnett (5 August 1896) that to perpetrate "a Clark Russel[l] puppet show . . . would be worse than starvation." Even Shaw had to confess that, despite his zeal to be kind. Using painterly images, he was compelled to observe that Russell's "landscapes are better than his figures—much what Conrad would write but without the personal note." The novel, Shaw also noted, as kindly as possible, betrayed evidences of being "not exhaustively planned in advance."*

Readers who have wondered about Shaw's curmudgeonly criticism later may look to the early book reviews for some of the reasons. He had used up his stock of genial patience on the mediocrities of the mid-1880s.———S.W.

A Novel By Mr. Julian Hawthorne

Mr. Julian Hawthorne's latest novel, like most works of art produced during a period of transition, not only begins in one fashion and ends in another, but preposterously exhibits the new fashion before the old, instead of the old before the new. It is as if a publisher not quite abreast of his time had commissioned Mr. James to write a novel, and, finding the last chapter inconclusive and unsatisfactory, had called in Miss Braddon to marry the lovers, kill the villain, and wind up the business on the strictest principles of poetic justice. A musician desirous of writing an overture illustrative of "Love—or a Name" might hit it off by composing a prelude in the style of Wagner with a coda in the style of Rossini.

The story opens in the Arcadia of modern noveldom, a New England village. In these outlands opportunities for persons of strong predatory instincts are so limited, that the choicer spirits emigrate in search of Tom Tiddler's ground. The average pressure of temptation is low, consequently the average level of character is apparently high. Contemplation of the village life is taken in doses by the American novelist as a corrective to the pessimism induced by the spectacle of rascality rampant in the great cities. Mr. Julian Hawthorne has only two honest people in his narrative; and they both hail from the Arcadian village of Hickory. They are of course the hero and heroine. The others are city bosses, prodigiously able as wire-pullers, and genial as private entertainers, but corrupt and indeed blackguard from the point of view of the public moralist. Apparently no man in America meddles with politics unless he has an axe to grind at them. Republican stinginess in what the Irishman who hired a bottomless sedan chair called "honour and glory," would seem to have overreached itself by leaving no inducement to legislators except money and the royalty of the railway board. The sovereign people has got itself under the thumb of the sovereign shareholder, who is, after all, a doubtful improvement on George III.

When Warren Bell leaves Arcadia and goes "ambitioning" in New York, he is a little sore and also a little relieved at having failed in his wooing of Nell Anthony, who has refused him on suspicion of having proposed more in duty than in love. He falls into the hands of a diabolic Monte Cristo named Drayton, who has laid a plot to overthrow the Republic and become benevolent despot of the United States. According to this plan, a semblance of the usual Presidents and parties is to be maintained; but the presidents are to be deadheads, to be manipulated, with the parties, by the omnipotent Drayton, who is personally of a retiring disposition and does not wish his name to appear. Foreseeing the need of a successor to himself, he selects Warren Bell, offering him a partnership in the scheme and the hand of his daughter Lizzie to boot. Warren, on patriotic grounds, accepts both; and he and Drayton set to work in the face of some opposition from Judge Muhlbach, the reactionist wire-puller. So far, there is every promise of a capital story, with plenty of motive and plenty of human material. But all is prematurely and violently wrecked by Nell Anthony. She, too, comes up to New York from Arcadia; and full soon she sets things to rights. An attempt of Judge Muhlbach to obtain a heavy fine for a short lease of a rising town lot, is penetrated and exposed by her with an economic insight so rare in one of her sex, years, and rustic breeding, that the defeated judge offers her his hand, which she indignantly refuses. She then proceeds to the residence of Drayton, who, after a faint resistance, confesses his plot, merely pleading that his intentions were good and that he would have taken care of Warren Bell's interests if she had not interfered. The other characters are soon disposed of. Lizzie is run down by a fire engine and slain. Drayton obliterates the countenance of her perfidious lover with a cut glass decanter, and then shoots himself. Warren Bell courageously marries Nell and retires from public life. "Be he where he may," says the author, "there is reason to believe that she whom we have known as Nell Anthony is with him." This conclusion is cheerfully intended; but in view of Nell's uncommon strength of character, it has something of the minor cadence in it.

There is a highly civilized wit and wisdom about the telling of this story that makes the barbarism of its winding-up quite astonishing. All interest and belief in the narrative vanish at the first pistol shot. In their place comes a wondering demand as to what Mr. Julian Hawthorne has to do with gunpowder and fire engines and such transpontine stage properties. There are still people who like a book in which for three volumes hardhearted relatives and designing villains block the heroine's way to the altar only to be arbitrarily removed in the last chapter by battle, murder, or sudden death: the sympathetic reader breathing more and more freely as the slaughter proceeds, and obstacle after obstacle is removed (in the Invinciblist sense of that verb) from the path of true love. But these unsophisticated persons are the gluttons of fiction. Mr. Julian Hawthorne's work appeals to the epicures. To even moderately cultivated palates, the crudities of old-fashioned romance have by this time lost their relish. There is no longer any need for the novelist to tie a very complicated knot in his story; but if he does tie one, he must unravel it fairly and not cut it by a suicide and a fatal accident. That Alexandrine method is a rough-and-ready one, and has done hard service in its day; but just at present, it is, as Mr. Julian Hawthorne's compatriots would say, "played out."

A Strange Voyage

Mr. Clark Russell's nautical novels are refreshingly briny and breezy results of the discovery of the picturesque. A very artful landsman, with the help of a gallery of flamboyant Turners and Admiral Smyth's "Sailor's Word Book," might manufacture one ocean landscape and one squall that might pass for a genuine Clark Russell; but he would not return to the subject again and again with the inexhaustible zest of the author of "The Wreck of the *Grosvenor*," "A Sea Queen," and other novels in which ships, sails, seas, and skies are word-painted over and over again until the reader is fain to cry "Avast!" and to make all snug by the simple expedient of skipping when he sees another description coming. Like Mr. Pecksniff's articled pupils, who were condemned to draw Salisbury Cathedral from every possible point of view, Mr. Clark Russell presents his ship in all weathers, at all hours, and from all quarters of the horizon. He describes the *Silver Sea*, in which "A Strange Voyage" was made, as she appeared from the shore in Plymouth Harbour, both at night and by day. Then he gets into a boat, and sketches her from the wavetops. Finally he goes aboard, and describes her from the deck; from the cabin; from foretop, maintop, and mizentop; in fog, storm, and calm; by moonlight and sunlight, temperate and tropical; in the Channel; in the Bay of Biscay-oh; in the trades; in the doldrums; in ballast and crank; afloat and aground; close hauled and running before a favourable breeze; and in many other highly technical predicaments, which cannot be referred to here without misgiving as to the accuracy of the language employed. And in all these aspects the ship is refulgent with the splendid colours that make a sea voyage a wonderful panorama to people of Mr. Russell's way of thinking. Mr. Russell is a literary Turner in his fondness for effects of light and atmosphere. There is another respect in which he resembles Turner. His landscapes are better than his figures.

The strange voyage is undertaken by a gouty gentleman in quest of health. A friend of his, a shipowner, lends him a ship, and accompanies him on his trip. The party consists of the invalid, his daughter, the shipowner, a colonel with his wife and daughter, and Mr. Clark Russell masquerading as Mr. Aubyn. Though their destination is the Cape, the men embark without a surgeon and the ladies without a maid. It would be hard to say which of these improbabilities is the harder to digest. The first startling incident that occurs is the rescue of a shipwrecked sailor, who turns out to be a Finn. Now Finns are supposed to bring ill-luck on board ship. In nautical novels they invariably do so. This particular Finn is an unusually objectionable person. He corrupts the crew, throws the captain overboard, runs the ship aground, maroons the pleasure party on a reef off the Mexican coast, and makes off in a boat with their portable property. For the rest we refer our readers to the novel.

In telling this tale Mr. Clark Russell has wasted his first volume in an attempt to interest the reader in the pleasure party by a deplorable comedy of manners, which is only successful from a realistic point of view inasmuch as it induces all the tedium of a real voyage. The shipowner and the colonel are bores; and superficial descriptions of bores are harder to bear than their originals in person. In short, the saloon of a passenger ship has not found its Moliere or its Sheridan in Mr. Clark Russell: and his book only becomes interesting when, in the second volume, the adventures begin. Then it becomes not only interesting, but exciting: so much so, that when the end of the third volume stops the way, the possibilities of the situation are not half exhausted, and the reader, with plenty of appetite left, vainly regrets all the space wasted at the commencement. The explanation suggested by the story itself is, that it was not exhaustively planned in advance, and that its details were invented from page to page. Intentions changed, forgotten, or found impracticable from bad economy of space, are traceable in many chapters. It is to be hoped that Mr. Clark Russell will not strand himself in this fashion when he embarks on his next novel. His sailing qualities are so excellent that his neglect to make the most of his three volumes of sea room is doubly aggravating.

REVIEWS

Shaw and the Nonconformist Conscience

J. L. Wisenthal. *Shaw's Sense of History.* Oxford: Clarendon, 1988. 186 pp. $45.00

The last ten years have witnessed such a proliferation of Shaviana that one can truthfully call them the Shaw Decade: one bibliography of Shaw's works, one of works about him; letters to the press, to Siegfried Trebitsch, to Alfred Douglas, to Frank Harris, and the last two volumes of the *Collected Letters;* the musical criticism, art criticism, and diaries; and, now emerging, the multivolume biography by Michael Holroyd. More than twenty volumes in all.

To these one may add J. L. Wisenthal's *Shaw's Sense of History,* another essential resource for Shaw studies and for scholars of Victorian culture. This is a book which provides further evidence that Shaw's plays and prose writings form a coherent worldview, a sense of history that spans past and present, as well as future, events. Wisenthal has succeeded in coming to terms with what he calls "Shaw's engagement with whole populations and historical epochs" in order "to demonstrate the importance of Shaw's interest in historical process, the design of history." No small task, considering Shaw's output. Yet Wisenthal's concise and lucid analysis fuses ideology and creativity to demonstrate how Shaw's historical attitudes are unveiled as much in *Caesar and Cleopatra, Saint Joan, "In Good King Charles's Golden Days," Man and Superman, John Bull's Other Island, The Man of Destiny, Major Barbara, Heartbreak House,* and *Back to Methuselah*—to name only the main plays—as in his letters, musical and theater criticism, *The Intelligent Woman's Guide, Everybody's Political What's What?,* and other writings.

Such a grand undertaking needs a grand perspective, and the locus from which Wisenthal views Shaw's work is the opposition of the two prevailing Victorian ideas of history: on the one hand, the sociopolitical meliorism of Thomas Babington Macaulay; on the other, the uncompromising will to change of that opponent of blind faith in progress, Thomas Carlyle. This historiographical context is essential since Shaw's plays, according to Wisenthal, move between "the antithetical Victorian intellectual traditions" these two thinkers represent. This interplay of polarities in Shaw's thought and work is followed through to "present history," and Shaw emerges not merely as the heir to Macaulay and Carlyle, or even their synthesis, but transcending them altogether by a leveling of past and present, and a leap of faith into the future.

Wisenthal examines three large questions which preoccupied the era in which the young Shaw thrived, and which deeply inform his work: the Great Man, progress, and the direction of English history. First, for Macaulay, there is no core of intense heroic soul to render human limitations insignificant; but Carlyle's heroes, writes Wisenthal, "are in touch with the profoundest truths of the universe, and any failings are therefore insignificant." Second, Macaulay's unqualified commitment to material, moral, and social progress is not at all Carlyle's idea of history as a series of constant changes. Finally, where Macaulay, writing in 1848, sees the last hundred and sixty years of British history as a time of "physical, moral and intellectual improvement," Carlyle sees roughly the same period as a godless era inaugurated by the restoration of the monarchy in 1660. As we shall see, Shaw assimilates these polarities, refutes them, and offers his own far-reaching alternative.

For Carlyle, the worship of the Great Man is a religious act: "Reverence for Human Worth . . . is the essence of all true 'religions',," he writes. So it is for Shaw, according to Wisenthal, in that great people inspire others to reach beyond themselves. "The apparent freaks of nature called Great Men mark not human attainment but human possibility and hope," he writes in his Preface to *Geneva*. Such are Caesar and Napoleon because they possess intensity of will. But Wisenthal is right to point out that this is not mere hero-worship. "There is no hope for civilization in government by idolized single individuals," writes Shaw—which did not prevent him from promoting Mussolini and Stalin at a time when he thought dictatorships necessary to bring about change. His idea of the Great Man gradually evolved from the power-hungry Napoleon of *The Man of Destiny* to the martyred mystic Saint Joan, who is, in Hegel's terminology, a "World-Historical Individual," a universal archetype rather than a mere political or religious figure.

If Shaw's Great Man incarnates an idea, so must a historical epoch. In 1949 Shaw saw the excesses of Victorian capitalism as "the most damnably wicked and ruinous episode in human history," but he saw the Middle Ages as "the record of a high European civilization based on a catholic faith." On the other hand, Shaw also uses *Saint Joan* to celebrate Renaissance individualism and nationalism, and to dramatize the waning of the Middle Ages as necessary to historical progress. Wisenthal is always careful to illustrate both sides of an issue and to place it in context—in this case World War I, the great disillusioning experience of Shaw's life. Joan may incarnate the Life Force, but she is also a prelude to the anarchy of war. "The whole value of Joan to us," said Shaw in a 1931 radio talk, "is how you can bring her circumstances into contact with our life and circumstances." For better or worse, Joan is an indispensable part of the historical continuum. Shaw believes in the recurring collapse of civilizations: one reaches its apex, then disintegrates. This suggests a cyclical view of history, recurrence rather than progress. In an irony that Shaw relished, Christianity, regarded as a heresy under the Roman Empire, became the established religion of Europe guilty of the same kind of excesses. Shaw fails to find in history any evidence of moral or intellectual improvement. The belief that there has been any progress, he writes, is the result of "the ordinary citizen's ignorance of the past combine[d] with his idealization of the present."

No progress—so far. But Shaw is deeply committed to the possibility of progress in the future. The pattern of recurrence and decline becomes a pattern of ascent when the context is expanded to include millennia. The decline of humankind is the progress of life, and so Joan's individualism is dangerous but desirable. "All progress is initiated by challenging current conceptions, and executed by supplanting institutions," writes Shaw in the Preface to *Mrs Warren's Profession*. Since Shaw sees the present from the vantage point of the future, the present becomes just another point in the historical continuum. According to Wisenthal, many plays with contemporary settings are really historical drama in modern dress that "reveal the essential historical forces of the present time." In fact almost half of Shaw's plays deal with "present history" in that they show us the contemporary world in relation to a historical background. The implicit assumption is that only the past can explain the present. For Shaw, the future, in a very real sense, is happening now.

After reading *Das Kapital* in 1883, Shaw saw Marx as the way of the future. Half a century later, he warned Churchill to beware Macaulay's idolatry "of an underlying divinity in the British character, and all the monstrous optimism which Karl Marx smashed like a conjuror kicking a very pretty lid off hell and shewing the horrible and grotesque realities beneath." Another sympathetic thinker was Hegel: Shaw called "We learn from history that men never learn anything from history" his "favorite Hegel epigram." Yet another was Henry Thomas Buckle, whose *History of Civilization* (1857–61) Shaw knew well, and for whom, writes Shaw, "progress depends on the critical people who do not believe everything they are told: that is, on scepticism."

Like Carlyle, Buckle, Hegel, and Marx, Shaw is a doubter, and for skepticism to yield alternatives for a better future, there must be change through action. Shaw's suggestion is the dynamic principle of the Life Force, of which the only reality is perpetual evolution. "Human society," he writes in *The Intelligent Woman's Guide*, "is like a glacier: it looks like an immovable and eternal field of ice; but it is really flowing like a river." The study of history is valuable insofar as we recognize that there are no permanent institutions or truths, that change is the law of existence. One must heed Lilith in *As Far as Thought Can Reach:* "I say, let them [men and women] dread, of all things, stagnation." This Shavian leitmotif—the evolutionary conflict between static death and dynamic life—has its parallel in the opposition of Macaulay's self-satisfied certainty to Carlyle's cyclical patterns of history.

Who are the skeptics whose changes keep the world evolving, who embody the Life Force? Historical development can take place only when thought, the first condition of historical change, is incarnated in people of action. The Serpent tells Eve in *In the Beginning,* "You imagine what you desire; you will what you imagine; and at last you create what you will." Wisenthal agrees with Martin Meisel that Shaw "presented ideas, embodied in men, as the realities of history, and will, not accident, as its driving energy." Wisenthal argues that these "world-historical individuals" need not be literally historical, but can be fictional, symbolic embodiments of historical forces manifesting themselves in the individual will. Shaw's plays offer countless examples.

But Shaw does not disregard facts altogether, and his history plays are very well researched: books on the American War of Independence for *The Devil's Disciple,* Mommsen for *Caesar and Cleopatra,* Gilbert Murray for *Androcles and the Lion,* a life of Napoleon for *The Man of Destiny,* the English translation of the transcripts of Jeanne d'Arc's trial for *Saint Joan*—"transcribed almost literally from the original documents," he admitted—and, yes, Macaulay's *History of England* for "*In Good King*

Charles's Golden Days." However, literature is a mirror that distorts history, and *Saint Joan,* for instance, corrects the misconceptions of versions of the saint by Voltaire and others, just as *Caesar and Cleopatra* is a response to Shakespeare and *The Man of Destiny* to Sardou. And Wisenthal makes the essential point that "historical" means more to Shaw than merely "factual," as when Shaw writes that the Epilogue to *Saint Joan* "is obviously not a representation of an actual scene, or even a recorded dream; but it is none the less historical." Conversely, as Shaw admits elsewhere, "Historical facts are not a bit more sacred than any other class of facts. In making a play out of them you must adapt them to the stage, and that alters them at once, more or less." All reports, histories, and dramatic representations, he continues, "are only attempts to arrange the facts in a thinkable, intelligible, interesting form." He explains it more clearly in a 1928 speech to the Royal Academy of Dramatic Art: "Now what the drama can do, and what it actually does, is to take this unmeaning, haphazard show of life, that means nothing to you, and . . . arrange it in such a way as to make you think very much more deeply about it than you ever dreamed of thinking about actual incidents that come to your knowledge."

Thus does Shaw assimilate the dynamics of historical epochs and extract from them archetypal characters, ideologies, and patterns which Wisenthal elucidates in an all-embracing yet comprehensive manner. Using what he sees as Shaw's own method in his history plays, he has juxtaposed pronouncements from wide-ranging sources in order to form a coherent, cohesive Shavian historical worldview. Woven into this complex tapestry of theories and ideas are the plays, not as mere evidence that there is method in Shaw's eclecticism, but to show how Shaw's worldview is the natural, almost inevitable result of a mind which knew what it was all about. In the final analysis, Wisenthal's Shaw combines a Tory-Romantic view of the past and a Whig-Utilitarian view of the present, while never losing sight of a hopeful future.

In "Bernard Shaw and the Heroic Actor" (A2962) in 1907, Shaw writes that "Shakespear's sympathies were with Plutarch and the Nonconformist Conscience, which he personified as Brutus." Wisenthal demonstrates that Shaw's lifework was indeed a struggle to do away with the old order and bring about a new one, a struggle which is not only at the heart of Shaw's idea of history, but which is also his personal philosophy and religion. The chief value of this study lies in its power to analyze and synthesize that struggle so that, after reading *Shaw's Sense of History,* one can never read Shaw the same way again.

Michel Pharand

Ways Pleasant and Unpleasant: Collected Letters Four

Bernard Shaw, Collected Letters 1926–1950, edited by Dan H. Laurence. New York: Viking, 1988. 946 pp. $45.00.

Shaw realized how much effort an edition of his correspondence could involve. When Hesketh Pearson forwarded Dodd, Mead & Company's proposal that Pearson edit a volume of Shaw's letters, Shaw replied on 18 January 1943: "But I strongly advise you to fight shy of the job, though it will be done someday by somebody. It would take as long as half a dozen biographies." Dan H. Laurence's four-volume selection of 2,653 letters, representing roughly one percent of Shaw's actual correspondence and perhaps ten percent of that which has survived, has taken twenty-seven years. Surely Shaw would find this gratifying, even if he were to learn that Laurence completed another monumental task, the Shaw *Bibliography*, while editing the correspondence.

Collected Letters 1926–1950 is less satisfying than the earlier volumes. In his introduction, after crowing a bit about the positive reception of earlier volumes and castigating reviewers for various long-forgotten criticisms, Laurence arouses suspicion concerning his criteria for selection. He states that he has "avoided as completely as possible the influence, in my work, of the perversity of thought that has been creeping into recent Shavian scholarship through a revisionist school of humourless pseudo-psychiatrists," and he makes it clear that "those who seek to uncover the dark Hyde in the present crop of letters are welcome to their searches." This challenge may explain why Laurence has included only the comparatively bland letters of Shaw to Molly Tompkins, has omitted the correspondence with T. E. Lawrence (except for one excerpt in a headnote), and has left out other letters that might offer revealing, if unflattering, glimpses of Shaw.

The possibility that Laurence has taken pains to present Shaw's better side, or even to suppress Shaw's worse side, will make it difficult to rely with confidence on this selection. From the 1939–45 correspondence, one would hardly know that there was a war on except for various personal inconveniences to Shaw. One reads of Shaw's tax burden, his efforts to exempt his domestic staff from war service, and his insistence that the war should not close the theaters or remove German music from the concert halls, but there are surprisingly few 1939–45 references to Hitler or to the progress of the war. Where are the letters giving Shaw's views on the beginning of the war or on the fall of Hitler? Shaw does mention the atomic bomb, but only to complain that the bomb has made it necessary for him to revise a preface. Either Shaw was uncharacteristically reticent once the war began or Laurence decided not to include his utterances, but the reader cannot tell. Still, there is enough in this volume to reveal Shaw's declining powers, his obstinacy in adhering to his admiration for the enemies of democracy, his lack of sympathy for the victims of various injustices, and his increasingly blatant contradictions in his letters.

The fourth volume shows Shaw as he suffered from what Mark Twain once called "the wanton insult of old age." Frequently disheartened by his waning powers, Shaw expressed his fear that he might have finished as a playwright, and he often joked about being in his dotage. In 1941, he complained seriously to H. G. Wells: "My imagination is nearly dead; I forget everything in ten minutes; and my weight has fallen to 9 stone; but I keep up a stage effect of being an upstanding old man." He added that "I havn't written a play for nearly two years. I am by no means sure that I shall ever write another." A great many of the letters reflect Shaw's growing discouragement with his ability to create or to speak to the modern age.

Shaw wrote to Hesketh Pearson on 4 September 1939 to address the discrepancy between Pearson's view of Dean Inge and Shaw's enthusiasm for him: "Remember: you have to account for my admiration of him." Pearson's task seems trivial compared with the challenge of accounting for Shaw's long-lived admiration of Mussolini, Hitler, and Stalin, particularly since Shaw's arguments frequently beg the question. Defending Mussolini's "conquest" of Ethiopia, Shaw argues that "European civilization must stand solid" against the uncivilized savage and complains about "futile squealing and atrocity mongering" against Mussolini. Defending Mussolini's regime against British protests, Shaw argues that "our attitude towards a new regime cannot be determined by the means employed to establish it," which seems uncomfortably close to claiming that the end justifies the means. To counter arguments that Mussolini has suppressed newspapers, suspended the Habeas Corpus Act, and persecuted individuals, Shaw cites British precedents instead of addressing the ethical nature of the acts themselves, as if an English wrong made an Italian right.

Shaw's statements about Hitler are equally problematic. He praises Hitler's "masterful" speeches, justifies the *Anschluss* as an inevitable result of the inequities of the Treaty of Versailles, describes Hitler's withdrawal from the League of Nations as a "masterstroke," and informs Lady Astor on 28 September 1939 that "nothing should be said about concentration camps, because it was we who invented them" during the Boer War. Although in August 1942 he says that Hitler has gone "off the rails," in October he calls Hitler "the greatest living Tory" and *Mein Kampf* (which Shaw was rereading carefully) "one of the world's bibles." In November he describes *Mein Kampf* as "a curious combination of an extraordinarily penetrating observation and comprehension of the political and psychological situation with epileptic phobias and conviction of the eugenic value of racial inbreeding," but earlier (in 1938) he has said, "I think we ought to tackle the Jewish question by admitting the right of States to make eugenic experiments by weeding out any strains that they think undesirable," so long as it is done "as humanely as they can afford to." What does a biographer make of Shaw's apparent unwillingness to realize that he cannot have it both ways?

Stalin elicited this comment from Shaw: "I still rank Stalin first, Roosevelt second, and the rest nowhere." Shaw dismissed Stalin's purges as somehow necessary to the Soviet experiment, which he continued to defend unwaveringly. Some of Shaw's extreme statements may be failed attempts at irony, but it is difficult to reconcile Shaw's political assessments with his supposed championship of human rights advertised on the dustcover of this volume.

During his later years, Shaw frequently refused to write letters on behalf of people trying to leave Russia or prisoners such as the American militant labor leader Thomas Mooney. Laurence, defending Shaw, claims that Shaw had become callous due to the incredible bombardment of letters asking for help, that Shaw did not want to seem discourteous to foreign hosts, and that Shaw felt that any intrusion by a foreigner would do more harm than good. However, this is unconvincing since Shaw, in the letter which Laurence introduces with his defense, makes it clear that he has little sympathy for the subject of the request. The defense becomes even less convincing when Shaw responds favorably to Werner Krauss, an actor who had participated in Nazi propaganda films, who asked Shaw to protest the injustice of trying Krauss as a Nazi collaborator after the war. Shaw writes that trials of collaborators are "a vindictive stupidity which cannot be justified on any ground."

Refusing a request to donate one day's royalties to a fund for Jewish refugees in 1939, Shaw asked, "Have we no desperate hangers-on to the Royal Literary Fund or the Pension Fund who need a benefit of this kind as badly as the Jews?" and wondered "Have you not yourself had to come to the rescue of individual refugees? If not you are luckier than I." Shaw's reaction to the opening of the Bergen-Belsen

Nazi concentration camp, where Anne Frank and almost forty thousand other prisoners perished, shifts emphasis from the Holocaust to an excuse for the Nazi regime: "Belsen was obviously produced by the incompetence and breakdown of the military command. The concentration camps are always left to the refuse of the officers' messes, for whom the job of feeding and sanitating the deluge of prisoners is too much. The result is always the same more or less." The volume's dustcover touts Shaw as among the earliest to denounce Hitler's treatment of the Jews, but in the only letter addressing the discoveries of Nazi treatment of prisoners, he seems to shrug it off by arguing that good help is hard to find.

Sometimes Shaw's contradictions are so blatant that they cast doubts on his integrity. To one correspondent he wrote that Fox Films had "backed out" of an arrangement for a German film version of *Pygmalion*, but two days earlier he had written to Augustin Hamon that Shaw had "got rid of Fox Films." Shaw's letters to Mrs. Patrick Campbell take so different a stance from his letters to her estranged husband George Cornwallis-West that Shaw appears to be trying, somewhat hypocritically, to ingratiate himself with both. Shaw wrote to Wilfrid Lawson on 21 August 1935 to praise Lawson's performance of Tarleton, but to Herbert Prentice (28 July 1935), Shaw had stated flatly that "Tarleton is hopeless." At one point, when Shaw claimed that he had destroyed his post-1885 manuscripts, Laurence commented that Shaw had produced "either an extraordinary case of forgetfulness or a colossal, self-protective lie." Shaw's letters include several other locutions of this order.

Despite the unpalatable features of the correspondence, the fourth volume reveals aspects of Shaw's final years that will interest his future biographers. Both before and after Charlotte's death in 1943, Shaw was the victim of a rogues' gallery of parasites. The Nobel Prize had destroyed any vestige of privacy for Shaw. He complained to Ada Tyrrell on 28 January 1928 that "those who see me now are those who shove and insist and will not take no for an answer," and he frequently suffered uninvited visitors and unsolicited letters. Shaw was generous with his money (he frequently tore up checks he received in repayment of loans and paid for the education of the children of several friends) and with his time (he frequently ushered others' works into print for no fee and spent many hours writing letters of advice and explanation). This made him an easy mark for several who wormed their way into his confidence.

G. S. Viereck, a free-lance journalist, published several fabricated interviews that Shaw frequently disavowed, even, in one instance, after Shaw had revised the proofs. (Shaw knew that Viereck, earlier a propagandist for the Kaiser, was a paid propagandist in the 1930s for Germany.) Lewis Wynne, after engaging Shaw in correspondence, forged several letters and manuscripts to market as Shaw's. Floryan Sobieniowski was so relentless a cadger that Shaw once complained that Sobieniowski would borrow the money for his own funeral "and then he won't die." Gabriel Pascal acquired screen rights for some plays and then produced them ruinously, his cost-overruns making *Caesar and Cleopatra* "the biggest financial failure in British film history." Sir Edward Elgar, urging "a domestic financial crisis," pried £800 from Shaw and then spent it on an automobile for the composer's attractive young secretary, on whom he doted.

John Wardrop and F. E. Loewenstein, both aspiring to control Shaw's literary affairs after Shaw's death, developed an intense rivalry. Wardrop helped edit *Everybody's Political What's What?* and had been led by Shaw to hope to become Shaw's literary executor, but Shaw became convinced that Wardrop would not do and offered instead to pay his tuition to law school. Wardrop's later demand for financial assistance to emigrate to America ultimately exasperated Shaw. Loewenstein, who helped to organize Shaw's files while trying to produce a bibliography, stole scores of Shaw's papers. Stephen and Clare Winsten also gained from Shaw's forbearance, publishing works by and about Shaw that Shaw refused to criticize publicly (Shaw also paid for the education of their son, Christopher). In other ways Nancy Astor and Blanche Patch also afflicted Shaw, the former constantly trying to intrude her self-imposed authority into Shaw's affairs and the latter trying to finagle Shaw into marrying her. (Laurence states that Patch had matrimonial designs on Shaw, but no letter bears on the issue.) Shaw had better luck fending off the insufferable Nancy and the importunate Blanche than he did in countering those bent on exploiting his manuscripts and copyrights.

Biographers will also welcome Shaw's reminiscences of earlier phases of his life and career. To an Australian cousin, Shaw wrote at length about his family background. To Edward Gordon Craig, Shaw recorded memories of Henry Irving and Ellen Terry. To other inquirers, Shaw responded with information about his meeting with Mark Twain, his early Fabian years, his schooling in Dublin, and his recollections of such persons as Edmund Gosse. Shaw's letters to his biographers supplement comments in earlier correspondence and also reveal his manner of dealing with his biographers.

Shaw devotes several letters to instructing actors, directors, and producers on the proper way to present his plays, focusing more on the treatment of earlier works than on work in progress. Several letters resist attempts to turn *Pygmalion* into an Eliza Doolittle/Henry Higgins romance, and Shaw is also adamant in his objections to setting *Pygmalion* to music. He criticizes performances of *The Devil's Disciple* that suggest a love interest between Dick Dudgeon and Judith Anderson. He refuses to authorize *The Chocolate Soldier* to the point of stopping it through the courts. His response to one production in a letter dated 29 October 1929 gives some sense of his usual attitude: "As to the broadcast of Brassbound, its infamy was such that I hereby solemnly renounce, curse, and excommunicate everybody who had a hand in it."

Despite such comments, Shaw was surprisingly flexible when it came to adapting his plays for moving pictures and radio broadcasts. He quickly realized the potential of talking films for playwrights and for politicians, considered the use of "canned" music as early as November 1926, and willingly rewrote the beginning of *Major Barbara* to make the stage play more effective on the screen. He appreciated that "in filming you can select all the perfect bits from your rehearsals," although "you must know which are the best bits," and he revealed his awareness of changes imposed by different conditions in his letter to BBC Producer Peter Watts on 3 October 1946: "Do not treat my printed text with blindly superstitious reverence. It must always be adapted intelligently to the studio, the screen, the stage, or whatever the physical conditions of performance may be." Worried about his financial position, particularly when wartime taxes became so debilitating that he had to live on an overdraft for the first time in his life, Shaw devoted several letters to questions about his commercial rights in films, the disposition of BBC recordings, and the provenance of television rights.

The letters also reflect the wide variety of Shaw's interests and provide flashes of Shavian prescience and wit. The letters include Shaw's utterances on Gene Tunney's boxing prowess, the dim hopes for an English National Theatre, a proposed revision of the national anthem, the proper design of bookcovers, the stylistic shortcomings of military historian Basil Liddell Hart, the Casement diaries controversy, BBC pronunciation, vivisection, international politics, immortality, music, and artificial insemination, among many other subjects. Writing to a cattle rancher, Shaw advises the humane use of paint rather than a branding iron. He tells E. Margaret Wheeler, who suspects that her eight-year-old daughter is really the biological child of another family, to leave well enough alone for the child's sake. He writes to Winston Churchill in June 1940 to advise him to "declare war on France and capture her fleet (which would gladly strike its colors to us) before [Hitler] recovers his breath." He comments of abortion, "like most operations it is not a fundamental cure: the trouble recurs." Of an argument concerning the role of women he notes, "the debate [turned] on whether a woman should spend her entire life in a nursery or in an office without ever taking a walk, each of you defending an idiotic position against an idiotic alternative."

Shaw wrote to St. John Ervine in 1936 that "when you have had as many biographies written about you as I have, you will learn that there is only one way to flatten out their distorting mirrors, and that is to write an autobiography or else get at the proof sheets of the biographers and rewrite them." At several points the letters are unreliable, particularly when Shaw's memory fails, when he contradicts himself, and when he wishes to gloss over matters deliberately, but such instances are fairly easy to spot at this point in Shavian scholarship, and Laurence identifies several. At the end of the volume, Lawrence provides a thorough and moving account of Shaw's last days that is a model of biographical writing.

To Arthur Davies of Santa Monica, California, who had asked "whether the appearance or existence of an apparition had ever been proved to Shaw's satisfaction 'beyond any doubt,'" Shaw responded on 21 January 1949: "Never. But I once walked into a room and saw myself sitting at an escritoire. As I stared, I vanished." As Shaw wrote to Mrs. Patrick Campbell on 12 July 1929, "even the wreck of G.B.S. must be more interesting than an average coaling schooner in full sail." The 740 letters of this volume fully justify this assessment.

Fred D. Crawford

Holroyd One

Michael Holroyd. *Bernard Shaw: A Biography. Volume 1: 1856–1898: The Search for Love.* New York: Random House, 1988. 486 pp. + viii. Illustrated. $24.95.

Michael Holroyd's *Bernard Shaw: A Biography* is the impressive result of fifteen years' research, reading, and writing. Holroyd's method is in the main chronological, though some backward and forward motion occurs as he traces some aspect or interest of Shaw over a period of time or presents a relationship with a lover, friend, or associate. Holroyd's grasp of Shaw's backgrounds is thorough and far-reaching. Such full knowledge is indispensable in writing about a figure like Shaw, who once asserted to Archibald Henderson—and with justice—that any complete account of him must also be a history of the age in which he lived, "a mere peg on which to hang a study of the last half of the XIX century." Shaw in his protean activities and achievements was something of a Renaissance man, and Holroyd's biography of him is on an appropriately large scale. Holroyd's is the first full biography of Shaw to follow Hesketh Pearson's *G.B.S.: A Full Length Portrait* (1942), Archibald Henderson's *George Bernard Shaw: Man of the Century* (1956), and St. John Ervine's *Bernard Shaw: His Life, Work and Friends* (1956). The Shaw Estate commissioned Holroyd to write a life of Shaw because a consensus had developed that such an enterprise was now necessary: a life to be written by one who had not known Shaw and a life that would consider Shaw's relevance to the later twentieth century. The appearance of a vast amount of new materials since Shaw's death also justified a new biography (many of these materials kept appearing as Holroyd was writing his first volume).

Holroyd's task was—and is—formidable, since Shaw was so many people and had so many careers, since he wrote enormously, and since the literature on him is extensive. The current volume is subtitled *The Search for Love* and is the first of three volumes (according to report, Holroyd has finished Volume II, *The Search for Power,* and has begun Volume III, *The Lure of Fantasy*). If the task has been daunting, Holroyd has completed it estimably. He has made Shaw accessible and interesting, and he has achieved the right tone in presenting him: admiration for Shaw's genius combined with a tolerant, ironic, sometimes laconic, sometimes enthusiastic approach to the man and his work. Holroyd's geniality combines the elements of sympathy and objectivity that most befit a biography of a still controversial literary figure, a figure who is arguably the greatest literary presence of the last hundred and twenty-five years. Holroyd's work on Shaw is likely to keep interest in him current and to lead many readers to a perusal—or a new perusal—of his work and to a determination to see as many of his plays as possible. Holroyd seems to me to have gotten Shaw "right," and we can look forward with satisfaction to the remaining volumes. The reader new to Shaw will find Holroyd's book persuasive, and the Shavian scholar will find many challenging insights and judgments.

The subtitle, *The Search for Love,* is in my view a bit misleading. I do not think that this search was Shaw's overpowering motivation during his first forty years, though of course it was one motivation. Rather, it was the search for fame or, simply, the need for self-expression: the compulsion to write at all costs and to make oneself heard as a meaningful voice. The perseverance to achieve success against all obstacles is, I think, the dominating character attribute that Shaw revealed consistently during these years. He evinced also a patience enabling him to survive all rebuffs and a confidence in his own abilities despite the contrary judgments of publishers' readers, John Morley, for example, advising him "to get out of journalism."

Though Holroyd has analyzed fully Shaw's adventures and misadventures with women (see below), it is, I think, his chief merit as chronicler to have been able to give us an acute sense of the frustrations, the agony, the heartache, and the discouragement underlying Shaw's attempts—and failures—to make himself heard during the period 1876–98. Shaw, in retrospect, regarded his long rise to fame indulgently, humorously, and ironically, though the facts as Holroyd marshals them belie the facade that Shaw placed on them. Shaw still hung on to a writing career after producing five novels that commercial publishers refused to touch. The novels can now be read without pain, in fact with pleasure, satisfaction, and stimulus. His novels are better than most of the fluff written at the time, better than most of the works he was condemned to review for the *Pall Mall Gazette*. Somewhat later, he also experienced even greater frustrations in achieving performances for his *Plays Pleasant* and his *Plays Unpleasant*.

In view of his eventual popularity, it is ironical that readers' reports on the novels generally agreed that Shaw possessed literary talent but that his fiction would not command the attention of many readers. Holroyd emphasizes that it was not only the influence of Henry George that turned Shaw to politics away from belles-lettres, but the failures of his novels as well. Correspondingly, fifteen years later, it was the American success of *The Devil's Disciple* that turned Shaw back to the theater and saved him from the tedium of a prolonged career as vestryman or other elected official. Shaw could now give up his intense career in practical politics as well as his career in literary journalism. Theatrical success would be sealed with the Vedrenne-Barker seasons at the Royal Court, 1904–7, to be described in Holroyd's second volume.

Romantic love and sexual adventure meant less to Shaw than his literary and political interests, and he regarded lovemaking and romantic gallantry as incidental diversions to his principal activities. But if the pursuit of women was not his commanding concern in the 1880s and 1890s, still he found time then for so many flirtations and romantic attachments that one can understand, after all, Holroyd's resort to his subtitle. Many of his freshest pages trace in rich detail the course of Shaw's encounters with women, as a result of materials made available since the biographies of Henderson and Ervine. The relationships with women were for Shaw always flirtations (or they began as such), but they varied in seriousness and Shaw's degree of commitment. There was the early but troubled relationship with Alice Lockett. There were some other relationships which Shaw took less seriously than did the women, those with Bertha Newcombe, Annie Besant, and Edith Nesbit (Bland). There were the two women who became his mistresses, perhaps concurrently, Jenny Patterson and Florence Farr. There was the woman he could not beguile with seductive words, Elizabeth Robins. There was the great actress, Ellen Terry, with whom he conducted an intense love affair by means of letters (they avoided meeting each other). There were women he liked to associate with who were at the time safely married: Ida Beatty, Eleanor Aveling, May Morris, and Janet Achurch. In the households of these married women, he became a constant visitor or "Sunday husband"; the men tolerated or resented his presence, Shaw being oblivious to the complex situations he was creating or else savoring them. As for Janet Achurch, Shaw tried to transform her into a splendid actress to whom he could entrust his plays, and he oversaw her life in the theater as he had Florence Farr's. Shaw reserved *Candida* for his Janet, but physical deterioration overtook her before she had an opportunity to play the part that Shaw had created for her. Shaw apparently delayed his own career as playwright because of his infatuation with Janet and a misplaced confidence in her. Whatever we may think of the marriage between Shaw and Charlotte Payne-Townshend (which terminates this first volume), there developed, Holroyd demonstrates, a sense of devotion and a seriousness toward her lacking in his other relationships thus far with women, except perhaps the epistolary one with Ellen Terry.

Fascinating as it is to learn the details of Shaw and the women in his life, his other activities are more significant and were also more significant to him. Holroyd is excellent in recapitulating them all for us and in presenting Shaw's many careers during his first forty years. Holroyd's discussion of the novels is excellent and illuminates for us Shaw in London in his twenties. *Love among the Artists*, in its rejection of rational values, was the most crucial of the five, Holroyd points out, and his discussion of *Cashel Byron's Profession* reveals that this work has many ramifications of meaning over and beyond the narrative itself. Holroyd also re-creates Shaw's early days as writer of musical pieces for the *Hornet* (1876–77; he ghosted for George Vandeleur Lee) and somewhat later for the *Dramatic Review* and other journals. He then discusses Shaw's work as reviewer for the *Pall Mall Gazette* (1885–88), mostly of ephemeral books. Holroyd gives us in fuller detail than customary a summary of Shaw's career as art critic for the *World* (1886–

88). He then presents sympathetically and perceptively Shaw, the music critic for the *Star* (1888–90) as Corno di Bassetto and for the *World* (1890–94) as G.B.S. Holroyd also gives us a full version of Shaw the disciple of Ibsen and the writer of his first book to achieve fame, *The Quintessence of Ibsenism* (1891). Then follows a discussion of his career as theater critic and as proponent of the higher drama for the *Saturday Review* (1895–98). Holroyd not only analyzes perceptively Shaw's literary, artistic, and aesthetic interests; he also encompasses with learning and authority Shaw's political ideas, his political activities, and his animating presence in the Fabian Society. Another notable aspect of Holroyd's book is his expert presentation of Shaw's relationships with prominent figures of the age, with William Archer, William Morris, Beatrice and Sidney Webb, and Henry Irving. Although Shaw sometimes seems like a pit bull snarling at an intruder in his comments upon Henry Irving, I am less sympathetic to Irving than Holroyd is, since Shaw was trying to make way for the drama of the future against the immovable obstacles in his way, of which Irving was one.

When he gets to the plays, Holroyd establishes succinctly the context for each of them. His interpretations are chiefly thematic and biographical, and his observations are for the most part pertinent. In the discussions of individual plays, one misses considered judgments of their present-day theatrical effectiveness and of their final worth as dramatic literature. This is not an unimportant consideration because the *Unpleasant Plays* have all had recent revivals, indicating perhaps that our contemporary audiences are more ready for *The Philanderer*, for example, than traditional academic critics and the theatergoers of the 1890s and the early 1900s may have been.

As for Holroyd's interpretations of Shaw's psyche and his works, some are brilliant and entirely tenable and some remain controversial, when a reader's sense of the facts may differ from the biographer's. I think that Holroyd makes too much of Shaw's alleged rejection by his mother as an explanation for what he sought in his relationships with women, that is, the nurturing mother and the approving presence that he had never known as a child. As for Bessie Shaw's alleged imperviousness to romance which Shaw emphasized in his accounts of her, Holroyd discounts Shaw's statements as a cover in order to silence speculation that he may have been the natural son of George Vandeleur Lee, an innovative musician who lived in the Shaw household after 1864 and whom Bessie apparently had known for some years previously. Holroyd's descriptions are sometimes exaggerated when he presents Bessie Shaw, for example, as having the "jaw of a prizefighter and a head like a football," or when he presents Yeats as "a stooping demonologist." Though the copious use of Shaw's own words contributes to the effectiveness of Holroyd's biography, there is finally too much quotation: long passages could be cut or paraphrased for a tighter organization (though the leisurely pace of the book is one of its merits). Without documentation it is sometimes misleading when Holroyd uses a passage from a later period in Shaw's life to elucidate some of his earlier activities. In a discussion of Shaw the hack reviewer (211), Holroyd uses a quotation from the Preface to *Man and Superman* ("Effectiveness of assertion is the Alpha and Omega of style"): an unsuspecting reader might think the passage came from one of these early reviews. In a passage describing Shaw's later political views (190), Holroyd quotes from "Fabian Essays Forty Years Later," but produces the opposite of his intended meaning because he quotes from a part of a sentence that contains a negative ("Morris was not right after all") but overlooks another negative in another part of the same sentence that he does not quote. William Morris, the revolutionary, may have been right after all: this is Shaw's meaning when he regards the economic debacle of the late 1920s and 1930s. As an admirer of Shaw's ability to write sustained discursive prose, I find this judgment of his style to be somewhat too sweeping:

> The effect of his prose is like alcohol upon the nerves: we are exhilarated, breathless, and, before the end, exhausted—and still the talkative spirit, the ascending wit, drive on. For it is a style that is always in top gear: emphatic, industrious, omniscient, studded with surprises, and better-trained for shorter distances than the long discursiveness that was to become a feature of his work.

Some of Holroyd's interpretations of the plays I find difficult to accept or understand. The statement that in *The Devil's Disciple* Dick Dudgeon is a realist, Anthony Anderson an idealist, and Judith a philistine is true only in some respects. It could as well be argued that Anderson becomes the realist in rescuing Dick and changing his own profession and that Dick becomes less of a realist as he surrenders to his own view of an exalted destiny. The observation that *Widowers' Houses* represents "realism without naturalism" is puzzling. This play, it seems to me, in its exposé of the seamy aspects of municipal housing, is—in the Zolaesque sense—the most "naturalistic" of all Shaw's plays. I find questionable the judgment that *Arms and the Man* conveys nothing of the horrors of war: how about Bluntschli the battered fugitive in Act I and the account of Stolz's death? I am not convinced that this play reveals "emotions [ostensibly in its author] that still responded to the adult world from the doorway of the nursery." To my mind the play is sophisticated in import rather than revealing its au-

thor as ingenuous, and Holroyd's interpretation seems to me somewhat facile if we can give any credence at all to Shaw's statements of
his serious purpose in his extended critique of the play, "A Dramatic
Realist to His Critics." I fail to see the basis, moreover, for the judgment that the prosaic Morell in *Candida* is Shaw's Pre-Raphaelite and
that Marchbanks is his Raphaelite. If the identifications of Marchbanks with Shelley and Yeats mean anything, certainly it is the young
man in his aesthetic appearance and aestheticist values who is the Pre-
Raphaelite. I am sure Shaw meant the term in the sense that Rossetti,
Morris, and Yeats embodied it. I do not understand why Marchbanks
is a Raphaelite or indeed the meaning of the designation as Holroyd
uses it. It is not clear to me either why Marchbank's denial at the end is
expressed, as Holroyd maintains, in the despairing note of Saint Joan.
Marchbanks now knows himself and his destiny as he had not known
it before, and he is ready now, Shaw implies, to be a mature poet. If he
has renounced sex at this point, there is no indication that he has
renounced the experience of the senses for good and all.

With respect to documentation, I think it unfortunate that Holroyd
did not give us some explanatory and informative footnotes as he did
in his monumental *Lytton Strachey*. These notes would undoubtedly
have cleared up some confusions, and they would have suggested
further ramifications of a subject difficult to incorporate at length in a
smooth-flowing primary text. Then, too, I would hope that Holroyd
will give us the benefit of his fifteen-year immersion in Shaw by indicating in full his sources following Volume III as he promises to do.
Though I have been reading in Shaw for many years, I nevertheless
found that a number of the quoted passages were new to me. Simply
for the satisfaction of my curiosity, if for no other reason, I would like
to know where they come from.

All cavils aside, I regard *Bernard Shaw: A Biography* as a marked
success. What I admire most is Holroyd's control of his subject: the
careful structure of his book, his measured and assured tone, his air of
confident authority, his ability to steer a clear path among a superabundance of sources. A biography of a man who lived so long, who
wrote so much, who engaged in so many activities, and who touched
modern life in so many ways would always threaten to get out of hand,
to become "a loose and baggy monster." Holroyd has mastered without strain an enormous corpus of multifarious materials. He has explored with astuteness and imagination the contours of a whole literary continent as it takes the shape of the life and work of one writer
and thinker. Holroyd's is an admirable work of synthesis, and we
remain much in his debt.

Frederick P. W. McDowell

John R. Pfeiffer*

A CONTINUING CHECKLIST
OF SHAVIANA

I. Works by Shaw

Shaw, Bernard. "As I See It," in *The Listener,* 19 January 1989, p. 27. Reprint of a 10 November 1937 essay for *Listener* in its "Diamond Jubilee Extra." One of seventeen pieces reprinted; others are by figures such as W. H. Auden, Edward R. Murrow, Dylan Thomas, Jacob Bronowski, and Malcolm Muggeridge.
———. *Bernard Shaw on Photography.* Edited by Bill Jay and Margaret Moore. Salt Lake City: Gibbs Smith, 1989. To be reviewed in *SHAW 11.*
———. *Bernard Shaw on the London Art Scene, 1885–1950.* Edited by Stanley Weintraub. University Park: Pennsylvania State University Press, 1989. "Of the 181 pieces on art collected in this volume, three appear here (from the original manuscripts) for the first time, and 170 have never before been reprinted after their first, often anonymous, publication." To be reviewed in *SHAW 11.*
———. "The Best Books for Children." *SHAW: Shaw Offstage: The Nondramatic Writings: Annual of Bernard Shaw Studies,* Volume Nine. University Park: Pennsylvania State University Press, 1989.
———. "Civilization and the Soldier." *SHAW: Shaw Offstage: The Nondramatic Writings: Annual of Bernard Shaw Studies,* Volume Nine. University Park: Pennsylvania State University Press, 1989.
———. "Dorothy Hickling, George Bernard Shaw; Portraits of George Bernard Shaw and Correspondence with Photographer," *Christie Auction Catalogue,* 10 November 1988, p. 48. "Three different portraits of Shaw, with correspondence relating to the success of the postcards [bearing GBS's photo], the use of photography for publicity, the relative costs of processes and photographers and the need to publicise and credit one's work, '. . . Bromoil means bankruptcy: it takes too long, and will drive you to Hampstead Heath to take tintypes. Of course if you have an

*Professor Pfeiffer, *SHAW* Bibliographer, welcomes information about new or forthcoming Shaviana: books, articles, pamphlets, monographs, dissertations, reprints, etc. His address is Department of English, Central Michigan University, Mount Pleasant, Michigan 48859.

independant [sic] income like Coburn & Baron de Mayer, that is another matter. . . .' (a lot) £600–1000."

———. *Fanny's First Play.* See *The Shewing-up,* below.

———. Five letters to Mary Hamilton, presented in "George Bernard Shaw and the Bishop's Daughter" by Helen M. Moore, *Carnegie Magazine* 59, no. 4 (July/August 1988): 22–30. The article prints six GBS letters to Hamilton (1878–1945), daughter of the Bishop of Ottawa. The earliest (29 November 1906) is in the Dan H. Laurence *Collected Letters.* Five more, dated 15 April 1907, 2 November 1908, 4 September 1917, 5 October 1918, and 23 November 1918, are published here for the first time. To frame the letters, Moore works with inferences drawn from the facts known about Hamilton's career as an actress who went to London, worked in the Royal Court Theatre, impressed Shaw, had parts in his plays, but returned disillusioned to Canada. None of Hamilton's letters is included here. The transcription of the GBS letter of 5 October 1918 erroneously says that Barker married an "Austrian authoress." She was actually an American, Helen Huntington.

———. *Interviews and Recollections.* Edited by A. M. Gibbs. Iowa City: University of Iowa Press, June 1989. To be reviewed in *SHAW 11.*

———. Letter to J. B. Priestley, in Vincent Brome's *J. B. Priestley.* London: Hamish Hamilton, 1988; p. 257. In a letter dated 1 August 1940 GBS refuses to join the Authors' National Committee for the war effort. See Brome in "Books and Pamphlets," below.

———. Letter to Paul Robeson, 13 June 1950. In Martin Bauml Duberman's *Paul Robeson.* New York: Alfred A. Knopf, 1988. See Duberman in "Books and Pamphlets," below.

———. Letter to T. E. Lawrence. See Wilson, Jeremy, in "Books and Pamplets," below.

———. "Orkney and Shetland." *SHAW: Shaw Offstage: The Nondramatic Writings: Annual of Bernard Shaw Studies,* Volume Nine. University Park: Pennsylvania State University Press, 1989.

———. *The Quintessence of Ibsenism,* in Charles R. Lyon's *Critical Essays on Henrik Ibsen.* Boston: G. K. Hall, 1987. Not seen. Lyons reprints at least part of *Quintessence,* along with all or part of William Archer's introduction to *When We Dead Awaken.*

———. Quoted on Wagner. In Rudolph Sabor's *The Real Wagner.* London: André Deutsch, 1987. Excerpts from "How to Become a Musical Critic" (1877) and "Tarnhelm" (1898).

———. *The Salt of the Earth.* Edited by Fred D. Crawford. *SHAW: Shaw Offstage: The Nondramatic Writings: Annual of Bernard Shaw Studies,* Volume Nine. University Park: Pennsylvania State University Press, 1989.

———. *Selected Short Plays.* Under the editorial supervision of Dan H. Laurence. Baltimore and Harmondsworth, Middlesex: Penguin Books, 1987. Includes *Bashville, How He Lied, Passion, Poison, and Petrifaction, Glimpse of Reality, Dark Lady, Overruled, Music-Cure, Great Catherine, Inca of Perusalem, O'Flaherty, Augustus Does His Bit, Annajanska, Village Wooing, Six of Calais,* and *Cymbeline Refinished.*

———. *Shaw's Music: The Complete Musical Criticism of George Bernard Shaw.* Edited by Dan H. Laurence. Three volumes, paperback. New York and London: Random House, June 1989. Reprint of the Dodd, Mead edition.

———. *The Shewing-up of Blanco Posnet and Fanny's First Play.* Baltimore and Harmondsworth, Middlesex: Penguin Books, 1987.

II. Books and Pamphlets

Alpern, Sara. *Freda Kirchwey: A Woman of The Nation.* Cambridge and London: Harvard
University Press, 1987. In a single reference we learn that in high school Kirchwey,
a reform journalist, "took as 'fathers' Galsworthy, Wells, and Shaw, a 'sort of un-
holy trinity'."

Anikst, A. "George Bernard Shaw." Translated by C. English. *Twentieth Century English:
A Soviet View.* Moscow: Progress Publishers, 1982; pp. 11–25. "Shaw was a socialist
who unconditionally condemned the capitalist order. His works can be regarded as
a satirical encyclopedia of the society in which he lived. His greatest gift consisted in
his ability to view reality critically." The essay's subheadings include "The Great
Scoffer," "The Thinker," "The Dramatist," "The Drama of Ideas," "The Para-
doxalist," "The Characters," "Romanticism or Reality?" and "The Heretic," from
which the quotation above is taken.

Auerbach, Nina. *Ellen Terry: Player in Her Time.* New York: W. W. Norton, 1989. A
paperback edition for $10.95.

Baker, Stuart E. "Shavian Realism." *SHAW: Shaw Offstage: The Nondramatic Writings:
Annual of Bernard Shaw Studies,* Volume Nine. University Park: Pennsylvania State
University Press, 1989.

Balashov, P. "George Bernard Shaw—Champion of the Truth." Translated by C. English. *Twentieth Century English: A Soviet View.* Moscow: Progress Publishers, 1982;
pp. 26–40. A very general account of GBS's literary career. "The writer remained
constantly concerned about the injustice of the existing order, and was forever
seeking ways to achieve truth and justice in social relations."

Basmadjian, Garig. "Candid Conversation." In *William Saroyan: The Man and the Writer
Remembered.* Edited by Leo Hamalian. Rutherford, Madison, and Teaneck, N.J.:
Fairleigh Dickinson University Press, 1987. One reference: When Saroyan was
asked who his influences were: "I loved Shaw, George Bernard, *The Prefaces.*"

Beerbohm, Max. *Letters of Max Beerbohm, 1892–1956.* Edited by Rupert Hart-Davis.
New York and London: W. W. Norton, 1989. GBS is well represented. There are a
number of letters to him, including the one in which Beerbohm expresses his
appreciation for Shaw's nomination of him to replace GBS as dramatic critic of the
Saturday Review in April 1898. There are also a few letters from GBS to Beerbohm.

Bentley, Eric. See Bloom, *Man and Superman,* below.

Berst, Charles A. See Bloom, *Man and Superman,* below.

———. See Bloom, *Saint Joan,* below.

Billington, Michael. *Stoppard, The Playwright.* London and New York: Methuen, 1987.
Billington refers to Shaw several times to elucidate Stoppard's theatrical tradition
and tactics. Both are fired by a response to public events; both constantly challenge
notions of what a play can do; *You Never Can Tell* and Stoppard's *Teeth* are examples
of the influence of dentistry on drama; both take popular theatrical tricks and
inject into them moral debate. They give mutually contradictory points of view with
uninflected fairness. Stoppard's naturalism comes by way of Ibsen, Chekhov, and
Shaw, among others.

Bloom, Harold, ed. *George Bernard Shaw's* Man and Superman. New York, New Haven,
and Philadelphia: Chelsea House Publishers, 1987. Includes "Introduction" by
Bloom (the only original piece; the others are reprinted), "The Theatre" by Eric
Bentley, "Shaw" by Louis Kronenberger, "*Man and Superman* and the Duel of Sex"

by Martin Meisel, "Heaven, Hell, and Turn-of-the-Century London" by Frederick
P. W. McDowell, "Don Juan in Hell" by Louis Crompton, "The Play of Ideas in Act
3 of *Man and Superman*" by Charles A. Berst, *"Man and Superman"* by Maurice
Valency, "Ann and Superman: Type and Archetype" by Sally Peters Vogt, and
"Comedy and Dialectic" by Nicholas Grene.

————, ed. *George Bernard Shaw's* Saint Joan. New York, New Haven, and Philadelphia:
Chelsea House, 1987. Includes "Introduction" by Bloom (the only original piece;
the others are reprinted), "The Saint as Tragic Hero: *Saint Joan* and *Murder in the
Cathedral*" by Louis L. Martz, "A Hagiography of Creative Evolution" by Louis
Crompton, "The Histories" by Margery M. Morgan, *"Saint Joan:* Spiritual Epic as
Tragicomedy" by Charles A. Berst, "The Saint and the Skeptic: Joan of Arc and
George Bernard Shaw" by William Searle, and "Shavian History" by Nicholas
Grene.

Boylan, Patricia. *All Cultivated People: A History of the United Arts Club, Dublin.* Chester
Springs, Pa.: Dufour, 1989. Not seen. Yeats and Shaw were early members of the
Club. As listed in *Publishers Weekly,* 9 June 1989.

Bradbury, Ray. "On Shaw's 'The Best Books for Children.' " *SHAW: Shaw Offstage: The
Nondramatic Writings: Annual of Bernard Shaw Studies,* Volume Nine. University
Park: Pennsylvania State University Press, 1989.

Brand, Gerhard. Reviews of Shaw's *Collected Letters, 1926–1950* and Michael Holroyd's
*Bernard Shaw: The Search for Love. Magill's Literary Annual, 1989, Essay-Reviews of 200
Outstanding Books Published in the United States during 1988.* Volume I. Edited by Frank
N. Magill. Pasadena and Englewood Cliffs, N.J.: Salem Press, 1989, pp. 84–93.

Brome, Vincent. *J. B. Priestley.* London: Hamish Hamilton, 1988. A number of GBS/
Priestley contacts are represented. In all, they show a view of Shaw that is interested
and respectful, and alternately amused, disgusted, exasperated, and realistic in
seeing him as human and limited. The account includes two letters from Shaw: 1
August 1940 and 16 January 1948, refusals in response to Priestley's invitations to
join the Authors' National Committee for the war effort and the British Theatre
conference.

Buckle, Richard. *George Balanchine, Ballet Master: A Biography.* New York: Random
House, 1988. One reference: Balanchine, in 1923, provided the choreography for
Caesar and Cleopatra for a Mikhailovsky Opera Theater production.

Buitenhuis, Peter. *The Great War of Words: British, American and Canadian Propaganda and
Fiction, 1914–1933.* Vancouver: University of British Columbia Press, 1987. Not
seen. Examines, among others, Shaw's writing against the war.

Bullock, Alan, and Stephen Trombley, assisted by Bruce Eadie, eds. "Shavian." In *The
Harper Dictionary of Modern Thought.* New and Revised Edition. New York: Harper
& Row, 1988. The complete entry: "Characteristic or reminiscent of the writings of
George Bernard Shaw (1856–1950). Nouns to which the adjective is frequently
applied are wit, irreverence, paradox, ebullience, insouciance."

Chaudhuri, Nirad C. *Thy Hand, Great Anarch! India: 1921–1952.* Reading, Mass.:
Addison-Wesley, 1988. Chaudhuri at ninety has been secretary to nationalist leader
Sarat Bose, political commentator for All-India Radio, author of iconoclastic portraits of Gandhi, Nehru, Churchill, and Mountbatten, and much interested in
literature. Here he reflects upon GBS's 1927 republication and endorsement of
William Archer's essays from a 1917 book containing anti-Hindu sentiments. Shaw
"had become almost an idol of educated Indians. . . . His Indian admirers were
driven to cry in agony: Et tu Brute!"

Christopher, Joe R. *C. S. Lewis.* Boston: Twayne Publishers, 1987. Christopher has an understanding of *Methuselah* and vitalism. In seven scattered references he connects Lewis with it, explicitly and implicitly, without giving anything more of an explanation of Lewis's opinion of GBS.

Crawford, Fred D. "Introduction: Offstage?" *SHAW: Shaw Offstage: The Nondramatic Writings: Annual of Bernard Shaw Studies,* Volume Nine. University Park: Pennsylvania State University Press, 1989.

———. "Shaw's Collaboration in *The Salt of the Earth.*" *SHAW: Shaw Offstage: The Nondramatic Writings: Annual of Bernard Shaw Studies,* Volume Nine. University Park: Pennsylvania State University Press, 1989.

Crompton, Louis. See Bloom, *Man and Superman,* above.

———. See Bloom, *Saint Joan,* above.

Daly, Gay. *Pre-Raphaelites in Love.* New York: Ticknor & Fields, 1989. Daly provides an account of the relationship of William Morris's daughter May and GBS. In 1892 May fell wildly in love with Shaw. He dropped her. She married Henry Halliday Sparling. GBS got sick. She took him into her home to nurse him. Their love was clear to her husband. Shaw left, but May's marriage was in great trouble because of the episode.

Danson, Lawrence. *Max Beerbohm and the Act of Writing.* Oxford: Clarendon Press, 1989. At Shaw's strong recommendation, Frank Harris turned Shaw's writing job for the *Saturday Review* over to Beerbohm in 1898. This account includes many references to GBS, including references to *Brassbound, Disciple, Heartbreak, Barbara, Superman, Misalliance, Mrs Warren, Plays, Pleasant and Unpleasant, Three Plays for Puritans,* and *You Never Can Tell.*

Dietrich, Richard F. *British Drama, 1890 to 1950: A Critical History.* Boston: Twayne Publishers, 1989. About a third of the pages of this volume are devoted to virtually all of the major works of GBS—perhaps a good gauge of his influence in this period. To be reviewed in *SHAW 11.*

Duberman, Martin Bauml. *Paul Robeson.* New York: Alfred A. Knopf, 1988. Robeson, the African-American actor, had a number of contacts with GBS, including one as late as 13 June 1950 when, declining his request for public support as a Progressive Party candidate, Shaw wrote him, "If you connect my name and reputation with your campaign . . . you will gain perhaps two thousand votes, ten of them negro, and lose two million. . . . Keep me out of it; and do not waste your time courting the handful of people whose votes you are sure of already. Play for Republican votes and episcopal support all the time; and when you get a big meeting of all sorts, don't talk politics but sing Old Man River." The letter is in the Robeson Archives.

Ducat, Vivian. "Bernard Shaw and the King's English." *SHAW: Shaw Offstage: The Nondramatic Writings: Annual of Bernard Shaw Studies,* Volume Nine. University Park: Pennsylvania State University Press, 1989.

Einsohn, Howard Ira. "The Intelligent Reader's Guide to *The Apple Cart.*" *SHAW: Shaw Offstage: The Nondramatic Writings: Annual of Bernard Shaw Studies,* Volume Nine. University Park: Pennsylvania State University Press, 1989.

Fairbanks, Douglas, Jr. *The Salad Days.* New York: Doubleday, 1988. One reference in this autobiography: Fairbanks admired T. E. Lawrence. He indicates that in the 1930s he made the brief acquaintance of Wells and Shaw, apparently by reading the books and plays. He does not say which ones.

Fisher, James. " 'The Colossus' Versus 'Master Teddy': The Bernard Shaw/Edward Gordon Craig Feud." *SHAW: Shaw Offstage: The Nondramatic Writings: Annual of Bernard Shaw Studies,* Volume Nine. University Park: Pennsylvania State University Press, 1989.

Ford, Ford Madox. *A History of Our Times.* Edited by Solon Beinfeld and Sondra S. Stang. Bloomington and Indianapolis: Indiana University Press, 1988. Autobiography containing two interesting references: "The Fabian Society of what were then called 'gas and water' Socialists, a singularly doctrinaire body which regulates its beliefs by statistics and was recruited almost exclusively from the blackcoated classes. Its most distinguished member was Mr. Bernard Shaw." A second reference: "The real poor among the labouring class took refuge, if they had any interest in politics at all, in either theoretic or violent anarchism. I have in my time seen bloodier contests than took place between Anarchists and Socialists in the eighties in public halls and parks but I have never seen one in which as great acrimony was displayed as on the occasion when in William Morris' little hall attached to his printing works on the Mall in Hammersmith, Mr. George Bernard Shaw who till then had been an Anarchist leader suddenly turned his coat and to that mild audience of red-tied aesthetes lectured on 'The Foolishness of Anarchism.' "

Gay, Peter. *Freud: A Life for Our Time.* New York and London: W. W. Norton, 1988. One reference: Freud quotes *Doctor's Dilemma* in reconciling himself to the death of his son Heinele: "Don't try to live forever; you will not succeed."

Grene, Nicholas. See Bloom, *Man and Superman*, above.

———. See Bloom, *Saint Joan*, above.

Hamilton, John Maxwell. *Edgar Snow: A Biography.* Bloomington and Indianapolis: Indiana University Press, 1988. One reference: Snow, a journalist and foreign correspondent, was particularly fond of GBS, to the extent that he and his wife Peg read *Intelligent Woman's Guide* to each other on their honeymoon.

Hampton, Aubrey. *GBS & Company: A Biographical Celebration in Two Acts Presided Over by Bernard Shaw.* Tampa: Organica Press, 1989. Copies may be ordered from Organica Press, 4419 North Manhattan Avenue, Tampa, Florida 33614.

Harben, Niloufer. *Twentieth-Century English History Plays, From Shaw to Bond.* Totowa, N.J.: Barnes & Noble Books, 1988. In the chapter "George Bernard Shaw: *Saint Joan*," Harben claims GBS is the originator of the modern approach to history plays. The essay notices *Man of Destiny, Good King Charles, John Bull,* and *Caesar,* and analyzes *Saint Joan* as a "major historical work of the twentieth century . . . [that] illustrates the new tradition of history play stimulated by Shaw, with his emphasis on discursive rational elements, an anti-heroic tone and diction, an overtly modern perspective and a consciousness of different possible views of an event."

Hill, Holly. *Playing Joan: Actresses on the Challenge of Shaw's* Saint Joan. New York: Theatre Communications Group, 1987. The author interviewed the following: Jane Alexander, Eileen Atkins, Elisabeth Bergner, Marjorie Brewer, Zoe Caldwell, Ann Casson, Constance Cummings, Judi Dench, Joyce Ebert, Pat Galloway, Ellen Geer, Lee Grant, Uta Hagen, Wendy Hiller, Frances Hyland, Barbara Jefford, Laurie Kennedy, Siobhan McKenna, Nora McLellan, Roberta Maxwell, Sarah Miles, Sian Phillips, Angela Pleasence, Joan Plowright, Lynn Redgrave, and Janet Suzman.

Holden, Anthony. *Laurence Olivier.* New York: Atheneum, 1988. Has references to Olivier's connections with *Caesar, Arms,* and *Doctor's Dilemma.*

Holland, Michael J. "Shaw's Short Fiction: A Path to Drama." *SHAW: Shaw Offstage: The Nondramatic Writings: Annual of Bernard Shaw Studies,* Volume Nine. University Park: Pennsylvania State University Press, 1989.

Horne, Alistair. *Harold Macmillan, Volume I, 1894–1956.* New York: Viking, 1989. One interesting reference notices that in 1886 and after, Lord Morley, head of the Macmillan readers, rejected four overtures by GBS, but commented, "the writer, if he is still young, is a man to keep one's eye upon." Of *Irrational Knot* (Shaw's second submission), the Macmillan reader wrote, "There is too much of adultery and like matters."

Hugo, Leon H. "The Black Girl and Some Lesser Quests: 1932–1934." *SHAW: Shaw Offstage: The Nondramatic Writings: Annual of Bernard Shaw Studies*, Volume Nine. University Park: Pennsylvania State University Press, 1989.

Kosok, Heinz. "John Bull's Other Ego: Reactions to the Stage Irishman in Anglo-Irish Drama." In *Medieval and Modern Ireland*. Edited by Richard Wall. Gerrards Cross: Colin Smyth, 1988; pp. 19–33, 138–39. The existence of the Stage Irishman had consequences for Anglo-Irish drama, long-lived ones that persisted after the Stage Irishman had died a satirical death in the portrayals of GBS, indeed until the late 1960s. Shaw had in fact gone a step further: "He made the ridiculous Englishman not only the laughing-stock of the Irish but also, and despite all this, successful. Broadbent, in *John Bull's Other Island*, holds the most absurd notions about Ireland and the Irish, but paradoxically this does not detract in any way from his popularity with the villagers of Rosscullen. . . . *This Other Eden* [by Louis D'Alton], as the title indicates, is clearly indebted to *John Bull . . .*, and Crispin the Stage Englishman who turns into a one-hundred-and-fifty-per-cent Irishman, is modelled on Shaw's Broadbent. If Shaw, to return to the starting-point of this paper, succeeded in terminating the life of the Stage Irishman, he at the same time gave the Stage Englishman another lease on life."

Kronenberger, Louis. See Bloom, *Man and Superman*, above.

Lawrence, T. E. *T. E. Lawrence: The Selected Letters*. Edited by Malcolm Brown. London: Dent, 1988. Index shows seven letters to GBS and about sixty to Charlotte.

Leary, Daniel. "The Time of His Life: A Shavian Influence." In *William Saroyan: The Man and the Writer Remembered*. Edited by Leo Hamalian. Rutherford, Madison, and Teaneck, N.J.: Fairleigh Dickinson University Press, 1987; pp. 69–76. Leary elucidates Saroyan's quotation: "Shaw . . . is the tonic of the Christian peoples of the world. He is health, wisdom, and comedy, and that's what I am, too. . . . If you must know which writer has influenced by writing when influences are real and for all I know enduring, then that writer has been George Bernard Shaw." Leary concludes: "While contemplating and balancing, the dramatist must distance himself through comic perspective to avoid his own paralysis and to prevent his audience from leaving. When we permit Saroyan's work to echo in the company of his fellow experimenters of all times, his new comedy gains in richness and significance. When we accept Shaw as Saroyan's major influence we are less inclined to dismiss his solution of togetherness as naive sentiment, more willing to envisage a world in which the children are at home, with the space and time to grow up."

McDonald, Jan. *The "New Drama" 1900–1914: Harley Granville Barker, John Galsworthy, St John Hankin, John Masefield*. New York: Grove Press, 1986. More than forty references to GBS.

McDowell, Frederick P. W. See Bloom, *Man and Superman*, above.

MacKinnon, Janice R., and Stephen R. MacKinnon. *Agnes Smedley: The Life and Times of an American Radical*. Berkeley and Los Angeles: University of California Press, 1988. Two references to GBS: The first runs through Chapter Seven, "Smedley as Eliza Doolittle, 1925–1927." In 1932 Smedley was host to GBS during his tour of the Far East. Includes photograph of GBS and Smedley in China.

Martz, Louis L. See Bloom, *Saint Joan*, above.

Meisel, Martin. See Bloom, *Man and Superman*, above.

Melville, Joy. *Ellen and Edy: A Biography of Ellen Terry and Her Daughter, Edith Craig, 1847–1947*. London and New York: Pandora, 1987; New York: Methuen, 1988. Much of Shaw's relationship with Terry and Craig is described here.

Miller, Agnes. See Stapledon, below.

Miller, Arthur. "Christian-Albrecht Gollub/1977." In *Conversations with Arthur Miller*. Edited by Matthew C. Roudané. Jackson and London: University Press of Mississippi, 1987. "Gollub: When did you first come into contact with literature? Miller: When I was turning twenty. G: What did you read at that point? M: A lot of Russians. And Shaw. G: What is it about Shaw that attracted you? M: Laughs. The irony of his plays. Terrific style and stylishness. And his ability to handle ideas—which I think is unapproachable."

———. "Philip Gelb/1958." In *Conversations with Arthur Miller*. Edited by Matthew C. Roudané. Jackson and London: University Press of Mississippi, 1987. Miller discusses Shaw's dramatic characters at some length, noting, for example, that "Shaw is impatient with the insignificance of most human speech, most human thought, and most human preconceptions. It's not that his characters are not people, it is that they aren't significant people the way people usually are. When you strip from the human being everything that is not of significance, you get a valid moment out of him, a valid set of speeches, a valid set of attitudes, but in the normal, naturalistic concept, they aren't real because the bulk of reality is, of course, its utter boredom, and its insignificance, and its irrelevancy, and Shaw is absolutely uninterested in that."

Mitchell, Sally, ed. *Victorian Britain, An Encyclopedia*. New York and London: Garland, 1988. Contains numerous references to GBS in addition to an entry for Shaw by Tamie Watters (see Watters, below).

Morgan, Margery M. See Bloom, *Saint Joan,* above.

Morris, William. *The Collected Letters of William Morris, Volume II: 1885–1888*. Edited by Norman Kelvin and Gale Sigal. Princeton: Princeton University Press, 1987. This volume has nearly fifty references to GBS. None in Volume I.

O'Brien, Philip M. *T. E. Lawrence: A Bibliography*. Boston: G. K. Hall, 1988; Winchester: St. Paul's Bibliographies, 1988. More than forty references to Shaw—some to Shaw pieces in Lawrence publications, and many in books and articles that connect Lawrence and GBS.

O'Neill, Eugene. *Selected Letters of Eugene O'Neill*. Edited by Travis Bogard and Jackson R. Bryer. New Haven and London: Yale University Press, 1988. Mentions *Methuselah, Doctor's Dilemma, Pygmalion,* and *Joan.* When asked to be a member of the Irish Academy being organized by Shaw and Yeats, among others, he said, "This I regard as an honor whereas other academies don't mean much to me. Anything with Yeats, Shaw, A. E., O'Casey . . . in it is good enough for me."

Owen, Bobbi. *Costume Design on Broadway: Designers and Their Credits, 1915–1985*. New York, Westport, and London: Greenwood Press, 1987. In a long "Index of Plays" many of the productions of Shaw's works, with the names of their designers, are included.

Person, Ethel Specter. *Dreams of Love and Fateful Encounters: The Power of Romantic Passion*. New York and London: W. W. Norton, 1988. Two references are to Shaw's famous epistolary romances, which seem to avoid much actual contact, and to his contribution to the love and power relationship's traditional representation in *Pygmalion.*

Peters, Sally. See Sally Peters Vogt in Bloom, *Man and Superman,* above.

Rayner, Alice. *Comic Persuasion: Moral Structure in British Comedy from Shakespeare to*

Stoppard. Berkeley: University of California Press, 1987. Not seen. From a review in *Theatre Research International* 14 (1988): 90–91. "A study of selected plays by Shakespeare, Jonson, Wycherley, Cumberland, Steele, Shaw [*Major Barbara*], and Stoppard, . . . examines the dialectic between 'use and delight,' the functions of comedy as social corrective and amusement, as morality and pleasure."

Rumbelow, Donald. *Jack the Ripper: The Complete Casebook.* New York and Chicago: Contemporary Books, 1988. Includes a number of references to GBS and excerpts from his pieces on the Ripper.

Saperstein, Lee W. "The Orkneys Revisited." *SHAW: Shaw Offstage: The Nondramatic Writings: Annual of Bernard Shaw Studies,* Volume Nine. University Park: Pennsylvania State University Press, 1989.

Schanke, Robert A. *Ibsen in America: A Century of Change.* Metuchen, N.J., and London: The Scarecrow Press, 1988. Shaw's role in the acceptance of Ibsen in America is noticed in several brief references.

Scott, Michael. *The Great Caruso.* New York: Alfred A. Knopf, 1988. Shaw knew Caruso and complained about a Caruso performance in a letter to the *Times.* Scott quotes Shaw to illustrate which voice properties have lost significance in an age that depends on electronic enhancement of the sound of the voice.

Searle, William. See Bloom, *Saint Joan,* above.

Slonimsky, Nicholas. *Perfect Pitch.* Oxford and New York: Oxford University Press, 1988. An autobiography of the Russian that includes a number of references to GBS. On *Methuselah,* and the recollection that his aunt Zinaïda Vengenova translated Shaw and Wells. She apparently met Shaw as well. He also invited Shaw to contribute a letter on musical subjects for his *Music Since 1900* (1937).

Stapledon, Olaf, and Agnes Miller. *Talking Across the World: The Love Letters of Olaf Stapledon and Agnes Miller, 1913–1919.* Edited by Robert Crossley. Hanover, N.H., and London: University Press of New England, 1987. One reference to GBS by Stapledon: "Do you know GBS? He is a tonic, nay more. He upsets all one's preconceived ideas about everything that matters."

Symons, Arthur. *Arthur Symons: Selected Letters, 1880–1935.* Edited by Karl Beckson and John M. Munro. Iowa City: University of Iowa Press, 1989. Contains occasional references to GBS. One: 28 April 1908: "The popular people you name (even Shaw) will be forgotten much sooner than they or anyone thinks. None of them have the one essential thing—the sense of beauty. That is what condemns Shaw forever."

Tahir, Laura. "*My Dear Dorothea:* Shaw's Earliest Sketch." *SHAW: Shaw Offstage: The Nondramatic Writings: Annual of Bernard Shaw Studies,* Volume Nine. University Park: Pennsylvania State University Press, 1989.

Tormé, Mel. *It Wasn't All Velvet: An Autobiography.* New York: Viking, 1988. One reference: In his "Afterthoughts" Tormé reflects that he is moved by a Shaw observation: "We are all amateurs: no one lives long enough to become a professional."

Tynan, Kathleen. *The Life of Kenneth Tynan.* New York: William Morrow, 1987. When Tynan became drama critic of the *Observer* in 1954, London tabloids "sneered at the 'new Bernard Shaw' tag" attached to him. This account has a number of comparisons of him with GBS, all respectful to both.

Valency, Maurice. See Bloom, *Man and Superman,* above.

Vogt, Sally Peters. See Bloom, *Man and Superman,* above.

Walker, Lester. *Tiny, Tiny Houses.* Woodstock, N.Y.: The Overlook Press, 1987. Provides a photograph and building plans for Shaw's writing hut at Shaw's Corner at Ayot St. Lawrence.

Watters, Tamie. "Shaw, George Bernard (1856–1950)," in *Victorian Britain, An Encyclopedia.* Edited by Sally Mitchell. New York and London: Garland, 1988, pp. 714–15. About three hundred words long. GBS is also mentioned in many other entries.

Weintraub, Stanley. "Ballads by Shaw: The Anonymous *Star* Versifier of 1888–1889." *SHAW: Shaw Offstage: The Nondramatic Writings: Annual of Bernard Shaw Studies,* Volume Nine. University Park: Pennsylvania State University Press, 1989.

Wilson, Jeremy. *T. E. Lawrence.* London: National Portrait Gallery Publications, 1988. A catalogue of the Gallery's Centenary Exhibition representing the life of Lawrence. It describes three GBS items: *Too True to Be Good* which incorporates a character based on Lawrence—"Private Meek"; a color reproduction of a 1932 GBS portrait by Dame Laura Knight; and a Shaw letter to Lawrence of 7 October 1924. Other GBS references, unindexed, dot the text.

Wisenthal, J. L. *Shaw's Sense of History.* Oxford: Clarendon Press, 1988. Shaw's idea of history as presented in his ten history plays is analyzed against a background of nineteenth-century theories of history. See review by Crawford, Fred D., in "Periodicals" below. Reviewed in this volume.

Woodress, James. *Willa Cather: A Literary Life.* Lincoln and London: University of Nebraska Press, 1987. Cather was very interested in theater and respected Shaw. Two references here have her reactions to *Devil's Disciple* and *Fanny's First Play.* A third gives Shaw credit for "the willful eccentricity of his plays."

III. Periodicals

Adams, Elsie B. "More on Shaw" (review of Harold Bloom, ed. *George Bernard Shaw's Man and Superman* and *George Bernard Shaw: Modern Critical Views*). *English Literature in Transition* 32, no. 2 (1988): 252–55.

Archer, Mark. Review of Michael Holroyd's *Bernard Shaw: The Search for Love. Drama,* no. 171 (1989): 51. Archer miscalls this *Bernard Shaw: The Pursuit of Love.*

Bemrose, John. "Dramatic Delights." *Maclean's,* 5 June 1989, pp. 54–55. Subtitled "Christopher Newton keeps a festival fresh," the article notes the beginning of the Shaw Festival's 27th season at Niagara-on-the-Lake, and Newton's influence on it. In a separate notice (p. 55), Bemrose reviews the Festival's GBS production for 1989, *Man and Superman*—a "superb production."

Berst, Charles A. "Scaling Everest: A Secondary Bibliography of GBS" (review of *G. B. Shaw: An Annotated Bibliography of Writings About Him* by J. P. Wearing, Elsie B. Adams, and Donald C. Haberman). *English Literature in Transition* 32, no. 1 (1988): 71–75.

Billington, Michael. "Devil of a Comic" (review of *The Best of Friends* at the Apollo). *Manchester Guardian Weekly,* 21 February 1988.

Bratton, J. S. Review of Thomas Postlewait's *Prophet of the New Drama: William Archer and the Ibsen Campaign. Victorian Studies* 31, no. 3 (Spring 1988): 464–65.

Burgess, Anthony. "The Life Force" (review of Michael Holroyd's *Bernard Shaw: The Search for Love*). *The Atlantic* 262, no. 4 (October 1988): 91–95.

Carpenter, Charles A. "Shaw (G.B.)," in "Modern Drama Studies: An Annual Bibliography." *Modern Drama* 31, no. 2 (June 1988): 219–21. About fifty entries, at least eleven of which have not been mentioned in the *SHAW* Checklists. Carpenter is a former Bibliographer of *The Shaw Review.* His annual bibliographical research on Shaw is indispensable.

Cohen, Edward H. "SHAW," in "Victorian Bibliography for 1987/Section VI." *Victorian Studies* 31, no. 4 (Summer 1988): 716–17. Nineteen entries, limited to Shaw studies related to Victorian contexts.

Craig, Patricia. "Lives and Letters" (review of Vivian Elliot's *Dear Mr Shaw*). *TLS*, 7–13 April 1989, p. 362.

Crawford, Fred D. Review of Michael Holroyd's *Bernard Shaw: The Search for Love*, and J. L. Wisenthal's *Shaw's Sense of History. Victorian Review* 15 (Spring 1989): 8–14.

———. "Shaw Works His Charm: A Biography Makes the Writer Accessible, but at What Cost?" (review of Michael Holroyd's *Bernard Shaw: The Search for Love*). *The Philadelphia Inquirer*, 16 October 1988, pp. 1F, 4F.

Crick, Bernard. "Michael Holroyd's 'Bernard Shaw'." *TLS*, 14–20 October 1988, p. 1147. Crick criticizes Holroyd's biography, *Bernard Shaw*, for not providing sources and notes in the first volume. See Holroyd, "Bernard Shaw," below.

———. "Skimping the Tar?" (review of Michael Holroyd's *Bernard Shaw: The Search for Love*). *History Today* 39 (January 1989): 49.

Davies, Robertson. "The Making of a 'Dublin Smartie' " (review of Michael Holroyd's *Bernard Shaw: The Search for Love*). *The New York Times Book Review*, 30 October 1988, pp. 1, 42.

Dukore, Bernard F. "Bernard Shaw's Dramatic Dialectic." *The World and I* 4 (April 1989): 546–59. "From Shaw's dialectical dramatic method, this essay will proceed to explore his social views, dramatized dialectically; then the religious ideas behind them, the role of emotion in his plays and finally, returning to the point of departure, the dialectical nature of his comedy." Dukore reminds us of the huge contribution to socialism GBS made for much of his life. In religion Dukore finds Shaw a "theistic existentialist."

———. "Dolly Finds a Father: Shaw's Dramatic Development." *Papers on Language and Literature* 24, no. 1 (Winter 1988): 81–90. "The earlier play [*You Never Can Tell*] about a Dolly who finds a father is a preliminary stage in Shaw's finding himself as a dramatist. The later play [*Major Barbara*] about a Dolly who does so reveals further strides as the author, while acknowledging his own genealogy, more fully secures his identity and finds his distinctive dramatic nature."

Everding, Robert G. "Bernard Shaw, Miss Alliance and Miss Cotterill." *English Language Notes* 25, no. 4 (June 1988): 73–81. "Indeed, to a greater extent than in his previous plays, *Misalliance* relied on myriad contemporary facts including a murder trial, the Suffragettes, the burgeoning sport of aviation, and an Edwardian fascination with new drainage systems. It was a biographical detail, however, that provided Shaw's greatest resource. Through his extraordinary relationship with Erica Cotterill, he found the emotional foundation for the Summerhays-Hypatia encounter as well as the impetus to formulate his modern views on courtship. More important, Shaw explored fully for the first time the parent-child relationship, a theme that would not only stand at the center of *Misalliance* but would also provide material for subsequent plays and essays."

Field, Michele. "Michael Holroyd." *Publishers Weekly*, 14 October 1988, pp. 45–46. An account of some facts of Holroyd's life and his experience writing a biography of Shaw.

Fisher, James. "Harlequinade: Commedia dell' arte on the Early Twentieth-Century Stage." *Theatre Journal* 41 (March 1989): 30–44. Treats Shaw briefly and finds "commedic" elements in *Caesar, Androcles, You Never Can Tell*, and *Passion, Poison, and Petrifaction*.

———. Review of Christine Dymkowski's *Harley Granville Barker;* Dennis Kennedy's

Granville Barker and the Dream of Theatre; Dennis Kennedy, ed. *Plays by Granville Barker;* and Eric Salmon, ed., *Granville Barker and His Correspondents.* In *Modern Drama* 31, no. 3 (September 1988): 465–68.

Fletcher, Ian. "Sonny and the Siren-Slaves" (review of Michael Holroyd's *Bernard Shaw: The Search for Love*). *TLS,* 16–22 September 1988, pp. 1007–8.

Gelderman, Carol. "Shaw on Anything and Everything" (review of Shaw's *Collected Letters, 1926–1950*). *American Theatre* 5, no. 7 (October 1988): 74–75.

"George Bernard Shaw" in "1986 Annual Review." *Journal of Modern Literature* 14, nos. 2/3 (Fall/Winter 1987–88): 380. Seven items from 1985 and 1986.

Grene, Nicholas. Review of *SHAW 7, Shaw: The Neglected Plays,* edited by Alfred Turco, Jr. *Notes and Queries* 36, no. 1 (March 1989): 119–20.

Gross, John. "From Young George to Mephistophelean G.B.S." (review of Michael Holroyd's *Bernard Shaw: The Search for Love*). *The New York Times,* 27 September 1988, p. C20.

Henderson, Bruce. "Two on Shaw" (review of *SHAW 6* and Harold Bloom's *George Bernard Shaw's Saint Joan*). *English Literature in Transition* 32, no. 2 (1988): 248–51.

Henry, William A., III. "From Crybaby to Curmudgeon" (review of Michael Holroyd's *Bernard Shaw: The Search for Love*). *Time,* 10 October 1988, p. 94.

Heron, Kim. "Did You Hear the One About the Fabians?" *The New York Times Book Review,* 30 October 1988, p. 43. Interview of Michael Holroyd on his writing a biography of Bernard Shaw.

Holroyd, Michael. "Bernard Shaw." *TLS,* 21–27 October 1988, p. 1175. Holroyd responds to Bernard Crick (see Crick, Bernard, above).

Jenkyns, Richard. "The Distant Shaw" (review of Michael Holroyd's *Bernard Shaw: The Search for Love*). *The New Republic,* 14 November 1988, pp. 38–41.

Kanfer, Stefan. "Better to Joke Than to Hang" (review of Shaw's *Collected Letters: 1926–1950,* with *Twain's Letters*). *Time,* 6 June 1988, p. 87.

Lahr, John. "Great Good Spirits" (review of Shaw's *Collected Letters: 1926–1950*). *The Listener,* 21 July 1988, pp. 19–20.

Laurence, Dan H. "The Early Life and Loves of Sonny Shaw" (review of Michael Holroyd's *Bernard Shaw: The Search for Love*). *Toronto Globe and Mail,* 1 October 1988, p. C21.

Lindop, Grevel. "Capital Dodges" (Review of the Royal Exchange Theatre, Manchester, production of Harley Granville Barker's *The Voysey Inheritance*). *TLS,* 26 May–1 June 1989, p. 582.

———. Review of the Royal Exchange Theatre, Manchester, production of *Arms and the Man. TLS,* 6–12 January 1989, p. 13.

McDowell, Frederick P. W. "Review Article: A Bernard Shaw Bibliography" (review of Dan H. Laurence's *Bernard Shaw: A Bibliography;* Dan H. Laurence, ed., *Shaw's Collected Letters: 1926–1950;* Dan. H. Laurence and James Rambeau, eds., *Bernard Shaw: Agitations, Letters to the Press;* Dan H. Laurence and Martin Quinn, eds., *Shaw on Dickens;* and Samuel A. Weiss, ed., *Bernard Shaw's Letters to Siegfried Trebitsch*). *Philological Quarterly* 66 (Fall 1987): 509–20.

Mason, Ronald. Review of *SHAW 5. Notes and Queries* 34 n.s. (September 1987): 421–22.

Maurer, A. E. Wallace. "G. Bernard Shaw: Losing or Saving Him" (review of Dan H. Laurence, *Bernard Shaw: A Bibliography;* and Stanley Weintraub, ed., *Bernard Shaw: The Diaries, 1885–1897*). *Review* 10 (1988): 220–39.

Moore, Helen M. See Five Letters to Mary Hamilton, in "Works by Shaw" above.

O'Brien, Conor Cruise. "Keeping Up with the Shaws" (review of Michael Holroyd's

Bernard Shaw: The Search for Love). *The New York Review of Books,* 24 November 1988, pp. 3–4, 6.

O'Neill, Michael C. Review of 1987 Shaw Festival production of *Major Barbara. Theatre Journal* 40, no. 1 (March 1988): 105–6.

Richardson, Betty. "And Now a Diary: More Achievements of Shaw Scholarship" (review of Stanley Weintraub, ed., *Bernard Shaw: The Diaries, 1885–1897*). *Papers on Language and Literature* 24, no. 1 (Winter 1988): 98–102.

Russell, John. "Shaw's Growth: A Paradoxical Portrait of the Artisan as a Young Man" (review of Michael Holroyd's *Bernard Shaw: The Search for Love*). *Chicago Tribune,* 25 September 1988, section 14, p. 7.

Sachsse, Rolf. " 'Sie sollten diesen Mist nicht mehr aufleben lassen . . .': Marginalien zu G. B. Shaw's Fototexten" [You must not revive this rubbish . . . : remarks on G. B. Shaw's writing on photography]. *Fotogeschichte* 8, no. 27 (1988): 35–39. In 1883 Shaw put an opinion of photography as art, which he later would change, into the mouth of Sidney Trefusis in *An Unsocial Socialist.* Lucia Moholy, in preparing *A Hundred Years of Photography* (1939), wrote GBS for permission to quote the opinion of Trefusis. He said no, unless she were willing to explain that he had repudiated it. She could not agree because she wanted the Shaw quotation to represent a moment in the historical development of the appreciation of photographic art. "For Lucia Moholy, whose book was intended to establish the basis of such a cultural-historical conception of the medium [of photography], its origin and effect, the views of Mr. Trefusis would have been welcome as an argument that had, by necessity, evolved historically, even though in the meantime it had become obsolete. For . . . Shaw, who had already begun his work on . . . *Shaw's Rhyming Picture Guide to Ayot St. Lawrence,* it was a painful reminder of an opinion that he thought had long become outdated, even though (originally) it had proven to be rather trenchant."

"Shaw, George Bernard (1856–1950)." In "Irish Literature/1900–1999."*1987 MLA International Bibliography of Books and Articles on the Modern Languages and Literatures.* New York: The Modern Language Association of America, 1988. Includes forty-eight entries, several of which have not appeared in this checklist.

Silver, Arnold. Review of *G. B. Shaw: An Annotated Bibliography of Writings About Him* by J. P. Wearing (vol. I) and Donald C. Haberman (vol. III). *Literary Research: A Journal of Scholarly Method and Technique* 12, no. 1 (1987): 48–51.

Sommers, Michael. "The Shaw Festival: A Balance of Risks and Old Reliables." *Theatre Crafts* 22, no. 7 (August/September 1988): 60–68. An account of the history and recent development, including 1988, of the Shaw Festival. Interesting details from the article include recent budget information: "The Festival's 1987 season saw an overall attendance figure of 87% capacity, with gross box office receipts of nearly $5.9 million, some $400,000 more than projected"; the establishment of the "Academy," the Festival's training program and workshop; and the Festival's interpretation of some of Shaw's plays, "removing them from the cliché of being British situation comedies, if you like, and attempting to put them into the surrealist area."

Weales, Gerald. "Inventing G.B.S" (review of Michael Holroyd's *Bernard Shaw: The Search for Love*). *American Theatre* 5, no. 10 (January 1989): 19, 56–57.

Weintraub, Stanley. "Crankily Buoyant to the Last" (review of Shaw's *Collected Letters, 1926–1950* and Vivian Elliot, ed., *Dear Mr Shaw: Selections from Bernard Shaw's Postbag*). *TLS,* 24–30 June 1988, p. 699.

Woodring, Carl. "Ricketts and *Saint Joan.*" *Columbia Library Columns* 37, no. 3 (May 1988): 25–33. Charles Ricketts designed sets for Wilde and Yeats, and for Shaw over a span of twenty years, including *Arms, Man of Destiny, Getting Married, Dark*

Lady, Fanny, Superman, Annajanska, and *Saint Joan.* The most elaborate and artisti-
cally successful collaboration of Ricketts and GBS was in the London production of
Joan (opening 26 March 1924). It was also the last. The article explains some of the
ramifications of Rickett's work on the production.

The Independent Shavian 26, nos. 1/2 (1988). Journal of the Bernard Shaw Society.
Includes "Shaw and Anarchism: Among the Leftists" by Richard Nickson, "Awful
Nomination, Anybody?" "What's in a Name?" by Bernard Shaw, "Exemplary Music
Criticism (Continued)," "AG and GBS: The Charwoman and the Gadfly" by Mau-
reen Murphy, "Unveiling of Plaque Re-opens Old Mystery" by Michael Godfrey,"
"The Battle of the Books," "Society-Philes" by David DeNicolo, "Editor to Editors"
by R. N., "A Self Introduction" by Bernard Shaw, "Our 'Communists' " by Bernard
Shaw, "Letter from London" by T. F. Evans, "GBS and the ABC Again" by Barbara
Smoker, "The Best of Friends," "Shaw's Man for Some Seasons," "Book Review
and Notes" by R. N., "Trilogy of Shavian Operas in New York Premiere" by
Donald V. Mehus, "News About Our Members," "Society Activities," and "Our
Cover."

The Independent Shavian 26, no. 3 (1988). Journal of the Bernard Shaw Society. Includes
"*Heartbreak House:* Between Modernism and Postmodernism" by Joseph Hynes,
"Shaw's Birthplace," "The *New York Times* and Arnold Daly's production of *Mrs
Warren's Profession*" by Sabah A. Salih, "Speaking Ill of the Dead," "Letter from
London" by T. F. Evans, "Authoritarian Democracy," "Book Review" by Rhoda
Nathan, "Unpublished Correspondence" by Bernard Shaw, "Book Review" by
John Koontz, "News About Our Members," "Kathleen Weatherley Bayfield," "Soci-
ety Activities," and "Our Cover."

IV. Dissertations

Gainor, J. Ellen. "Shaw's Daughters: Discourse of Gender and Female Identity in the
Work of George Bernard Shaw." Princeton University, 1989. *DAI* 49 (June 1989),
3732–A. "The demonstration of his adherence to Victorian concepts and beliefs
calls into question his reputation as progressive."

"Section One, 'Shaw's New Women,' explores his figuration of this late
nineteenth-century character and shows that Shaw conformed to patterns of plot,
characterization, and narrative focus identified by feminist critics of novels of the
period. Section Two, 'Shavian Androgyny,' examines Shaw's concern with the
gender indeterminacy prevalent in the *fin de siècle.* Shaw's cognizance of scientific
and artistic interest in the image of androgyne and its social manifestations de-
volved, however, to a biased dramatic representation of only masculine, cross-
dressed women. Section Three, 'Shaw's Daughters,' focuses on the relation of
literary paternity to the theme of father/daughter love and instruction. Shaw's
daughters mature into women caught between their male 'engendering' and the
procreative function they must fulfill. Shaw's assumption of a male base for human existence, and his conflicting sense of women's roles and potential, shape his
dramaturgy and throw into relief his assumptions and attitudes unexamined in
previous studies."

Lee, Josephine D. "Language and Action in the Plays of Wilde, Shaw and Stoppard."
Princeton University, 1987. *DAI* 48 (March 1988), 2345–A. "Discusses the relationship between linguistic style and action in three British playwrights. . . . The earnest

attitude postulates that language must imitate a reality existing apart from words; the dandiacal attitude, on the other hand, plays freely with language for its own sake. The tension created through the conflict of these two ideas of language is the central interest of these plays. . . . Although Shaw apparently takes an earnest approach to language, his characters do not always follow his lead. Shaw justifies his stylistic experiments with a variety of earnest reasons; in such optimistic plays as *Major Barbara* and *Man and Superman* Shaw presents style as an effective means of establishing real power, and as a manifestation of the Life Force evolution towards the Superman. However, in *Heartbreak House*, doubts about style predominate; Shaw deflates poetic dialogue with an awareness of the dangers of excessive language."

Turner, Tramble Thomas. "Bernard Shaw's Influence on Sean O'Casey's Later Plays." The University of North Carolina at Chapel Hill, 1987. *DAI* 48 (March 1988), 2347–A. O'Casey's letters, *Autobiographies,* and later plays emphasize or reflect the importance to him of *John Bull, Dramatic Opinions and Essays,* and *The Intelligent Woman's Guide.* They shaped his approach to drama, to Irish nationalism, and to political, religious, and economic themes.

V. Recordings

Caesar and Cleopatra, Pygmalion, and *Saint Joan.* Available as numbers VV 7028, VB 6018, and VH 3003, respectively, as videocassettes, from Merit Audio Visual, P.O. Box 392, New York, New York 10024. Phone: (212) 267–7437.

Enser, A. G. S. *Filmed Books and Plays: A List of Books and Plays from Which Films Have Been Made, 1928–1986.* New York: Gower, 1987. For Shaw are listed *Androcles, Arms, Caesar, Disciple, Dilemma, Catherine, How He Lied, Barbara, Millionairess, Pygmalion,* and *Joan.* "Film" here must be narrowly defined and exclusive of videotape.

"Shaw, Bernard," and "Shaw, George Bernard." *InfoTrac Database.* Belmont, Calif.: Information Access Company. Disc [1988 only]. Includes about twenty items, several of which (reviews) have not appeared in the *SHAW* Checklists.

"Shaw, G. B.," and "Shaw, George Bernard." In *Words on Cassette, 1987/88, A Comprehensive Bibliography of Spoken Word Audiocassettes.* New York and London: R. R. Bowker, 1987; pp. 834–35. Includes *Shaw on War, Caesar, Heartbreak, John Bull, Barbara, Misalliance, Pygmalion,* (two versions), *Joan,* and "The Seven Ages of George Bernard Shaw" by Margaret Webster. Entries furnish production and cast credits as well as publisher and cost.

CONTRIBUTORS

Fred D. Crawford, co-editor of *SHAW,* is Associate Professor of English at Central Michigan University. He becomes General Editor of *SHAW* with the next volume.

Howard Ira Einsohn is librarian and part-time instructor at Middlesex Community College, Middletown, Connecticut.

Robert G. Everding is Dean, College of Visual and Performing Arts, Humboldt State University, Arcata, California.

James Gindin, a leading Galsworthy scholar, is Professor of English at the University of Michigan.

David Huckvale is artistic director of the Shaw Festival at "Shaw's Corner," Ayot St. Lawrence, an independent lecturer, musician, and broadcaster, and a tutor for the Open University.

Betty Hugo is Senior Lecturer in the Department of English, University of Pretoria, South Africa. She is currently working on Siegfried Trebitsch's translations of Shaw's plays.

Leon H. Hugo is Professor of English, University of South Africa, and a member of the *SHAW* Editorial Board.

Frederick P. W. McDowell is Professor Emeritus of English at the University of Iowa and a member of the *SHAW* Editorial Board.

John R. Pfeiffer is Professor of English at Central Michigan University and Bibliographer of *SHAW.*

Michel Pharand teaches in the Department of Comparative Literature at The Pennsylvania State University.

Stanley Weintraub, co-editor of *SHAW* and editor since 1956, is Evan Pugh Professor of Arts and Humanities at The Pennsylvania State University. He moves from the general editorship to the Editorial Board with the next volume.

Samuel A. Weiss, editor of *Bernard Shaw's Letters to Siegfried Trebitsch,* is Professor of English at the University of Illinois at Chicago.

Thomas R. Whitaker is Professor of English and Theater Studies at Yale University.

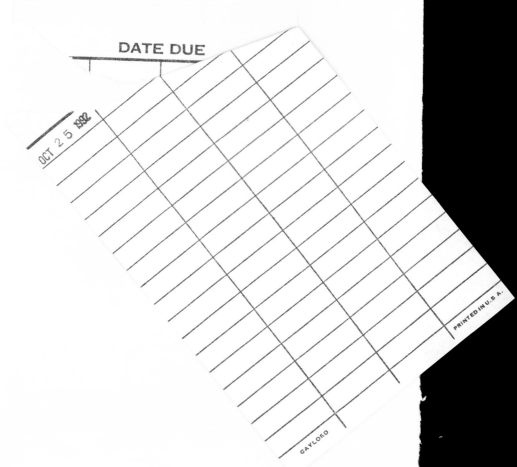

DATE DUE

OCT 2 5 1992

GAYLORD   PRINTED IN U.S.A.